INDONESIA

Number 114   October 2022

Published by Southeast Asia Program Publications • Cornell University Press

Submissions: Submit manuscript as double-spaced document in MS word or similar. Please format citation and footnotes according to the style guidelines in *The Chicago Manual of Style*, 17th edition.

Address: Please address all correspondence and manuscripts to the managing editor at sg265@cornell.edu. We prefer electronic submissions.

Reprints: Contributors will receive one complimentary copy of the issue in which their articles appear.

Abstracts: Abstracts of articles published in *Indonesia* appear in *Excerpta Indonesica*, which is published semiannually by the Royal Institute of Linguistics and Anthropology, Leiden. Articles appearing in this journal are also abstracted and indexed in *Historical Abstracts* and *America: History and Life*.

Subscription information: Contact subscriptions@dukeupress.edu for more information. Digital subscriptions for individuals and institutions are handled by Project Muse (muse@jhu.press.edu).

INDONESIA online: All *Indonesia* articles published at least five years prior to the date of the current issue are accessible to our readers on the internet free of charge. For more information concerning annual print and online subscriptions, pay-per-view access to recent articles, and access to our archives, please see: seap.einaudi.cornell.edu/ indonesia_journal or http://ecommons.cornell.edu

Managing Editor   Sarah E. M. Grossman

ISBN 978-1-5017-6999-3
ISSN 0019-7289
©2022 Cornell University

Table of Contents 114

Kartini, *Inlandsche kunstnijverheid* and Dutch Imperial Policy in the East Indies, 1898–1904

Joost Coté

In August 1903 a Dutch language colonial newspaper, *De Sumatra Post*, opened a brief report on what it identified as the first signs of a new colonial policy with the words: "The wind is currently blowing in the direction of encouraging a native craft industry."[1] It described a proposal, initiated by the colonial Director of Native Education and Industry, Mr. Jacques Abendanon, to promote Native arts and crafts as a means to address "the declining welfare" of the Javanese. It was to launch a two-year training program in technical drawing for talented Native school teachers who would be reassigned to the training schools for Native colonial officials and school teachers to develop their knowledge of and interest in stimulating a "Native arts industry." It was the first policy outcome flowing from the first official public exhibition of "Native arts and crafts" in the colony held the previous year in the colonial capital, Batavia.

A significant "player" in events that had led to this moment was Raden Ajeng Kartini (b. 1879), daughter of the *bupati* of Japara, a regency that included a major traditional wood crafting center. Largely self-educated since leaving the local European elementary school in 1892, and well-read in contemporary Dutch literature and colonial

Joost Cote is Senior Research fellow in history at Monash University.

[1] *De Sumatra Post*, August 5, 1903: "Aanmoediging der inlandsche kunstnijverheid" (Encouragement of native arts and crafts).

affairs, before the end of the century she had already ventured into the "public arena" of imperial discourse.[2] Kartini expressed herself an admirer of Abdul Rivai, the pioneer Malay language journalist and editor of the first Malay language paper, *Bintang Hindia*, and advocate of Western education as the pathway for Indonesians to progress.[3] At the same time she shared the political consciousness of the first generation of an emerging Western-educated class of Indigenous colonial officials, indignant at their treatment by supercilious colonial officials.[4] Her correspondence with politically influential Europeans makes clear how she sought to exploit the "green shoots" of what appeared to be a rejuvenated colonial policy. Her declared aim was to begin to educate Europeans and colonial policy makers in their understanding of "the Native" and to promote the potential opportunities that a new colonial policy might make available.

In the context of what appeared to be a new European interest in Native craft, Kartini's involvement was premised on the hope that this could be one means by which Europeans might come to appreciate "the soul of the Javanese."[5] The extensive Kartini archive documents her direct and indirect involvement in the exhibitions mounted in the Dutch metropole, in the colony and internationally, between 1898 and 1903.[6] It also makes clear her strategic association with several key Europeans who were directly involved in the promotion of Native arts and crafts in the colony and in the Netherlands. It reveals the difficulty she had in keeping up with the sudden European demand for local Native wood and other crafts once the "flood gates" were opened, as well as the unwanted attention and criticism that her involvement brought her.

Situating her voice in this brief "moment" of European and colonial media interest in Native arts and crafts reveals the unbridgeable gap that persisted between Kartini's presentation of craft as a "living" manifestation of the Javanese and the European/ colonial perception of it as an object and "colonial product." Shortly after her untimely death in September 1904, the possibility of a coincidence between these two views that may have momentarily appeared to exist was swiftly and conclusively rejected in the formulation of an official colonial *Inlandsch nijverheid* policy. In the immediately

---

[2] Apart from her involvement in the 1898 National Exhibition of Women's Work, she had also contributed an article that year to the prestigious ethnographic journal *Bijdragen tot de Taal-, Land- en Volkenkunde*, published 1899, officially listed as authored by her father. See Coté, *Kartini*, 790–92.

[3] H. Pols, *Nurturing Indonesia: Medicine and Decolonisation in the Dutch East Indies* (Cambridge: Cambridge University Press, 2018), 21–45; H. Poeze, "Early Indonesian Emancipation: Abdul Rivai, Van Heutsz and the Bintang Hindia," *Bijdragen* 145, no. 1 (1989): 87–106. Kartini was in touch with students of the Doktor Djawa medical training school, referencing Agus Salim, a later nationalist leader, who she learned had recently made a "powerful nationalist address" to students, and who she hoped would work with Rivai to "awaken his race compatriots to work together for their people . . . towards a mutual objective: the raising up of the native race." Kartini to Mej. Bosch, July 5, 1903 (unpubl.) See also Kartini to Mev. Abendanon, July 24, 1903.

[4] Kartini had direct extensive evidence of the growing "displeasure" within the echelon of Javanese colonial administrators through her family. Her uncle had outlined these concerns in 1896 in *Tijdschrift voor het Binnenlands Bestuur*. She had access to the views of her younger generation via her brother, Sosrokartono, one of the few Javanese men at the time to study in the Netherlands, who had had delivered a "Javanese manifesto" of demands in 1899, which she largely replicated several years later in a document titled, *Geef de Javaan Opvoeding*. See Coté, *Kartini*, 805–25.

[5] Kartini employs this phrase in a letter to Mej. Bosch, July 5, 1903 (unpublished) discussed later.

[6] These are, respectively, in the Netherlands, The Hague 1898 and 1900 and 's-Gravenhage 1902; in Java, Batavia 1902 and Semarang, 1903; in France, Paris, 1900; and Japan, Osaka, 1903. Later her sister Roekmini was directly involved in the 1906 Surabaya ad Semarang 1908 craft exhibitions.

following years, it became apparent that more direct means to reveal "the soul of the Javanese" were necessary.

Exhibitions of Native Craft in the Context of an Imperialism

By the latter years of the nineteenth century the phenomenon of the exhibition had become firmly enmeshed in the need to showcase the imperial nation in a competitive imperial context.[7] At the same time, within the nation itself, the exhibition also gained growing political and cultural significance in focusing its citizens' attention on the value of its colonial resources and its contribution to its imperial prestige. In the Dutch context, the latter years of the nineteenth century and early years of the twentieth was a period that saw the "successes" of its violent military operations in finally securing control of the archipelago, and concomitant political pressure from Dutch capital eager to invest in and exploit these newly pacified regions of its empire.[8] There were also demands from within the East Indies colony itself for political and economic reforms on the part of a growing, newly arrived, settler community, and voiced in the metropole by "returnees" after having made their fortunes in the colony. Expressed via numerous public organizations that emerged in the course of the second half of the century, these metropolitan political, economic, academic, and literary—and revivalist religious and missionary—discourses concerned with the colonies,[9] together, contributed to the formulation of the new direction in imperial policy at the beginning of the new century. Formulated as a so-called "ethical policy," this was enunciated by the nation's first "democratic" (universal male franchise) elected, government, led by populist Christian party but supported across the political spectrum.[10]

M. Bloembergen identifies the 1883 Amsterdam International colonial and export trade exhibition as embedding the practice of a "Native exhibit" in Dutch *tentoonstellingen*.[11]

---

[7] E. Locher Scholten, "Dutch Expansion in the Indonesian Archipelago around 1900 and the Imperial Debate," *Journal of Southeast Asian Studies* 25, no. 10 (1994): 91–111; M. Kuitenbrouwer, *Nederland en de opkomst van het moderne imperialisme* (Amsterdam: De Bataviaasche Leeuw, 1985).

[8] On the contemporary response to the "conquest of Aceh," see P. Bijl, *Emerging Memory: Photographs of Colonial Atrocity in Dutch Cultural Remembrance* (Amsterdam: Amsterdam University Press, 2015), ch. 1, 43–84. The dramatic defeat of Dutch force in Lombok in 1894, and the widely celebrated victory in 1895, crystalized this emerging "military fascination." See J. van Goor, "De Lombok expeditie en de Nederlandse nationalism," in *Imperialisme in de marge: De afronding van Nederlands-Indië*, ed. J. van Goor (Utrecht: HES, 1986), 19–70.

On the economic pressure, see A. Taselaar, *De Nederlandse koloniale lobby: Ondernemers en de Indische politiek 1914–1940* (Leiden: CNWS, 1998), part 1, 31–92.

[9] H. J. van den Doel, *De Stille macht: Het Europese binnenlands bestuur op Java en Madoera, 1808–1942* (Amsterdam: Bert Bakker,1994), ch. 3, 107–38; W. Otterspeer (ed.), *Leiden Oriental Connections* 1850–1940, (Leiden: Brill, 1989); J. Bell, *Nederlandse literatuur in het fin de siecle: Een receptive-historische overzicht van het proza tusen 1885 en 1900* (Amsterdam: Amsterdam University Press, 1993), 265–326. Numerous societies existed with economic and academic interests in the colonies disseminating views via journals. One explicitly nationalist organization was the *Algemeen Nederlandsch Verbond*, publisher of *Neerlandia*, to which Kartini was invited to contribute. Its objective was "awakening a sense of tribal unity and create a sense of tribal solidarity amongst all those [people of Dutch origin] who now live far from each other" (1896): hppts://www.dbnl.org/tekst/_nee003189601_01/_nee003189601_01_0171.php.

[10] See E. Locher Scholter, *Ethiek in fragmenten: Vijf studies over het koloniale denken en doen van Nederland in de Indonesische archipel (1877–1942)* (Utrecht: HES, 1981).

[11] M. Bloembergen, *Colonial Spectacles: The Netherlands and the Dutch East Indies at the World Exhibitions, 1880–1931* (Singapore: Singapore University Press 2006), ch. 2, 50–105.

At this exhibition a reconstructed Native *kampong* was featured that included specially imported "Natives" playing various, prescribed "traditional" roles. For a Dutch public in the Netherlands, removed from the immediacy of colonial conditions, exhibitions of "performing Natives" in reconstructed villages, and now, gradually, also static displays of their "work," may have seemed more "real" than images offered by existing literature, ethnographic displays, or dramatic media reportage of wars. It may also have stimulated greater curiosity in the "exotic Native." However, their impressions of "the Native" after such an exhibition visit in Europe, was perhaps no more "unreal" than that held by urban colonial settlers, given the exclamations of "surprise" reported in accounts of the first exhibition of Native *kunst* in the colony.

The 1883 exhibition, largely displaying the results of amateur ethnographic collections already accumulated in the metropole,[12] expressed a new "scientific" dimension in the representation of "the Native." These exhibits were now classified according to Western ethnographic categories, thereby further objectifying both objects and their creators, while further highlighting the powers of Western civilization.[13] At the 1889 *Exposition Universelle* in Paris, French organizers demanded that Dutch curators apply even more stringent "scientific" requirements to substantiate that exhibition's global objective of projecting the civilizational role of imperial rule. They were required to reference an anthropologically "proven" human evolutionary framework in their representations of the colonized Native, preferably reinforced with the addition of craniological measurements.[14]

In the event, however, the Netherlands exhibit in 1889 was less "scientific" than the French organizers had wished, it appeared to have retained a more popular tone, to which the reception given it by the French *belle monde* arguably contributed.[15] For some members of the public, the performances of "real natives" there appeared like an exotic variation of the recently popularized folk theater performances.[16] Bloembergen cites a report of spectators being stimulated by a "lascivious curiosity"[17] as they watched "sixty genuine inhabitants of Java and Sumatra . . . displaying their arts and crafts along with music and dance." Altogether, the Dutch pavilion was reported as "radiating a congenial, warm atmosphere," so much so that the Native exhibit in "[o]ur little colonial corner" in Paris could just as well have been a "little village in Zeeland."[18] All this, Bloembergen suggests, while it may have extended a metropolitan European public's awareness of

[12] P. ter Keurs, "Introduction: Theory and Practice of Colonial Collecting," in *Colonial Collections Revisited*, ed. P. ter Keurs (Leiden: CNWS Publications, 2007), 1–15. A majority of chapters in this volume point to the link of metropolitan collections with the regional military campaigns.

[13] Bloembergen makes this case in *Colonial spectacles*, 116–18. For an overview of the contemporary "scientifization" of the study of the Native, see Otterspeer, *Leiden Oriental Connections*.

[14] Bloembergen, *Colonial Spectacles*, 153. See also F. Gouda, *Dutch Culture Overseas: Colonial Practice in the Netherlands Indies 1900-1942* (Amsterdam: Amsterdam University Press, 1995), 42–46. For an account of "racial science" in the Dutch colonial context, see F. Sysling, *Racial Science and Human Diversity in Colonial Indonesia* (Singapore: NUS, 2016).

[15] Bloembergen cites descriptions by French writers Emile Zola and Edmond de Goncourt. Bloembergen, *Colonial spectacles*, 139.

[16] See D. J. Fisher, "The Origins of the French Popular Theatre." *Journal of Contemporary History* 12 (1977): 461–97; A. Bonnell, *The People's Stage in Imperial Germany* (London: Taurus Academic Studies, 2005).

[17] Bloembergen, *Colonial Spectacles*, 107–8.

[18] Bloembergen, *Colonial Spectacles*, 107, 156.

the Indigenous inhabitants of their empires, did so only by enveloping "the Native" in further layers of exoticism, while allowing European spectators to "absolve themselves" from confronting the reality of colonialism.[19]

The Exhibition of Women's Work, 1898

In this respect, the Exhibition of Women's Work held in The Hague in 1898 to which R. A. Kartini contributed, was nothing new.[20] It, too, had a Native village with "performing Javanese" where "the visitor could step outside and find some relaxation." Here they could taste Indonesian food, observe marriage ceremonies, watch Javanese women doing batik work, and come "under the spell of the gamelan music."[21] As at the 1889 exhibition, this was rather more a distraction from the exhibition's political intent, in this case a focus on the importance of the economic and political role of women in a modernizing Dutch nation. Now, it was suggested, European women might also contribute to the imperial role of the "fatherland," albeit limited in the first instance to the care of disadvantaged females in the settler community. Kartini, by then an avid reader of contemporary feminist literature,[22] expressed her support for this feminist cause by her contributions related to batik intended to draw attention to work of Javanese women. However, as she was to discover, the European feminism of the day did not yet extend to an appreciation of the "living Native women" as a "real person."[23]

Vereeniging Oost en West

Rather unexpectedly perhaps, the 1898 women's exhibition did generate a new organization that specifically concerned itself with the promotion of arts and crafts produced by "the Natives of our colonies." It grew out of what had reportedly been a less than exciting element of the 1898 exhibition, the *Oost-Indië zaal*, the room devoted to the display of Native objects. It was the display to which Kartini and her sisters, encouraged by their father and brother, had contributed, but was in fact, like similar displays, dominated by "war booty," objects collected during colonial military operations and items collected from the living rooms of a Dutch urban bourgeoisie.[24] Although Kartini had expressed her dismay at the lack of attention her contribution on batik had

---

[19] Bloembergen, *Colonial Spectacles*, 163. See also M. Bloembergen, "Exotisme en populaire antropologi: Een Javaanse dorp op de wereldtentoonstelling in Parijs (1889)," *Nederlands Kunsthistorisch Jaarboek* (2002), https://brill.com/view.journals/nkjo/53/1/aericle-p251_11.xml?language=en.

[20] J. Coté, "Celebrating Women's Labour: Raden Ajeng Kartini and the Dutch Women's Exhibition, 1898," in *Een vaderland voor vrouwen/A fatherland for women: The 1898 "Nationale tentoonstelling van Vrouwennarbeid" in retrospect*, ed. M. Grever and F. Dieteren (Amsterdam: IISG/VVG, 2000), 119–35; M. Grever and B. Waaldijk, *Feministische openbaarheid: De Nationale Tentoontelling van Vrouwenarbeid in 1898* (Amsterdam: IISG/IIAV, 1998). (Trans. *Transforming the Public Sphere: The Dutch National Exhibition of Women's Labour* [Durham: Duke University Press, 2004]).

[21] M. Grever, "Reconstructing the Fatherland: Comparative Perspectives on Women and 19th-Century Exhibitions," in Grever and Dieteren, *Een vaderland voor vrouwen*, 22–23. See also Grever and Waaldijk, *Feministische openbaarheid*, 182–92.

[22] Most notably this included, *Hilda van Suylenberg* (Cecile Goekoop), *Barthold Meryam* (Cornelie Huygens), *Verbonden Schakels* (Hélène Mercier). See Coté, *Kartini*, 840–43.

[23] Kartini to Stella Zeehandelaar, May 20, 1899; Coté, "Celebrating Women's Labour."

[24] Her father, Raden Mas Adipati Sosroningrat, had arranged a public viewing of the contribution of woodcarving, paintings, and the representations of various the stages of batik making before these were

received,[25] this organization was soon to catapult her into the arena of the new European interest in "the Native."

The curator of the *Inlandsche afdeeling* of the 1898 women's exhibition and now president of the *Vereeniging Oost en West*, the East-West Association, Mevrouw Zuijlen–Tromp,[26] intended the new organization as a means to "educate" the Dutch public about their East and West Indies colonies. In part, this was to be achieved through the display and sale of "Native arts and crafts."[27] To inaugurate this objective, a series of small exhibitions were held, the first of which was an exhibition of Native weaponry retrieved from colonial military operations and largely drawn from the earlier display. This was immediately topical at a time when the Dutch public were following with great interest the annals of the "successful" colonial war against Acehnese and Balinese rulers. The second was an exhibition of metal craft, including copper items. The third in 1901 focused on "East Indies weaving, Javanese batiks and East Indies furniture," contributed by returned former colonial residents domiciled in The Hague. In particular, the inclusion of Native batik and woven items engaged with the revival of interest in "women's craft work" in the Netherlands and the recent experimentation in reproducing batik that was developing on the sidelines of the Dutch arts and crafts movement.[28]

The catalogue for the 1901 exhibition in The Hague confirmed that this display of colonial "collectables" was largely the product of colonial "souveniring" rather than of direct contact with the practitioners of these "Native arts and crafts."[29] Nevertheless, a detailed sixty-page overview of *Inlandsche kunstnijverheid* in the East Indies gave some indication of a new interest that differed from earlier ethnographic and museumized frames of reference within which native artifacts had typically been presented previously. It was prepared by G. P. Rouffaer, secretary of the Koninklijke Instituut (Royal Institute), for *Oost en West* of which he was member and based on his work in cataloguing the institute's resources and two earlier research field trips to the Indies.[30] His account, which

sent. Kartini's brother, Sosrokartono, who had recently arrived in the Netherlands to study, assisted in setting up the exhibition. Grever and Waaldijk, *Feministische openbaarheid*, 182n121, 182.

[25] Kartini to Stella Zeehandelaar, May 25, November 6, 1899, March 14, 1902; to Mev Abendanon, December 21, 1901. Only much later was her account of the batik making process, "Het blau maken," formally acknowledged by GP Rouffaer. See Coté, *Kartini*, 788–90.

[26] Colonial-born Mevrouw G. A. Zuylen-Tromp (1863–1951) was the wife of a retired colonial military officer. Her colonial experience expressed itself in a concern for Javanese women as "the victims of bad European attitudes and poor Indo-European leadership." Grever and Waaldijk, *Feministische openbaarheid*, 186.

[27] A further important initiative discussed at early meetings was to educate the young generation in Europe through commissioning appropriate schoolbooks. *Voorloopige Notulen, Oost en West, 1900*, Archief Koninklijke Vereeniging Oost en West, Special Collections, Leiden University.

[28] The display of "native weaponry" and the exhibit of Native metal craft were defined as displays of Native male craft, while the third, woven materials, was specifically designated as a focus on "female" craft. *Inleiding, Tentoonstelling van Nederlandsch Oost-Indische Kunstnijverheid (Derde Groep) te 's-Gravenhage in de Gothische Zaal van het Paleis op de Kneuterdijk*: Catalogus, 24 Juli tot 1 October 1901 ('s-Gravenhage: Boek en Handelsdrukkerij).

[29] The catalogue lists 638 items of woven cloth exhibited of which, other than several donated by Dutch museums, were all provided by European (women) owners in the Netherlands. The only reference to Kartini's region was to several batik of Chinese origin from Semarang.

[30] "F. G. P. Jaquet, Rouffaer, Gerrit Piter (1860–1928)," *Biografisch woordenboek van Nederland*, http://resoiurces. huygens.knaw.nl. In 1903, he contributed to the establishment of, and chaired the organization overseeing, *Oost en West* Native arts and crafts permanent exhibition and shop, Boetan discussed later. N. J. Krom, "Herdenking van Dr GP Rouffaer," *Bijdragen* 84, no. 2/3 (1928): 218.

marked the beginning of his own rise as the Dutch expert on Indonesian woven cloth, gave evidence of a new privileging of Native craft practice that was lacking in earlier ethnographically oriented writing.[31] Whether this was evident to the exhibition goer, they were certainly being made aware of the new association's objective of drawing attention to an imperial message regarding the power and extent of the Dutch domination of the archipelago by the broad regional representation of the Indies the display provided.

The 1902 Oost en West Tentoonstelling in Batavia

Given its focus, and its extensive membership of former and currently resident colonials,[32] it is not surprising that a colonial branch of Oost en West was soon established (March 18, 1901) and that it planned for an exhibition in the colony itself for the following year. The colonial branch was headed by colonial government officials, H. J. W. Van Lawick van Pabst and J. E. Jasper. The former, the colony's Chief Inspector of (agricultural) Cultures, listed among the founding members of Oost en West (O&W), gathered at its inaugural meeting in The Hague in 1899 while he was on furlough in the Netherlands was appointed the colonial branch president.[33] The colonially born Jasper, a *controleur*, later to become the recognized authority on Javanese arts and crafts in the colony, as Rouffaeur was in the Netherlands, had previously been appointed to report on *Inlandsch kunstwerk*.[34] The local O&W branch was strongly supported by the Director of Native Education, Industry and Religion, Jacques Abendanon, as well as by several prominent colonial businessmen, including Victor Zimmermann, who appears in the history as an enthusiastic Native arts aficionado and promoter.

Abendanon, a Netherlands-educated lawyer, had been resident in the colony since 1875 and had had a long legal career prior to his appointment as director of Native Education and Industry. He had also been closely involved in the more recent modernization and repurposing of the Bataviaasch Instituut, the colony's major scientific institution of which he had briefly been secretary.[35] Here he had worked enthusiastically in redeveloping its museum and scientific journal, before taking up his new role to implement a new "Native policy."[36] In this capacity (1900–5), both in his official role and privately together with his wife Rosa (Rosita), the "idealistic director"

---

[31] Later to become recognized as an "expert" on Javanese batik, this was Rouffaer's first public report of his research, later expanded in a 1914 publication (with H. H. Juynboll), *De batik kunst in Nederlandsch-Indië en haar geschiedenis op grond van materiaal aanwesig in 's Rijks Ethnographisch Museum en andere openbare en particuliere verzamelingen in Nederland*. As the title indicated, this was however based solely on a study of "materials present in the Royal Ethnographic museum and other public and private collections." However, in this publication he did reference Kartini's 1898 account of batik making.

[32] *Voorloopige Notulen*, 1899.

[33] Van Lawick van Pabst was *Hoofd Inspecteur der Cultuurs*, Head Inspector of (commercial) Agriculture. He is mentioned as a regular visitor to the Japara *kabupaten* by Kartini, first in a letter to Abendanon, November 24, 1901. He worked more closely with her after the Batavia exhibition. Kartini to Mev, Abendanon, September 2, December 12, 1902.

[34] See S. van Doorn, *Johan Ernst Jasper, Indisch ambtenaar: leven en werk 1874–1945* (n.p, 1998).

[35] For a recent critical study of the legacy of the colonial museum see MK Rizqika, "Beyond the Collections: Identity Construction at the National Museum of Indonesia", in *Cultural Dynamics in a Globalised World*, ed. M. Budianta, M. Budiman, A Kusno, and M. Moriyama (London: Routledge, 2018), 217–23.

[36] For Abendanon's career see H. van Miert, *Bevlogenheid en onvermogen: Mr. JH. Abendanon (1852–1925) en de ethische richting in het Nederlandse kolonialisme* (Leiden: KITLV Press, 1991).

coopted the enthusiastic Kartini in pursuit of his progressive policies to develop *Inlandsch onderwijs* (Native education) and *Inlandsche nijverheid* (Native industry).[37] It was in this context that Kartini was to gain her enduring public profile and become a central figure in the context of the history of the "ethical policy," not least as a result of Abendanon's later publication of an edited collection of her correspondence with the Abendanons in 1911.[38]

The first major exhibition of Native arts and crafts in the colony was assembled by the Afdeeling Nederlands-Indië van de Vereeniging "Oost en West" (the colonial branch of the metropolitan Dutch Association) and opened in Batavia in June 1902 under the patronage of the wife of Governor General Rooseboom.[39] While the four men mentioned above were its key organizers, behind the scenes the wives of Abendanon and Lawick van Pabst were actively engaged in curating the displays.[40] In the colonial capital the exhibition of Native arts and crafts appears to have been as popular as the one held the previous year in the imperial capital, raising considerable funds for the organization, and significantly increasing its membership, including that of Kartini and her sisters.[41] Its public, however, was significantly different as, besides Europeans, all of whom can be expected to have had direct experience of *Inlanders*, if primarily as servants, there were large numbers of Indonesian and Chinese visitors from better-off urban families.[42]

The catalogue prepared for the exhibition by Jasper reveals its content was similar to the earlier O&W exhibitions in the Netherlands in focusing primarily on metal and woven items and a smaller number of items of *houtsnijwerk* (wood carvings). The first category, which Jasper acknowledged he was personally most interested in, amounted to five hundred *kopergiet* (copper-based) items. There were 110 woven items, including *kappa, slendang, Lokcwans, pelangis* and batiks,[43] and a small (fifty-one) collection of wooden *kunstsnijwerk* (woodcraft). While the largest single contributor to the exhibition

---

[37] The term "idealistic director" was used by colonial critics of his attempt to expand Javanese access to Dutch language education. He and his wife had met Kartini in 1900 during the director's meeting with her father regarding his tour of Java to consult with regional Javanese rulers on their views on education. Recounted by Kartini in a letter to Rosa, August 8–9, 1901.

[38] The first publication of an edited collection of her letters was published in the colony in 1911: J. Abendanon (ed.), *Door duisternis tot licht: Gedachten over en voor het Javaansche volk van Raden Adjeng Kartini* (Semarang, Surabaya: Van Dorp, 1911). Numerous reprints of the 1912 edition appeared in the Netherlands, with a "special edition" appearing in 1924.

[39] Although it appears to have been the first official *tentoonstelling* that included "native craft items" in the colony, the collection and sale of such items at commercial *tentoonstellingen*, such as at the one in 1893, had taken place earlier. Among the hundreds of items that received prizes in 1893, the *Bataviaasch Nieuwsblad* lists numerous Native craft items, such as "cigar holders" from Bantam, sarong from Lasem and Pekalongan, and various copper items. *Bataviaasch Nieuwsblad*, December 16, 1893.

[40] The *Soerabijasche Handelsblad*, June 12, 1902, reported that "the talent for decorating" by Abendanon's and van Lawick van Pabst's wives had succeeded in recasting the exposition buildings into "artistic rooms of Native art."

[41] Their father and uncle were already listed in 1900 among the colony-resident members of the Dutch-based organization.

[42] An entry fee was charged on a sliding scale according to race, highest for Europeans, less for Chinese and 50 cents for *Inlanders*.

[43] There were fifty-five individual contributions by Javanese, including from the Raden Ayu Patih of Surabaya. Contributors representing Surabaya's Javanese and Arabic haji community were listed separately. There is no reference to a Kartini/Japara contribution.

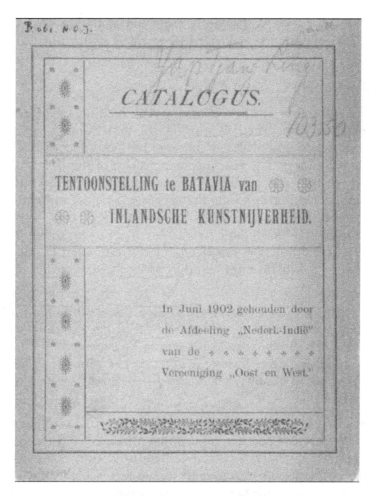

Cover of the catalogue for the exhibition in *Catalogus van de tentoonstelling te Batavia van inlandsche kunstnijverheid* (Batavia of Native arts and crafts) (Batavia: Javasche Boekhandel & Drukkerij, 1902). Source: Leiden University Digital Collection (Shelfmark Br N 02-356), https://scharrelaar-p3.leidenuniv.nl/view/item/1055221?solr_nav%5Bid%5D=79102bbf58fdb2eb41d9&solr_nav%5Bpage%5D=1&solr_nav%5Boffset%5D=10#page/1/mode/1up.

was a European,[44] there were also a large number of non-European contributors. Prominent among the latter in all categories listed in the catalogue are the names of Chinese donors, as well as those of a large group of Indonesian and Arabic merchants from Surabaya,[45] indicating that a viable craft market already existed in Java by this time. This was further emphasized by the catalogue's notice that "all items in the catalogue with prices indicated" were for sale. With this exhibition *Oost en West* made clear it intended to be a major player in this colonial market for "authentic" Native craft

[44] This was F. F. Römer of Surabaya, who provided 223 items, all of which were for sale. *Oost en West* provided seven items, two from Ambon and one from the west coast Sumatra.

[45] The largest Chinese contribution (sixty-seven items) was made by Lim Ting Bo of Surabaya.

to support its activities in the Netherlands. Engaged as its key supplier in relation to woodcraft, as her correspondence makes evident, was R. A. Kartini.

Positioning Native Craft in Colonial Policy

In opening the exhibition in Batavia on the fifth of June 1902,[46] the president, van Lawick van Pabst, was concerned to emphasize that the exhibition, ostensibly to celebrate Native craftwork, was primarily intended to provide a platform for promoting a new direction in colonial policy. The special objective of the *tentoonstelling*, he stated, was "to show that the native is capable of doing more than just planting rice or lazing about [*luieren*]; that he can make objects that give evidence of a great and deep feeling for art, for what is beautiful." He hastened to add, however, that "Admittedly much of what is produced would not be suitable for display in a European boudoir" but this was largely because "to date little effort has been made to see what he, unaided, is capable of; to appreciate what his artistic ability could produce *under intelligent guidance*."(italics added)[47]

A local press report more succinctly elucidated the exhibition's underlying aim as being to "advance the knowledge of our wonderful [*schone*] colonies and especially, to increase the welfare of its inhabitants." This would be achieved by a threefold strategy: "To awaken interest in [the Native craftsman's] work, to ensure him with a wider market, and to provide information about what he produces; this is the triple objective of this exhibition."[48]

Both summaries of the exhibition's aims projected a new engagement with "the Native" in terms of what the new colonial policy direction indicated would be in the Natives' best interests. Initially, Van Lawick pointed out, achieving the economic implications of the promotion of Native craft would face several practical impediments, notably the high cost of transportation and the poor payment currently received by craft workers for their product. More significant were impediments that could be categorized as related to "colonial relations." These were, firstly, the reluctance of Native crafters "to send goods, to entrust their works to complete strangers, to send these so far away." This, van Lawick believed, would be erased over time with greater interaction between European consumers and Native creators that would flow naturally from increased promotion and sales.[49] Most significant, therefore, was the need to direct and "enable these [craft]people to produce objects which could also be used by European society which is rarely the case for items currently being produced."[50]

A common response to this first formal display of Native craft presented in the urbanized environment of Batavia, which continued to appear in colonial press reports over the following weeks, were the expressions of amazement at what "the Native" could

---

[46] *Bataviaasch Nieuwsblad*, June 5, 1902.

[47] *Het Nieuws van den dag voor Nederlandsch-Indië*, June 5, 1902. "Intelligent guidance" can be understood as "European direction."

[48] *Het Nieuws*, June 5, 1902.

[49] *Het Nieuws*, June 5, 1902. These problems were also regularly referenced in Kartini's correspondence as she became increasingly involved in supplying craft to *Oost en West* in Batavia.

[50] *De Locomotief*, June 9, 1902; *Soerabijasch Handelsblad*, June 10, 1902.

produce! One extensive report on the exhibition commenced the second installment of a series of articles on the exhibition with: "One question which many attending the exhibition will be asking themselves is: 'How is it possible that natives in their pokey little quarters and with their primitive tools are able to produce all these beautiful things?'"[51] It was a question, this writer emphasized, that was prompted by "our" (that is, the urban European colonial population's) generally felt surprise at witnessing this "expression of the native's artistic feeling," which the opportunity to closely inspect the objects now revealed to them for the first time. The "surprise" expressed itself in patronizing terms: that the "genuine native art" on display was "so wonderfully beautiful [*zoo practige mooi*] that one involuntarily develops respect for the natives who have achieved . . . such heights *without the least guidance*" (italics added).[52] Elsewhere this writer, commenting on the display of weaving, expressed the view that these were "so fine and artistically worked that they will bring joy to many a [Dutch] female heart." Similar responses were typically followed with the recommendation that it therefore behooved Europeans to develop a greater interest in the life condition of these "unfortunate *Inlanders*."

Extending the apparent success of the exhibition, in February of the following year, O&W opened a sales room (*verkoopzaal*) for Native craft in Batavia. This also served as a collection and supply depot for its larger venture in the Netherlands, *Boeatan*,[53] the Native arts and crafts shop it opened in the Den Haag in November that year. Both shops were also intended to provide a permanent facility for the viewing, purchase, and general promotion of Native arts and crafts, and to provide an ongoing presence for these objects in the European space between the series national and colonial regional exhibitions it also planned to organize.[54] Media coverage of this new venture in the colony continued the patronizingly extravagant praise for the talent that "lay hidden amongst the natives." Visitors and potential purchasers at the shop, one report exclaimed, would have "had no idea of" what awaited them and would now "have to come to recognize" that they needed to change their opinion about *de inlander*.

> The so often depreciated native, who many regard as beings that existed so far below them that there could not even be a basis of comparison, is in fact not so dumb, so stupid, of so little worth, as so many imagine; and when one thinks of the primitive tools with which so many objects of artwork are undertaken, when we see the work of their hand, of their sense of artistry and determined perseverance, our admiration demands we inspect their work more carefully.[55]

---

[51] *Bataviaasch Nieuwsblad*, June 5, 1902, "De tentoonstelling van Inlandsche nijverheid en kunstnijverheid by H."

[52] *Bataviaasch Nieuwsblad*, June 30, 1902. The writer later noted: "Any visitor to the tentoonstelling will have to admit that in Java real artists, can be found, who with a little guidance could surprise the whole of Europe. Some copper pieces are really sublime in their execution and one does not need to be an expert . . . to recognise this."

[53] The name adopted is the Malay/Indonesian word "buat[an]" "work," "product."

[54] *De Locomotief*, July 13, 1903, reporting on this adds that the shop had recently provided exhibits for a Ministry of Industry initiated *tentoonstelling* in Groningen, in the north of the country. As Groot details, Boeatan also acted as an important space where Dutch women crafters interacted with and displayed their own craftwork. M. Groot, "Crossing the Borderlines and Moving the Boundaries: 'High' Arts and Crafts, Cross-Culturalism, Folk Art and Gender," *Journal of Design History* 19, no. 2 (2006): 128.

[55] *De Preanger Bode*, February 13, 1903, "Inlandsche Kunstnijverheid." Some days later, *De Locomotief* (February 17, 1903) headlined the "great interest" (*Grote belangstelling*) this shop in Rijswijk was already attracting, including large purchases by an international travel agent.

While such patronizing comments as these pointed to a "new awareness" of the colonial subject in the colony, they did not necessarily express an appreciation of the product: the dominant theme of otherwise positive press reports was that, in order now for a Native arts and crafts industry to flourish, it needed to conform to the tastes of the European consumer. [56]

Kartini and Inlandsche kunstnijverheid

In his speech opening the *tentoonstelling*, Van Lawick regretted that currently, in Europe, "while they may have magazines full of Japanese and Chinese articles, we will look in vain for typical Indies items which will surely be much more to their taste." The future of a "Native craft industry," therefore, would only "blossom when led in the right direction by Europeans [to produce] items that would look good in a European home."[57] One anonymous critic of this view, who may or may not have been concerned with protecting the 'authenticity' of Javanese craft, rejected the notion out of hand: such a policy would result in the production of items, such as "the deformed and tasteless copper flowerpots and vases that looked like nothing on earth", that were already appearing, and otherwise products that were totally unsuited to the materials from which they were made. This criticism, evidently by a recent European arrival looking down his nose at these colonials, concluded: "How someone could suggest that such hybrid monstrosities could be sold in Paris is a complete mystery to us. People that say this have probably never been to Paris."[58]

However, it is apparent from her correspondence with Rosa Abendanon that Kartini was not averse to the suggestions of that "clever" Mr. van Lawick.[59] Reflecting her enthusiastic insertion into the growing European interest in Native arts and crafts in the colony are her own suggestions for woodcraft that would most interest Batavian customers. After having initially been approached by Rosa in March 1901 on behalf of the well-known Dutch ethnographer A. W. Nieuwenhuis, who required "photograph boxes" for his collection of ethnographic photographs that he was taking back to the Netherlands, Kartini's involvement had progressively evolved. In August 1901 it was suggested she might contribute to an appropriate wedding gift from the colony for the Dutch queen.[60] In the latter part of 1901 Kartini reports on the constant flow of individual

---

[56] Even if, as in the case of a detailed report on the small Japara collection at the 1902 exhibition in the *Soerabaijasch Handelsblad* (June 12, 1902), the beautiful (*fraai*) woodcarving was admired for the execution of the carving (the "buiging der uitbeitelingslijnen"), this admiration did not necessarily extend to the "product" itself.

[57] *Het Nieuws van den dag voor Nederlandsch-Indië*, June 5, 1902. He had also emphasized that "we have to make our mark in Batavia, if only to uphold the honour of our colonies."

[58] *Het Nieuws*, June 9, 1902. Evidently more interested in Indigenous arts than European consumption, the author commenced his short article by describing how five hundred Inlanders paid a "dubbeltje" (50 cents) "to take a look at what Pak Ras and Ekowinangoen and their colleagues had produced." Ekowinangoen, a contributor to the 1902 exhibition, was recognized, also by Kartini, as the leading woodcraft artisan in nearby Kudus.

[59] Kartini to Mev. Abendanon, June 10, 1902.

[60] Kartini to Mev. Abendanon, August 1, 1901, June 2, 1902. This had earlier been suggested in January 1901. The reference was to carved photograph frames. Reference in correspondence to the craft items arranged, designed, or proposed by Kartini are too extensive to be reported on here. They can be readily located via keyword search of the digitalized open access edition of her writing.

woodcraft orders from the Abendanon's Batavian acquaintances for craft items from Japara for whom she was thinking up new ideas and designs. By January 1902 this was becoming a problem:

> There has been a torrent of requests recently—it is a great pity that our clever craftsman does not have some working capital. The consequence of this is, amongst other things, that it is not possible to have any woodcarvings in stock. Everyone who comes here wants to buy this and that, but must constantly leave disappointed.[61]

These "problems" came to a head when she was asked to provide craft for the 1902 *tentoonstelling*. Although receiving no acknowledgement for her intense involvement as a supplier, as it were "behind the scenes," Kartini expressed her intense delight at the exhibition's success. As she had already conveyed in earlier correspondence in relation to individual "orders," in line with its organizers she saw that this new interest in Native craft could be utilized to promote a new interest in "her people." Soon after the exhibition's opening, she wrote enthusiastically to Rosa Abendanon:

> . . . how we would love to see the exhibition! We are following everything that is being reported in the newspapers with great interest. How our hearts beat and our eyes shine since we only read so many good things about it! All of you have shown such zeal for your noble work and we wish you all, and especially our people in whose interests the work has been undertaken, the warmest best wishes for the brilliant success of the exhibition. . . . To hear of the enthusiasm of the European public for the craft and art of our people made us feel so good! We are so very proud of our people, so little known and appreciated![62]

To Abendanon's son, Eddy, Kartini exclaimed: "Hooray for the native arts and crafts: they are heading towards a fine future! I can't tell you how grateful and happy I am about this. We so love and admire our people, we so love to feel proud of them. Our people are so little known and . . . so misunderstood."[63]

After the exhibition, O&W decided to implement a regular system to enroll Kartini in the marketing of craftwork. Following initial visits in August and September 1902 from the key promoters of the exhibition, van Lawick and Victor Zimmerman,[64] van Lawick, Kartini was informed that O&W wanted to engage her on a more permanent basis to coordinate the growing flow of orders and to be responsible for arranging the payments to the Japara craft workers to ensure an orderly and regular craft

---

[61] Kartini to Mev. Abendanon, January 10, 1902. The Abendanons continued to be major "customers," as made evident when Kartini continues: "I therefore appreciate the fact that you send money in advance when you order anything. Of this I give the woodcarver a portion of what he requires in advance to buy wood and pay his assistants. But if it becomes too busy these advances will add up significantly, which I cannot afford."

[62] Kartini to Mev. Abendanon, June 10, 1902.

[63] Kartini to EC Abendanon, August 15, 1902.

[64] In her letter to E. C. Abendanon, Kartini says of Mr. Zimmerman, a prominent businessman and contributor to the exhibition that "he was in ecstasy about what he saw here of the artistic work produced by this so often scantily regarded brown race." She notes that besides woodcarving, goldsmithing, and textile crafts were also being undertaken locally. She expands on Zimmerman's visit later in a letter to Mev. Abendanon, August 4, 1902.

production.[65] As van Lawick had alluded to in his speech at the exhibition, Kartini now also had to involve herself with other practical issues related to the developing Native craft market. These included dealing with the postal office in receiving and ensuring timely payments for craftsmen, liaising with the woodcraft center on payments and production times, and having to constantly deal with reports of damage resulting from the transportation of goods by the railways.[66]

For Kartini, conforming to a European consumer focus was a pragmatic solution to educating Europeans about the Javanese while simultaneously contributing to improve Javanese economic conditions. Throughout the extensive corpus of correspondence with Rosa Abendanon dealing with the preparation and supply of items of woodcraft, Kartini proposed new ideas for items that would suit the European home for which she provided local crafters with the designs. These included products that clearly met her own needs and tastes as a sophisticated representative of a new generation of Western-educated Javanese, such as bookcases to house her growing collection of Dutch literature and writing tables such as the one at which she would sit at late into the night, writing extended letters to advance her "campaign."

At the same time, now caught up in the sudden colonial interest, and herself becoming increasingly directly involved with the Japara craft people, she also became more aware of the deep spiritual significance attached to their work. Early in 1902 she herself refers to media commentary regarding the "corruption [that] has entered the Japara woodcarving industry because the daughter of a highly placed Native officials continually requests the woodcarvers to follow European models and motifs."[67] Shrugging this off, she comments somewhat patronizingly on the "superstitious beliefs" of woodcarvers who resisted the new ideas, and who, she reports, "were terrified that the wayang spirits would be angry with them" when asked to carve them, until they were reassured by her father, using his prestige as the *bupati* to silence this protest.[68] Gradually, however, these and similar blithe comments in letters to European acquaintances about "her people" as "simple creators," creating "beautiful objects" with "extremely primitive implements," terms that she appears to have intentionally inserted to reflect European public opinion, gave way to expressions intended to convey feelings that suggest that she too was on a path of (self-)discovery.[69] Learning about her own people for one who happened "to be the child of a father to whom power and prestige had been granted," was humbling. It led her to exclaim at last: "What right did we have to accept that token of respect

---

[65] Kartini to Mev. Abendanon, September 2, 1902. She subsequently suggested to Mev. Abendanon that she organize her private orders as well: "Why don't you draw up a list of what you would like to order? Your order will then be the first attended to . . . But at the moment we honestly cannot do anything for you" (September 22, 1902).

[66] As well as such issues beyond her control, was the pressure of ensuring orders were filled on time since otherwise, as she explained to Mev. Abendanon, "if [a] particular work is not completed in time then your little girl is the one who will get it in the neck" (September 22, 1902).

[67] Kartini to Mev. Abendanon, March 5, 1902.

[68] Kartini to Mev. Abendanon, March 5, 1902. She continues: "Only when Father assured them that Father would take all responsibility and that the fury and revenge of the gods would only affect him, only trouble him, and not them, who were only carrying out orders, were they prepared to do it. How amusing it was! It goes like this in many things." She also refers to superstitious fear in relation to being photographed.

[69] In June she writes to Rosa about visiting "Native houses" "to gather ideas." Kartini to Rosa, June 10, 1902.

[the worker crouching on the ground before her] from someone whom we regarded as a hundred times our superior. I hated myself."[70]

As Kartini's association with O&W intensified in the course of 1902, Director Abendanon suggested she write an article about the Japara wood carving center, for which he would provide accompanying photographs. It would serve to enlighten a metropolitan Dutch readership about the origins of the products they were now seeing in *Boetan*. Kartini's publication, *Van een vergeten uithoekje* (From a forgotten corner), written by this already published Dutch language author well-read in contemporary modern European literature,[71] conveyed the exhilaration a (European) visitor would derive from seeing firsthand the Japara artists in action. Published in January 1903, it appeared in *Eigen Haard*, a well-respected, culturally attuned, feminist oriented, illustrated periodical devoted to the arts, literature, and "the modern."[72] It was to be the first "participant observer" account of native woodcraft practice. Such an article had previously been requested of her by Mev. Ter Horst-de Boer,[73] founder of *De Echo*, a new colonial weekly for colonial (white) women, with whom Kartini had already published several short stories.[74]

The article in *Eigen Haard* appeared at a significant moment, both in the evolution of a new European interest in "native craft" and in Kartini's personal life. The narrative copiously referenced the Batavia *tentoonstelling*, and for O&W, it provided an extravagant advertisement for its "marketing" of Native craft and its aims to promote an "understanding" of the colony.[75] For Kartini, it provided the opportunity to celebrate the art and character of her people in the full glare of the gaze of an enraptured metropolitan, and specifically culturally progressive and feminist European readership.[76] More immediately relevant for Kartini was that it came at a time when her association with the influential socialist MP, Henri van Kol, was leading to parliamentary consideration of her request to study in the Netherlands. This connection had also led to an intimate correspondence with his wife, the author and noted feminist Nellie van Kol, who

---

[70] Kartini to Mev. Abendanon, August 24, 1902 She concludes her reflection with "And this is how a member of the 'aristocratic brood' thinks; no wonder it is coming to bed down with the social democrats." This references her contact with Henri van Kol, leader of the Dutch Social Democratic party in regard to her plan to study in the Netherlands. Later, when contemplating her impending marriage and elevation to Raden Ayu, she insisted, "I do not want my foot kissed. I have never allowed anyone to do this to me." Kartini to Mev. Abendanon, August 25, 1903.

[71] See Kartini's article and her endorsement in *Eigen Haard* in Coté, *Kartini*, 769–78. See the bibliography of books cited in letters in Coté, *Kartini*, 840–48.

[72] Eigen Haard, Koninklijke Bibliotheek, https://www.kb.nl/themese/tijdschriften/eigen-haard.

[73] Kartini to Mev. Abendanon, September 22, 1902.

[74] Ter Horst–de Boer had already published two of Kartini's short stories, in 1899 and 1900 (Coté, *Kartini*, 735–68). See also Ter Horst's Kartini's obituary. J. Coté, "Kartini in Her Own Words: *Inside Indonesia*," April 2021, https://www.insideindonesia.org/kartini-in-her-own-words. Ter Horst was later to found a craft atelier to produce "authentic Native craft" for the European market. See Inge van Vught, "Dragers van Verhalen: Een kunst-en cultuurhistorisch onderzoek naar zes boekbanden vervaardigd in Nederlandsch-Indië voor de Europese markt tussen 1910 en 1940," 20–21, scriptie inge_van_vugt_definitef_scripttiearchief.pdf.

[75] Given his involvement, Kartini's article also provided useful publicity for the promotion of Abendanon's progressive Native education and industry policies, both of which eventually failed to gain political support.

[76] Prior its publication, both the colonial and metropolitan press covered the story of Kartini's (and Roekmini's) plans to study in the Netherlands, which information was reiterated in references to the article appearing in *Eigen Haard*: e.g., *Algemeen Handelsblad*, October 16, 1902, January 14, 1903, and January 16, 1903; *De Sumatra Post* July 15, 1902 and February 17, 1903; and *Het Nieuws van de Dag*, February 16, 1903.

prefaced Kartini's article in Eigen Haard with a powerful endorsement of her study ambitions. This was also the first public revelation of Kartini in the metropole, and, reiterating Nelli's comments, the periodical's editor welcomed Kartini and her ambitions into the embrace of her well-to-do readers.[77] It was publicity she later came to regret and may well have contributed to the dramatic turn that Kartini's life was to take soon thereafter.[78]

Toward Policy Settings: Native Craft in Its Imperial Setting

Two years previously, at the 1900 *Exposition Universelle* in Paris, criticism had been expressed in some Dutch reports on the Dutch pavilion's display of Native arts and crafts of the East Indies[79] that it was "cold and colourless." While "showing some respect for ancient temple architecture, there was a certain disregard for the rest."[80] What was lacking, according to this critic, was any reference to a "living" community in the Indies, and what there was had been framed in an overarching archaeological and ethnographic perspective imposed by French organizers. But, wrote this critic, an "exhibit of cultural artefacts" was "an entirely different thing than an ethnographic one." For this writer the Dutch exhibit in Paris failed to reflect the new direction that was now being taken by the government of the Netherlands Indies, which was now "striving for its [the colony's] well-being, for its industries, its cultures and everything related to these. The beautiful exhibits relevant to this have been hidden away, as if the [Dutch exhibition's commissioners] were ashamed of it."[81]

The substance of this report, that the 1900 Dutch colonial exhibit failed to give visitors any idea of the colony's "life," referenced the new lens through which *Inlandsch kunstwerk* was beginning to be appreciated, also in the colony itself. However, this criticism had a distinctly utilitarian edge: it reflected a concern that the exhibition had failed to project an image of the vital and the potential economically productive nature of the colony. To underline his point, this critic made reference to changes recently initiated at the Colonial Museum of Haarlem, a public education institution established at the initiative of the Maatschappij ter Bervordering van Nijverheid, the society for the promotion of industry.[82] This institution had recently transformed itself into a museum of colonial products based, he emphasized, "on principles of the natural sciences rather than ethnological ones." Had it not done so, the writer continued

> it would have become hopelessly lost, buried in ethnography, whereas now it has been able to develop its own specific role and is able to live with the changing colonial needs. . . . In a world struggle on the industrial stage, these relics [i.e.,

---

[77] For the text of their endorsement in *Eigen Haard*, see Coté, *Kartini*, 739–41.

[78] While her public profile no doubt assisted in her gaining Dutch government approval of her scholarship, the publicity may also have influenced the Regent of Rembang in proposing marriage.

[79] Described in *Wereld-tentoonstelling te Parijs in 1900: Afdeeligen van Nederland en de Koloniën*, Verslag van de Centrale Commissie, 1897, https://digital collections.universiteitleiden.nl/view/tem/1014075?.

[80] *Een bezoek aan de Parijsche wereldtentoonstelling van 1900*, 5, 6, https://digitalcollections.universiteitleiden.nl/view/item/1053683?.

[81] *Een bezoek*, 15. In this, the same report noted, other imperial powers were no different. The Dutch exhibit committee also did not include a representative of the East Indies.

[82] The connection is highlighted by Bloembergen, *Colonial Spectacles*, 125.

artefacts presented from an ethnological or museumological perspective] are indeed of little significance. They are so dead that they have little relevance to the present day, and even less of the future of a country or a colony.[83]

At the exhibition the Haarlem Colonial Museum mounted in 1902, this new perspective was clearly on display. Although an official "Guide for Visitors" provided the public with a special four-page introduction to the *Inlandsche kunst en kunstnijverheid*,[84] (Native arts and artistic craft work) the exhibition catalogue itself simply listed Native products alphabetically in a cumulative list together with "colonial products produced by Europeans," among which they were displayed in the hall. They were categorized as items of metal, varnish, carved ivory and wood, platted and basket work, and woven (batik and embroidery) items. Among the display of the latter were also examples of "Dutch batik technique."

In July the following year, at a national, government-initiated exhibition in Groningen where Oost en West was prominent, the Haarlem Museum announced it had achieved a breakthrough in its laboratory experimentations to produce "genuine batik" in the Netherlands. Its new product far surpassed earlier poor quality coloring of European machine fabrication. It claimed it was now able to replicate the "sharpness of color" the Native product achieved using natural elements. The museum's report emphasized how its experiments had been motivated by the recent interest in Native batik generated by the research of Royal Institute secretary, Rouffaer.[85] It was believed that, with European technology now having succeeded in replicating the original, the new Dutch or "Haarlem batik-technique" product could now be sold widely in the colony, benefitting "the Native" by making the cheaper imported product widely available. This "breakthrough" reinforced the notion that under European direction, Native craft had commercial potential, in the production of which Natives could possibly also participate, if market requirements could be met.

At the same time, the "new batik" was also an indication of how the wider Arts and Crafts movement in Europe was playing a role in identifying "Native craft," in this case batik, as an item of relevance to the modern world. A review of the Groningen craft exhibition noted the comments of the influential English arts and crafts writer Walter Crane, who, in praising the Dutch innovation, commented on the importance of the recent European interest in Native crafts as helping to stimulate the revival of decorative arts in Europe. Expanding on this theme, the reviewer continued, that research into the application "of this old Javanese method" now made it possible for "each decorative artist" in the Netherlands to

> reproduce his drawings permanently on silk, linen, parchment, leather, etc., without the intervention of a factory or paint shop. May many now feel called, as independent workers, to practice batiking with all its elements so that the Dutch

---

[83] *Een bezoek*, 16.

[84] *Gids voor de bezoekers van het Koloniaal Museum te Haarlem, Het Museum* De Bussy: Amsterdam 1902. (https://digital colllections.universiteitleiden.nl/item1053948#). The guide was specifically prepared for school children who were now also learning more about 'their' colonies from newly produced schoolbooks advocated by *Oost en West*.

[85] Quoted in *Bataviaasch Nieuwsblad*, July 22, 1903, "Haarlemsche Batikkunst: Proeven van Nederlandsche Batik."

arts and crafts will continue to be enriched by this new branch which is capable of producing as beautiful products as the Javanese art of batik making.[86]

In particular, as M. Groot has elaborated, the new interest in batik had encouraged revisiting the disappearing craft activities of Europe and the participation of women in craftwork.[87] However, these "discoveries" had not greatly diverted Europeans' attention *toward* the existence of "the Native" as creator, or to encouraging Europeans in the metropole to encompass the reality of Native life and culture in *their colony* more generally. Nor, as will be discussed below, did a new perspective on "Native products" necessarily imply new economic opportunities for Javanese producers.

OSAKA 1903

Bearing on the potential implications of a "Native arts and crafts policy" in the colony, was also the dimension of international imperialism and trade competition. The Fifth National Industrial Exhibition in Osaka, Japan, in 1903 that was belatedly expanded to become an international exhibition proved to be an ideal occasion for showcasing Dutch imperial policy at an international forum. While there was not yet a new colonial policy in place—only a general announcement of a proposed colonial "ethical policy" that would properly reflect the Christian nation—the presentation of "Native arts and crafts' at Osaka was intended to demonstrate the progressive nature of the Dutch colonial regime while simultaneously emphasizing the significance of the colonial economy. Here, in its Asian setting, although representing little more than decoration within an aggressively economic focus on colonial resources, "Native arts and crafts" could be effectively deployed as a platform for the exercise of imperial Dutch "soft power."

There had been little time to put the colonial element of the Dutch exhibit together,[88] but Dutch exhibition organizers considered the Netherlands as already ahead of the other ten foreign nations at Osaka in being able to remind a new generation of Japanese how once the Netherlands had been regarded by their ancestors as "the most prominent nation in Europe." Now, it was confidently assumed a rapidly modernizing Japan "would love nothing better than to renew and strengthen the centuries old friendship, the cooperative trade, and to increase and broaden both our shipping links."[89] With this in mind, Dutch exhibition organizers hoped that the display of colonial products at Osaka would also be a means of educating Dutch business interests on the economic importance of Japan as the market for its colonial resources where hitherto Japan had typically only been included in a category of "Sundry other countries [*sic*]" in official colonial reports.[90]

[86] *Bataviaasch Nieuwsblad*, July 22, 1903, "Haarlemsche Batikkunst."

[87] M. Groot, "Crossing the Borderlines." See also T. Eliëns, M. Groot, and F. Leidelmeijer (eds.), *Avant Garde Design: Dutch Decorative Arts 1880–1940* (London: Phillips Wilson, 1997).

[88] Organizers complained that there had been insufficient time for local experts in Batavia to collect and properly describe a range of representative items. Kartini also alluded to this in her brief reference to her possible contribution for the exhibit. The delay in having the Dutch exhibit ready for the March opening was also blamed on the slow pace of Japanese workers (*langzaamheid der Japansche werklieden*), which meant it was not ready for public viewing till April. H. Rud Du Mosch, "Verslag eener reis naar Japan," http:// digitalcollections.universiteitleiden.nl/viww/item/1052694?. The writer was deputy chair of the East Indies committee that prepared the colonial exhibit at Osaka.

[89] Du Mosch, "Verslag eener reis naar Japan."

[90] Du Mosch, "Verslag."

To consolidate the "soft power" impact of the substantial Dutch exhibition, a fifty-page English language introduction to the catalogue provided a detailed overview of the colony's resources and commercial life. This, according to the English-language *Japan Weekly Chronicle*, would be "of great use to Japanese merchants who now have, in an encyclopedic form, a list with particulars and statistics of the principal products, mineral and agricultural, of the numerous islands of the archipelago."[91]

Among the exhibits of "colonial resources" listed were items of Native arts and crafts donated by Oost en West and Mr. V. Zimmermann, the key nongovernment promoters of Native arts and crafts in the East Indies colony since the 1902 Batavia *tentoonstelling*.[92] Among these items were some originating from Japara and that Kartini referenced as having specifically arranged for sending to the 1903 Osaka exhibition.[93] The *Chronicle* described Oost en West, which had contributed "between five and six hundred items," as a society "established for the purpose of the betterment of the natives of the Dutch East Indies."[94] Its items were interspersed around the large Dutch exhibition hall, providing "a valuable introduction to the natives themselves" in a way that gave "the stranger to the colonies some idea of the extent of the native skill in handicrafts."[95] The display included many of the articles previously part of the Batavia exhibition, with an emphasis on items for everyday use, such as wooden boxes, jewelry, "and other things delightful to the feminine heart, whether she be savage and simple, or civilized and gentle."[96]

Educating the Colony: The Semarang Craft Exhibition, 1903

In 1903, as the reference at the beginning of this article suggests, there were indications that "a new wind was blowing" in the colony. It was also the year that Kartini was required to withdraw from her hectic involvement in the activities of Oost en West as a consequence of her impending marriage. She handed responsibility for her projects—the ordering of craft work and the newly established classroom—to her sister Roekmini. After initially expressing the pain she felt now confronted by her broken dreams following confirmation of the marriage, she soon assured friends of her determination to make use of the new opportunities that her prospective elevation to *Raden Ayu* would now provide.

Confident of the full the support of her intended, the Regent of Rembang, Kartini outlined to Rosa her proposal for the establishment of a purpose built, Native-led, craft workshop and training center, headed by the leading Japara craftsmen, Mas Singgwirio, with whom she had worked closely over the preceding eighteen months.[97] She was assured by M. C. Brandes, chief executive of the Cultuur Maatschappij, Der Vorstenlanen, a leading colonial financial and business entity with whom she discussed

---

[91] "At the Osaka Exhibition," *The Japan Weekly Chronicle*, May 20, 1903.

[92] Du Mosch, "Verslag," 16–22.

[93] Kartini to Mev. Abendanon, December 12, 1902.

[94] "At the Osaka Exhibition."

[95] "At the Osaka Exhibition."

[96] "At the Osaka Exhibition."

[97] Kartini to Mev. Abendanon, August 1903. He unfortunately died soon thereafter.

the plan, that funding would be "no problem."[98] Her new project clearly fitted the "new direction" being proposed by the Director of Native Industry as indicated by the 1903 press release.

Although her untimely passing in September 1904 meant her plan was not able to be realized, before her marriage in November 1903 she was engaged in one further significant project initiated by O&W: the first of its series of regional colonial craft expositions. This was to be held in Semarang in July, in premises provided by the prominent Semarang publisher, C. H. T. van Dorp,[99] a progressive publishing and newspaper company founded in the 1850s with an established interest in "Native affairs."[100]

In advance of the exposition's opening, Semarang school teacher Mejuffrouw W. J. (Mieneke) Bosch, or Mientje, as Kartini soon came to address her as, made contact with Kartini. This was perhaps not so surprising since, apart from Kartini now being well-known publicly as an enthusiastic promoter of local woodcraft and author of the recent article in *Eigen Haard*, Bosch would have heard about her locally in Semarang from her school teacher colleague at HBS Semarang, Mr. Both, who had taught Kartini French, as well as from the Semarang Resident P. H. Sijthoff, where Kartini had been a frequent guest.[101] Not long before the Resident had included her in the official European welcoming party on the occasion of the visit to Semarang of the Susunan of Solo.[102]Bosch herself had a public profile in Semarang beyond her position as HBS teacher,[103] including offering private French classes for the city's young ladies, advertisements for which appeared regularly in the local press. She was also locally active in charity work and as treasurer of the newly established local branch of the Koninklijke Natuurkundige Vereeniging, the nature conservation society.[104]

Mien had first intended to visit Kartini in Japara in June 1903 to view with her the craft workshops she had written about and which had supplied items for the exposition, but they first met in Semarang.[105] It must have been a mutually rewarding meeting, and the following month, in correspondence Kartini referred excitedly to many aspects of her personal life that would interest the school teacher, emphasizing topics such as her

[98] Kartini to Mev. Abendanon, August 25, 1903. Brandes had been appointed to the executive committee overseeing the *Mindere Welvaart Onderzoek*, the official inquiry in to the economic condition of the Indigenous population (*Soerabaijasch Handelsblad*, December 30, 1902). The *Sumatra Post* published a brief obituary in 1918: M. C. Brandes (*De Sumatra Post*, July 20, 1918).

[99] Kartini to Mev. Abendanon, July 4, 1903.

[100] See "Gedung van Dorp masa ke masa," https://festivalkotalama.com/artikel/gedung-van-dorp-masa-ke-masa/. It had pioneered publication of Malay and Javanese-language books and the first Malay-language newspaper, *Slompret Melajoe* (1860–1911) and later (1911) published the first edition of Kartini's letters.

[101] The level of intimacy in that connection is apparent from Kartini's descriptions of her visits to Semarang in correspondence with Mev. Abendanon, and in more detail in Roekmini's correspondence with Annie Glaser (unpublished). Heer Both had replaced Annie Glaser, the local Japara teacher that Abendanon had appointed to assist Kartini in preparing for her teacher certificate studies.

[102] Bosch had been the only teacher representative in the city's formal welcoming entourage that included the entire upper echelons of the local colonial administrative and business personnel.

[103] Bosch's appointment in August 1903 was featured in multiple newspaper reports referring to local public concern about lack of staff for the HBS.

[104] *Bataviaasch Nieuwsblad*, October 5, 1903. The paper also reported how she was a very welcome visitor to the Pangungsen Landkolonie, a local colonial welfare project. (*Bataviaasch Nieuwsblad*, July 16, 1903).

[105] Kartini to Mej. Bosch, June 8, 1903 (unpublished). Kartini arranged to meet a week later in Semarang when she was there staying with her brother.

recently established classroom and her brother's academic success in the Netherlands.[106] But Kartini's main objective lay in asking Bosch for her "assistance to make our beautiful art known and develop."[107] Unfortunately, Kartini had been ill when Bosch did visit Japara, as she had so much wanted to "tell you about our people and to show them to you when you were here; to know the soul of our childlike people and come to love them. That inner soul we had so much wanted to reveal to you."[108] She was thus now all the more grateful to Mien Bosch for being willing to "assist us to make our arts known," a promise that Bosch soon fulfilled with an enthusiastic article published in the local press.[109]

A few days later, Kartini wrote again to Mienetje about a "collection of Japara craft pieces I have just sent off" to the van Dorp showroom, urging her to quickly take a look and write to her soon with her impressions, expressing the hope of coming to Semarang soon to see the exhibition for herself.[110] However, on the very day she sent off the items of Japara wood carving to Semarang, her father confirmed his approval of her marriage about which she had had intimations already in June.[111] She was now committed to preparing for the marriage and unable to visit in person to see her people's craft on display before a European assembly.

Mieneke Bosch's response to Kartini's request, undoubtedly influenced by her introduction to the "real world" of Japara, expressed something new in the colonial rhetoric surrounding *Inlandsche kunstnijverheid*. Her review of the Semarang exhibition published soon after it opened gave extravagant praise to the artistry and craftsmanship on display, focusing largely on the wood carvings from Japara. In describing the beauty of the carved wayang figures, the Naga, and the general impression of foliage and bird life inserted into the carvings, Bosch expressed her wonder in "Arts and Crafts" terms at "this extraordinary folk art" that clearly revealed the "artists who carry these images in their soul, [and] have recreated them with masterly inspiration."[112]

Bosch's article commenced by drawing a contrast between what appeared to be a general colonial European public perception that such craft was a disappearing tradition, a key trope in the current media discourse on the "declining welfare of the native", and its obvious survival and relevance to contemporary Native life in the Javanese

---

[106] Kartini to Mej. Bosch, July 5, 1903 (unpublished).

[107] Kartini to Mej. Bosch, July 5, 1903.

[108] Kartini to Mien, July 5, 1903. She was entertained by her sister, Roekmini.

[109] Mien continued the acquaintance after Kartini's marriage and visited her in Rembang the following year. Kartini to Mej Bosch, June 15, 1903, 9 July 1904 (unpublished).

[110] Kartini to Mej. Bosch, July 8, 1903 (unpublished). Other than woodcraft, Kartini also prepared tortoise shell and Japara *dringen* (silk cloth), the sale of the latter she requested Mien to arrange on her behalf and for which she had written a brief description. Kartini to Mien Bosch, July 16, 1903 (unpublished).

[111] This sequence of events is detailed in Kartini's letters to both the Abendanons from June 22, 1903. In her letter of July 16 to Mien, Kartini apologizes for the gap in her correspondence, promising to explain the reason (i.e., the marriage plans, although this is not mentioned) when she would be in Semarang staying with her brother.

[112] "Inlandsche kunstnijverheid te Semarang (Geschreven voor de Locomotief)," *De Locomotief*, July 11, 1903. Although unsigned, her authorship can be deduced from its praise to Kartini and Kartini's later expression of appreciation of her article in *De Locomotief* in her July 16 letter in which she thanks Mien for the "beautiful article" in which she could "feel the thoughts of the writer" (Kartini to Mej. Bosch, July 16, 1903 [unpublished]).

heartland. In urban Semarang, she commented, "old Semarangers" would typically say "One doesn't see this anymore," "It is impossible to get them," "It seems that this [craft making] is finished." In contrast she recalled her visit to village Java where "everywhere one sees beautiful homes whose interiors are decorated with wood carving." While this was most evident in the case of the Japara *kabupaten,* with its beautiful interior paneling (*prachtige lambriseering*), in fact "even in the most isolated *desa,* so much effort and cost is expended on decorating their houses."[113] Nevertheless, Bosch spoke of the importance of "rescuing" this traditional art form, while at the same time warning that any revival needed to guard against the introduction of "all kinds of European motives which, unfortunately too often have served to spoil beautiful batik work."

Besides recognizing the efforts of Mev. Abendanon and Oost en West for their work in advancing the appreciation of Native arts and crafts, the article paid particular homage to the work of the "Japara Raden Ajengs."[114]

> The committed efforts of the daughters of the regent of Japara who with heart and soul are working to promote the beautiful Javanese wood carving art and who, as a consequence of this, have become the energetic coworkers of Oost en West. Because they, by their circumstances and location, are able to exercise much influence on the simple artists in more isolated desas, it is of significance to get to know their perceptions and principles regarding the direction in which the revival of arts and crafts need to be directed.

Reporting on the unfortunately absent Kartini, the writer recounted how during this time

> Lady Kartini, the oldest daughter of the Regent of Japara, is tirelessly thinking about and weighing up ideas about new forms, new models and will not rest until she has brought the woodcrafter to consider broader approaches, while constantly stressing to him the respect that exists for the Javanese motifs. She therefore asks politely in a note to the public to have patience with Singowirio because there is only one master of the *art,* and only one thinking head which finds its inspiration in his heart, as he expresses it in his poetic way of speaking. Others simply work according to a pattern, they are no more than clever workers and their appearance is so different to that of the creator of the *art,* whose eyes sparkle with a mysterious gleam.

Although not free of the now recognizable colonial overtones that had characterized so much of the commentary in the colonial press, her admiration for *Inlandsche* arts was also clearly concerned to position Javanese arts in the context of the European arts and crafts movement. This she made evident in referencing the recent 1903 publication by Dutch artist, writer, and English arts and crafts enthusiast Etha Fles.[115] As her characterization of the interiors of village homes "decorated with wood carving" might

---

[113] The article notes the widely accepted assumption that "one feared that this original art would die out if there was not powerful support either in the Indies or from Europe."

[114] The plural here references the important role of Roekmini, who escorted Bosch when Kartini was ill.

[115] Margaretha Yekia Johanna Fles, "Inleiding tot een kunstgechiedenis," https://www.resources.huygens. knaw.nl/vrouwenlexicon/lemamata/data/Fles. Fles is regarded as a "pioneer advocate of modern art" and supporter of the socialist ideals of John Ruskin and William Morris and a "community arts movement." She had participated in the preparation of the Dutch exhibit of arts and crafts at the 1900 Paris exhibition. Bosch

already suggest, Bosch insisted that the encouragement of Native arts and crafts needed to operate along the lines of the

> modern idea of decorative arts which fortunately is becoming more and more prevalent . . . [This] was no doubt also lying unconsciously in the soul of these Javanese Raden Ajengs. Now that they have devoted themselves to secure the blossoming of this *art* and find new channels for its expression, they have readily been able to appropriate these [modern] perceptions.[116]

Although she admired Kartini "[a]s a passionate advocate of her national art, . . . concerned to ensure that this remains purely Javanese," Bosch also stressed, echoing William Morris's principles, "[i]t must be an art *industry*, applied art, which will contribute to the beauty of the whole, and absolutely not be another useless object, only destined to be admired behind a glass cover."

Imagining a Native Industry 1904

Unlike the consumer- and policy-focused Oost en West organization, Bosch's review of the craft exhibition represented an appreciation of an Indigenous art form inspired by the discourse of the contemporary European arts and crafts movement. It paid homage to its Javanese creators, situating Kartini as a pioneer in uncovering this art form to a European gaze. However, for colonial policy makers and the scientists at the Haarlem museum, as much as for the Vereeniging Oost en West and the planners for the Dutch exhibits at international exhibitions, the central interest remained the possible value of craft work as a form of Native "industry" and a focus of paternal colonialism.

In 1904 the potential policy and practical issues of a "Native industry" had yet to be teased out. Were Native arts and crafts to be encouraged to become a productive economic activity? If so, was it to be an avenue for the expression of Native skill, initiative, and autonomy, or an arena of European skill enhancement and cooption? Were Natives capable of conducting an industry in modern terms? Would it indeed answer to the needs of "Native welfare" as represented by the new "ethical policy," or represent an effective contribution to the colony's natural and human resources? These were now the themes of several major inquiries in both the colony and the imperial center in the context of elaborating a new colonial policy.

The first inquiry into the possible solutions to improve the "less than optimal Native welfare" was the *Mindere Welvaart Onderzoek*, commenced in 1902. It was initially focused on investigating ways to improve Javanese agricultural practices. Extending for more than a decade, the *Onderzoek* continued producing numerous, largely inconclusive reports on many economic and social topics concerned with Native welfare.[117] Of more immediate consequence were two inquiries undertaken in 1904 by "colonial experts," one in The Hague, chaired by Conrad van Deventer, the other, a local inquiry undertaken by

---

notes that Fles had compared Javanese art with that of the Greeks, but Bosch believed a more appropriate comparison was with the human representation manifested in Egyptian art.

[116] Throughout the article Bosch emphasized (through the use of italics) that she considered Native craft as *kunst'*—art.

[117] Van den Doel, *De stille kracht*, 230–38. It published its first cumulative reports on regional assessments of Native "handel en nijverheid"—trade and industry—in 1906.

the Director of Native Industry, Jacques Abendanon. Both aimed to identify a moral and, at the same time, practical basis for an improved Native economy in the context of an expanding colonial investment. Each drew on similar assumptions about "the Native's" innate abilities, even if coming to differing policy outcomes.

In the course of 1904, Abendanon, as Director of Native Industry, held a series of local conferences to assess local support for his policy objectives aimed at stimulating a Native craft industry as a strategy for addressing declining Native welfare. One of the many such conferences was held in Semarang in April 1904. The two-day meeting, reported in detail in the local press,[118] was held at the official residence, the *Kabupaten*, of the regent of Semarang and attended by an estimated forty regional businessmen, colonial officials, and several high-ranking Javanese including the regents of Semarang, Demak, and Kudus. The conference was chaired by the Semarang resident, Piet Sijthoff, who had shown himself a firm supporter of Kartini's efforts to promote Japara craft work.[119]

The Semarang meeting was preceded by a viewing of a small but elegant exposition of Native craft mounted by the Regent. Although this clearly was not the focus of the majority present, it was evidently of interest to Abendanon, who made a point of spending a full hour before the meeting to view and discuss the items on display. As reported, the two-day meeting was characterized by a robust exchange of views between three interest groups: regional European businessmen mainly engaged with colonial commercial agriculture, several regional colonial officials, and the director. Their disparate views, as reported in the press and later summarized in Abendanon's official report, constituted a representative cross-section of the contemporary colonial response to the general question as to how the issue of Native industry, now the focus of a colonial "welfare policy," might be addressed.

It was clear that Abendanon had arrived at the Semarang meeting with an explicit agenda with which he hoped to convince the region's private and official government representatives. To the latter he suggested they immediately institute a regional survey, "whether this be in terms of the availability of particularly good raw material, or the particular ability of local craft workers" that could provide a rational basis for a promotion of Native industries in the region. This would ensure that "no artificial promotion of an industry would result but rather that a more rational distribution of economic activity across the region" could be implemented. Preempting an obvious objection that *Inlanders* would not be able to compete in a world market, he clarified that any such industries would have to find their market locally, for instance to serve the needs of urban Semarang. He also made it immediately clear to business interests present that it was not the government's intention to provide interest-free loans to European firms merely so that a few more Natives could be employed. What he wanted to see develop was a *vereeniging van inlandsche nijvaren*, an association of Native industries, much like the arrangement made by European colonial investors, so that "with an advance from government funds," several industries that were in the interests of local Javanese communities could be developed. Among these could be craft industries.

[118] "Indische Nijverheid," *De Locomotief*, April 16, 1904.

[119] Sijthoff had attended Kartini's wedding in November the previous year. Despite his support for her efforts, he had officially advised against supporting her request to study in the Netherlands and had always urged Kartini to marry.

Those identified by the newspaper as offering the most strident opposition to the propositions Abendanon was attempting to have accepted were a junior but well informed local *controleur*, A. H. J. G. Walbeehm, and a high-profile local European entrepreneur, C. C. Zeverijn. Walbeehm, whose past appointments since entering civil service in 1889 were mainly in the region, was convinced he had a better grasp of what was in the Native's best interest than the director. This, he made clear, was based on his record of public involvement in "the Native question" regularly cited in press commentary.[120] Zeverijn was a prominent entrepreneur, past treasurer of the Semarang Chamber of Commerce, and at the time principal of agent of the Cultuur Maatschapij Der Vorstenlanden, headed by M. C. Brandes, the group of European entrepreneurs and financiers exploiting agricultural production in the principalities of Yogyakarta and Surakarta. He was also directly engaged in an experimental project to improve irrigation in the territory of the Solo sultanate and was a leading figure in the Vereeniging van Europeese Landhuurders (Association of [European] land renters), the European entrepreneurs involved in renting Javanese kampong land to control the production and commercialization of agriculture in the region.[121]

During the first day's meeting Walbeehm held the floor to present a bleak outlook regarding the future of "native industries." Echoing others, he pointed to the poor quality and potential over-production that would result from promoting Native industries that would "spoil the market," or alternatively, artificially increase prices so as to disadvantage the Native consumer. Previous trials to teach Natives better production methods had failed because "*inlanders* did not even stay for two days with this instructor," according to Walbeehm. He was adamant therefore that "no *inlanders* should ever be appointed at the head of an enterprise, or even to have a senior position." He asked rhetorically: "How could one expect, where civilized European nations were only able to achieve this in three hundred years, that natives could achieve this [establishing industries] in only a few years. You could not turn a native into an independent industrialist even in ten or twenty years"

The second day was dominated by the Semarang Chamber of Commerce and presided over by Mr. Zeviers. Responding to Walbeehm's conclusion of the previous day, Abendanon opened that day's meeting with a question:

> Was it considered possible to train young Natives to work in the area of trade so that, for instance, first as clerks or office scribes, they could be prepared to independently establish themselves as small traders and shopkeepers. If so, would the establishment of a basic trade school be necessary for this? And what subjects would need to be taught at such a school.

Led by Zeviers, the businessmen made clear that, from their experience, Natives themselves accepted as given that the highest level they could manage was that of a *mandur* (foreman); even if provided with government loans, as Abendanon suggested, they would never be able to compete with "the Chinese or haji"—here referencing

---

[120] Walbeehm's first appointment was as *aspirant controleur* on November 23, 1889 in Pati. In 1898 he had been appointed to conduct a regional ethnographic study of the local Javanese dialect and his "Javaase Sprakkunst" was reviewed in *De Locomotief*, February 7, 1898. He was a descendent of an Indies family whose name appears in the colonial press from as far back as 1847.

[121] *De Locomotief*, July 26, 1900; *Batavia Nieuwsblad*, July 7, 1902; *De Locomotief*, September 27, 1904.

Arab—businessmen. To protect a Native industry, for instance fisheries, by imposing tariffs would only provide them with jobs at the expense of their own people as consumers. In this context the example of imported batik was raised: to attempt to protect the Javanese batik industry with a higher import tariff would require a duty of between 300 and 400 percent, which, the "concerned" businessmen agreed, would again simply disadvantage the Native consumer.

> The only thing that could eventually be done would be to begin making batik in the Indies by the same means as in Europe, that is by machine. But the raw material would still need to be imported from Europe and the European machine would be doing the work. So the only thing that would be achieved would be that some natives would be receiving a day wage as a factory worker while, for this, the rest of native society would be having to pay more for their item of clothing.

Another heated discussion arose in relation to whether, as an example, Javanese should be encouraged to engage in the sugar industry as independent farmers. This was also strenuously opposed on the grounds that this would likely ruin the European-controlled sugar industry because "leaving this to the care of native sugar farmers would produce hotbeds of plant diseases (*broeinesten van plantensziekten*) the result of which would be that the European sugar industry, which surely is important for a large segment of the population, would be threatened."[122]

At the end of 1904, Abendanon presented his official report to the colonial government in which he acknowledged the general opposition of the colonial entrepreneurial lobby to his ideas.[123] Nevertheless, he persisted with his view in identifying Native craft production as constituting a viable Native industry. He recommended the establishment of vocational training centers and a continuation of exhibitions and markets to promote Native crafts, along the lines initiated by Oost en West, and a policy recommendation preempted in the 1903 press announcement cited at the beginning of this essay. Abendanon's proposals were fulsomely endorsed by van Lawick and Jasper, who appended separate reports to the director's submission.[124] Even they, however, were divided on whether "the Native" would be capable of sustaining a viable industry that met European standards by themselves, both urging the necessity of "European guidance."

The recommendations Abendanon presented in his report were rejected. It was evident that his views went far beyond what the business lobby, and a colonial public, could find acceptable or even envisage. This was not only because of the general assumption of Native incompetence, but of the threat "the Native" might pose to the

---

[122] On the discourse within and with regard to the contemporary colonial sugar industry, see J. Coté "'A Teaspoon of Sugar . . .': Assessing the Sugar Content in Colonial Discourse in the Dutch East Indies, 1880 to 1914," in *Sugarlandia Revisited. Sugar and Colonialism in Asia and the Americas 1880–1940*, ed. Ulbe Bosma, Juan A. Giust-Cordero, and G. Roger Knight (New York: Berghahn Books, 2007), 113–44.

[123] J. Abendanon, *Rapport van den Directeur van Onderwijs, Eerendienst en Nijverheid betreffende de maatregelen in het belang van de Inlandsche nijverheid op Java en Madoera in verband met de moederland voor dit doel beschikbaar te stellen fondsen* (Batavia: Landsdrukkerij, 1904). See also van Miert, *Bevlogenheid en Onvermogen*, 70–79.

[124] J. E. Jasper, "Nota van de controleur bij het Binnenlands Bestuur …over het opbeuren van Inlandsche nijverheid" (1904); H. J. W van Pabst van Lawick, "Bijlage111. Nederlandsch-Indiesche Vereenging Oost en West" (1904).

colonial economy, as businessmen at the Semarang meeting had suggested. Beyond their concern about possible loss of market share or damage to agriculture was more importantly an unspoken concern that promotion of Native industry threatened their access to cheap labor.[125] This was made clear by the second report commissioned in 1904 in the Netherlands to consider Native policy. It was overseen by one of the architects of a new "ethical" colonial policy, the former Semarang private company lawyer and sugar industry investor, now "colonial specialist," Conrad van Deventer. Appointed to head a parallel "desk" inquiry in the imperial capital, in his "Overzicht" (summary) of several separate extensive reports by recognized colonial experts, van Deventer concluded that the only practical solution to address Native welfare was to engage the Native in a more vibrant European colonial economy—that is, as labor.[126]

Conclusion

This article has set out to sketch the contours of one "moment" in the much longer and more complex trajectory of the history of the evolution of a modern Indonesian consciousness. It has intentionally aimed to give space to some of the representative voices of this moment of "living history" when most were silenced and unseen. It was a moment when, at least for Kartini, the "green shoots" of European interest in Native arts and crafts might have suggested the beginnings of a new era in colonial relations that she had been eager to help foster. This was of course, not be.

After the resignation of a disillusioned Abendanon in 1905, who however continued his work in Europe,[127] it was in particular J. E. Jasper who continued to effectively pursue a program of promoting local Native arts and crafts exhibitions. The highlight of Jasper's career was the publication in the Netherlands between 1912 and 1916 of a five-volume scholarly account of Java's rich arts and crafts heritage, *Inlandsche kunstnijverheid in Nederlandsch-Indië*, authored with the assistance of Mas Pirngadie, a much-valued Javanese employee at the Bataviaasche Genootschap museum.[128] Although there is no evidence that Kartini's proposed craft factory in Rembang eventuated, her older brother, Boesono, with Jasper's cooperation maintained a craft training *huisvlijt* school after his appointment as Regent of Ngawi.[129] Roekmini and the two younger sisters, Kartinah and Soematri, who also remained involved with the promotion of Japara crafts, including working with Oost en West to provide for their colonial and European market arts and crafts market. In 1906 Roekmini wrote excitedly of her involvement in curating her contribution of Japara craft at the first *Jaarmarkt-tentoonstelling* (annual market and

---

[125] For an extended assessment of Abendanon's educational and industry policy in the context of and subsequent policy debates, see van Miert, *Bevolgenheid en onvermogen*, 68–81.

[126] C. van Deventer, *Overzicht van den economischen toestand der Inlandsche bevolking van Java en Madoera*, ('s-Gravenhage: Martinus Nijhoff, 1904); Mr. D. Fock, *Beschouwingen en vorstellen ter verbetering van den economischen toestand der Inlandsche bevolking van Java en Madoera* ('s-Gravenhage: Martinus Nijhoff, 1904); E. B. Kielstra, *Financiën van Nederlandsch-Indië* ('s-Gravenhage: Martinus Nijhoff, 1904). It also included a report by batik expert G. P. Rouffaer, "De voornaamste industrieën der Inandsche bevolking van Java en Madoera, aanhangsel tot het overzicht van . . . Mr C.T. van Deventer."

[127] Van Miert, *Bevolgenheid en onvermogen*, ch. 5 and 6.

[128] Jasper's interest in the arts extended beyond Indonesia, with articles on Islamic art, Chinese ceramics, Indian weaving, and arts and crafts in British India. See van Doorn, *Johan Ernst Jasper*.

[129] Roekmini to Annie Glaser, May 30, 1906 (unpublished).

exhibition) held in Surabaya in 1906 and 1908 organized by Jasper. This, like the original exhibition in Batavia, provided both a "showing" and a point of sale for local craft.[130] In 1907 Jasper proposed using the profits from the exhibition to establish a craft school for "Native girls" focusing on teaching the skills of batik, weaving, and plaiting, for which he had asked the three sisters to be the teachers.[131]

Meanwhile, the three sisters also continued to advance the more explicitly political objectives of Kartini's original vision. Although now removed from the kabupaten following the death of their father, R. M. A. A. Sosroningrat, in 1908, they were at the forefront of an emerging "movement amongst educated Javanese"[132] to promote the interests of the Javanese people. In July, the Semarang newspaper *De Locomotief* carried a "Call to Young Java" signed by "the three raden ajengs of Japara", Summarized in numerous other colonial and Netherlands media, the *Arnhemsche Courant*),reported to its readers in the Netherlands, that the three "pioneers" (*baanbrekers)* had been issuing this circular "on a large scale" using a "snowball method" to promote the idea of forming an organization "through which the new generation of Javanese intellectuals (*de Jong Javanen*) could express their demands for emancipation more forcefully."[133] The stated aim of their circular was to establish an association of educated Javanese with the view to produce its own publication in which

> We could publicize our holy struggle, that of the development (*opheffing*) of our people; in which we could discuss our weak points and the means by which these could be improved, in which we could take a stand against the less than friendly expressions published in the press . . . [which are] so offensive to our national feeling [*ons national ge*voel] such as: the Javanese are untrustworthy.[134]

According to other Javanese contributors to the colonial press supporting this idea, what was needed was to "bring people together as up to now no bond exists, no shared feeling exists amongst us, we hardly know each other, we ourselves don't even know what strengths lie sleeping within our people."[135]

To underline the seriousness of the *raden ajengs* in "wanting to break with the old traditions, adats, in so far as these might prove to be an obstruction to the appropriation

[130] "Roekmini to Mev. Abendanon, March 7, 1906," in *Realizing the Dream of R. A. Kartini*, ed. Joost Coté (Athens, Ohio: Ohio University Press, 2008), 122; "Roekmini to Mev. Abendanon, October 28, 1906," in Coté, *Realizing the Dream*, 125; Roekmini to Annie Glaser, May 30, 1906 (unpublished). J. E. Japer, *Verslag van de eerste Jaarmarkt-Tentoonstelling te Soerabaya* (Semarang: G. C. T. van Dorp, 1906); "De jaarmarkt tentoonstelling," *Soerabaijasche Handelsblad*, May 7, 1906.

[131] Roekmini to Mev. Abendanon, December 2, 1907. The plan was postponed till after the 1908 tentoonstelling, but the sisters' involvement did not eventuate due to Roekmini's marriage the following year.

[132] "Java Vooruit," *Algemeen Handelsblad*, August 5, 1908. For the text of the circular and Roekmini's own comments, see Roekmini to Mev. Abendanon, June 17, 1908.

[133] *Arnhemsche Courant*, September 25, 1908. The *Courant* begins its article with "The victory begins at Japara," a mock reference to a possible Indonesian insurrection, although it reports favorably on the content and intentions of the sisters' circular.

[134] *Arnhemsche Courant*, September 25, 1908. This sentiment echoes that expressed by Kartini in her correspondence with Mienke Bosch cited earlier.

[135] *De Sumatra Post*, July 15, 1908, citing other colonial papers. The later *Courant* article referencing the already announced Javanese "Bond" predicted that "much good will flow for the development of the Javanese from the establishment of this organisation working in cooperation with the government which these days is also wanting to go in this direction."

of enlightened ideas," the *Courant* explained to its readers how the eldest, Roekmini, had recently married a non-aristocrat but modern thinking *wedono* who shared her ideas about working for the advancement of Java.[136] In the end the Japara sisters' *Java Vooruit* initiative was overtaken by a much more ambitious and more securely embedded proposal: to establish an association of Javanese intellectuals, *een Javaanschen Bond*, soon to be known as Budi Utomo.[137]

And so the long journey to "Merdeka!" began.

---

[136] See Roekmini to Mev. Abendanon, June 17, 1908, September 26, 1908. The point being highlighted was that Roekmini, as a daughter of a *Raden Ayu*, R. A. Moerjam, was expressing modern "democratic tendencies" by "marrying down."

[137] Fulsomely reported in the *Preanger Bode*, October 6, 1908, and *Bataviaasche Nieuwsblad*, October 8, 1908. See also Roekmini to Mev. Abendanon, September 26, 1908.

The Indonesian Central Government in Local Conflict Resolution

Lessons from the Reconciliation of Nahdlatul Wathan

Saipul Hamdi and Kevin W. Fogg

In September 2019, some five thousand people from towns and villages across the island of Lombok came to demonstrate at the provincial office of the Ministry of Law and Human Rights in Mataram, West Nusa Tenggara, over a dispute between two factions of an organization. While a large demonstration by an Islamic group is not exceptional in Indonesia, it is noteworthy that this action took the form of a protest against a symbol of the national government—instead of the apparatus of the rival organization. From the start of the *Reformasi* period, the two factions of the Islamic organization Nahdlatul Wathan have been in continual conflict, but this had long taken the form of violence and competition in nongovernmental forums. Since 2019, the conflict—and eventual reconciliation—has moved largely into arenas mediated by the Indonesian national government.

This article discusses not just why the two factions of a mass Islamic organization that split in the 1990s would reconcile now, but specifically why they would actively

Saipul Hamdi is a senior lecturer in Sociology at the University of Mataram in West Nusa Tenggara, Indonesia. Kevin W. Fogg is Associate Director of the Carolina Asia Center at the University of North Carolina at Chapel Hill. We thank Sarah Grossman and an anonymous reviewer from the journal *Indonesia* for their feedback.

seek central government intervention in their reconciliation and follow government guidance for that intervention. This case extends our understanding of social conflict resolution in post-authoritarian Indonesia, in addition to its contribution to the study of Islamic organizational life and of society on Lombok.

In the transition out of the authoritarian Suharto regime in Indonesia, social conflict emerged across the archipelago. Small-scale violence lingered for decades after the transition to the *Reformasi* era, even as large-scale violence subsided.[1] The case study in this article looks fundamentally unlike most of the conflicts that have been the focus of previous scholarship, and its resolution also points toward a shift in the role of the state in Indonesian society.

This study challenges some of the stereotypes about religious violence in Indonesia since 1998, because although the dividing lines on Lombok were clearly between two different communities organized around religion, the religion in question was the same: Islam. This makes the case markedly different from the work of Ward Barenschot or Christopher R. Duncan on North Maluku, Lorraine Aragon or Dave McRae on Central Sulawesi, and even John T. Sidel's broad thesis about the motivating factors that pushed Muslims into various forms of nativist and religious violence around 1998.[2] Within Sidel's framework, the social conflicts around Nahdlatul Wathan most closely align with the form and context of "riots," happening in provincial towns and cities where the "institutions of Islamic learning, association, and political activity enjoyed a special claim on the public sphere."[3] Still, these conflicts were not just a groundswell of discontented and disempowered Muslim masses looking for an outlet; they were openly and unambiguously part of a power struggle between known rival sets of elites.

Thus, this case fits the traditional definitions of neither ethnic nor religious violence—as were the focus of so much attention in the first decade of this century.[4] Rather, Nahdlatul Wathan on Lombok represents a pure case of social conflict. Although it was deeply ingrained and resulted in loss of life, much property damage, and a very tense environment for over two decades, it did not fall along the lines that have been most commonly tracked by scholars. In that way, it bears some greater similarities to the political schisms of the last several decades, such as the multiple splits within the political parties Golkar and PPP.[5]

[1] Patrick Barron, Sana Jaffrey and Ashutosh Varshney, "When Large Conflicts Subside: The Ebbs and Flows of Violence in Post-Suharto Indonesia," *Journal of East Asian Studies* 16 (2016): 191–217.

[2] Ward Barenschot, "Patterned Pogroms: Patronage Networks as Infrastructure for Electoral Violence in India and Indonesia," *Journal of Peace Research* 57, no. 1 (2020): 171–84; Christopher R. Duncan, *Violence and Vengeance: Religious Conflict and Its Aftermath in Eastern Indonesia* (Ithaca, NY: Cornell University Press, 2013); Lorraine Aragon, "Communal Violence in Poso, Central Sulawesi: Where People Eat Fish and Fish Eat People," *Indonesia* 72 (2001): 45–79; Dave McRae, *A Few Poorly Organized Men: Interreligious Violence in Poso, Indonesia* (Boston: Brill, 2013); John T. Sidel, *Riots, Pogroms, Jihad: Religious Violence in Indonesia* (Ithaca, NY: Cornell University Press, 2006).

[3] Sidel, *Riots, Pogroms, Jihad*, 101.

[4] Edward Aspinall, "Ethnic and Religious Violence in Indonesia: A Review Essay," *Australian Journal of International Affairs* 62, no. 4 (2008): 558–72.

[5] Aisah Putri Budiatri, *Faksi dan Konflik Internal Partai Politik di Indonesia Era Reformasi* (Jakarta: Yayasan Obor, 2018); Firman Noor, "Leadership and Ideological Bond: PPP and Internal Fragmentation in Indonesia," *Studia Islamika* 23, no. 1 (2016): 61–103; Marcus Meitzner, "Indonesian Parties Revisited: Systemic Exclusivism, Electoral Personalisation and Declining Intraparty Democracy," in *Democracy in Indonesia: From Stagnation to Regression?*, ed. Thomas Power and Eve Warburton (Singapore: ISEAS, 2020), 191–209.

This case study of Nahdlatul Wathan not only compliments the current scholarship on the nature of social conflict in Indonesia, but also challenges previous studies about conflict resolution in the archipelago. The bulk of the scholarship has emphasized the centrality of non-state actors to effective resolution.[6] In one of the most exhaustive surveys on violence from 1996 to 2006, Yuhki Tajima argued that overreliance on the state during the New Order period had led to much of the conflict after the fall of authoritarianism, because groups could no longer rely on the state as a mediator.[7] In a related vein, Patrick Barron, Sana Jaffrey, and Ashutosh Varshney have argued that the post-1998 state has been most effective at keeping a lid on major armed conflict but has not been effective at promoting or facilitating real reconciliation between conflicting groups.[8] These studies point alternatively to the state's lack of authority with the conflicting parties or the state's lack of capacity to facilitate conflict resolution.

Reconciliation, or *islah* to use the Arabic term that has been adopted for this Islamic context, is a key step in the process of conflict resolution. Reconciliation is not a box to tick, but rather a process that must be followed by the agents of a conflict to facilitate further steps in resolution. Reconciliation overlaps with the process of healing the wounds and trauma of society, seeking justice and truth and mutual forgiveness between the victims and perpetrators of violence.[9] David Bloomfield, Teresa Barnes, and Luc Huyse note that reconciliation can require several decades or even generations.[10] In this case, the supposed *islah* has come after one generation, but has also appeared very quickly after a reconciliation pushed onto the organizational elites by the government. This raises questions about whether it is actual reconciliation within society, or merely a kind of new equilibrium among power players. This study builds on and speaks to broader themes raised in earlier studies by Saipal Hamdi and Hamdi and Bianca J. Smith[11] in relation to conflict and the reluctance to reconcile within NW.

Nahdlatul Wathan in 2021 is an example of the central government having not only the authority and the capacity to negotiate a resolution between the parties of a longstanding social conflict, but also the interest to do so. This reflects a change from the last twenty years, and it suggests a more assertive central state in Indonesian society.

---

[6] See, for example, the authors in part III of Charles A. Coppel, ed., *Violent Conflicts in Indonesia: Analysis, Representation, Resolution* (London: Routledge, 2006); Suprapto, "Religious Leaders and Peace Building: The Roles of Tuan Guru and Pedanda in Conflict Resolution in Lombok—Indonesia," *Al-Jāmi'ah: Journal of Islamic Studies* 53, no. 1 (2015): 225–50; and Alexandre Pelletier and Jessica Soedigdo, "The De-escalation of Violence and the Political Economy of Peace-Mongering: Evidence from Maluku, Indonesia," *South East Asia Research* 25, no. 4 (2017): 325–41.

[7] Yuhki Tajima, *The Institutional Origins of Communal Violence: Indonesia's Transition from Authoritarian Rule* (Cambridge: Cambridge University Press, 2014).

[8] Barron, Jaffrey, and Varshney, "When Large Conflicts Subside."

[9] David Bloomfield, Teresa Barnes, and Luc Huyse, *Reconciliation after Violent Conflict: A Handbook* (Stockholm: The International IDEA, 2006), 11–14.

[10] Bloomfield, Barnes, and Huyse, *Reconciliation*, 22.

[11] Saipul Hamdi, *Nahdlatul Wathan di Era Reformasi: Agama, Konflik Komunal, dan Peta Rekonsiliasi* (Yogyakarta: Kurnia Kalam Semesta, 2014), "Politik Islah: Renegosiasi Islah, Konflik, dan Kekuasaan dalam Nahdlatul Wathan di Lombok Timur," *Kawistara* 1 (2011): 1–14; Saipul Hamdi and Bianca J. Smith, "Sisters, Militias and Islam in Conflict: Questioning 'Reconciliation' in Nahdlatul Wathan, Lombok, Indonesia," *Contemporary Islam* 1, no. 6 (2012): 29–43.

Nahdlatul Wathan: A Mass Islamic Organization Split in Two

The organization Nahdlatul Wathan has been the dominant nongovernmental institution on the island of Lombok since Indonesian independence.[12] The central figure of this movement was Tuan Guru Kyai Haji Muhammad Zainuddin Abdul Majid (1908–97, hereafter Tuan Guru Zainuddin), who was educated in Mecca before returning to Lombok and founding a school in Pancor in 1935, with the name Nahdlatul Wathan Diniyyah Islamiyyah (Revival of the Nation Islamic Religion, hereafter NWDI). Through the example of its high standards and modern format, and through the powerful charisma of its founder, this school grew in the 1940s into a network of schools spreading out from East Lombok, planted by Tuan Guru Zainuddin with alumni of the mother school as the staff. In 1953, the network formally established an organization, called Nahdlatul Wathan (Revival of the Nation, hereafter NW).

From the 1950s to 1999, NW's influence over Sasak Muslims was unrivaled. This was largely embodied in Tuan Guru Zainuddin, who was inexhaustible in his educational and propagation efforts. He also involved himself directly in politics, both supporting candidates and (during the 1950s and 1960s) serving as a national legislator himself. One Swedish anthropologist visiting Lombok in the 1970s estimated that the anniversary celebrations for the founding of NWDI would draw half a million people to Pancor each year—one quarter of the Muslim population of the island![13] By the 1990s, Nahdlatul Wathan had established over six hundred Islamic schools across Lombok, each operating quasi-independently but under the direction of Tuan Guru Zainuddin's leadership and instruction.[14]

The ubiquity of NW did not mean that it was without internal conflict, and two serious issues arose in the 1970s. First, the leadership of the organization chose to align politically with Golkar, the Suharto regime's ruling party, after the party restructuring process of 1973. This led many within the organization to dissent, with the argument that NW should be supporting the Islamic political party. The dissenters were promptly exiled from the organization by Tuan Guru Zainuddin—providing an organizational precedent for excommunication over political questions. The second conflict was both an organizational and a family conflict, and it connects more directly with later conflicts within the organization. Tuan Guru Zainuddin had up to four wives at a time, as is permitted under Islamic law, but only ever had two children—both daughters. The elder daughter is Sitti Rauhun and the younger daughter is Sitti Raihanun, and they were born to different mothers. In 1969, Tuan Guru Zainuddin moved to hand off the day-to-day leadership of NW to his son-in-law by his elder daughter, Sitti Rauhun. That move ended calamitously with an extraordinary organizational congress called in 1977 at which Tuan

---

[12] The history recounted here is based on the authors' own research. Prominent sources from within the organization that have surveyed the organizational history include H. M. Yusuf, ed., *Sejarah Ringkas Perguruan N. W. D. I. & N. B. D. I. dan N. W.* (Pancor-Selong, Lombok Timur: Pengurus Besar Nahdlatul Wathan, 1976); H. Abdul Hayyi Nu'man, *Maulanasysyaikh TGKH. Muhammad Zainuddin Abdul Madjid: Riwayat Hidup dan Perjuangannya* (Pancor, Lombok: Pengurus Besar Nahdlatul Wathan, 1419 H/ 1999 M); and Mohammad Noor, Muslihan Habib, and Muhammad Harfin Zuhdi, *Visi Kebangsaan Religius: Refleksi Pemikiran dan Perjuangan Tuan Guru Kyai Haji Muhammad Zainuddin Abdul Madjid, 1904–1997* (Ciputat: Logos, 2004).

[13] Sven Cederroth, *The Spell of the Ancestors and the Power of Mekkah: A Sasak Community on Lombok*, Gothenburg Studies in Social Anthropology 3 (Goteborg, Sweden: Acta Universitatis Gothoburgensis, 1981), 85.

[14] Noor, Habib, and Zuhdi, *Visi Kebangsaan Religius*, 221.

Guru Zainuddin lambasted his son-in-law for subverting the proper purposes of the organization and removed him from leadership.

From 1977, Tuan Guru Zainuddin again ran NW (and the mother school, NWDI), although he integrated his son-in-law by the younger Sitti Raihanun as formal organizational head and later drew in representatives of Sitti Rauhun's family, too (she divorced the man who had been exiled from the organization and remarried another, more religious figure). Rivalries and tension between the two daughters, their husbands, and children continued from the 1980s to the 1990s. When Tuan Guru Zainuddin passed away in 1997, the heir to organizational leadership was unclear, as some of the likeliest candidates passed away around the same time. NW held an organizational congress in July 1998—at the peak of Indonesia's political *Reformasi*, after President Suharto had resigned in May—when against all expectations the leader chosen as the new organizational head was Tuan Guru Zainuddin's younger daughter: Sitti Raihanun.

The election of Sitti Raihanun was highly controversial and was immediately rejected by several other leaders within the family and within the organization—both because it favored one side of the family and because it elevated a woman to a place of spiritual leadership.[15] During the organizational congress itself, a large voting bloc walked out and boycotted the vote before Sitti Raihanun secured the final victory. One of her uncles who had been running the school NWDI declared himself the organizational leader, but confusion and dissention continued to reign. Eventually in September 1999, those who rejected Sitti Raihanun's leadership held a "Reformasi" congress at which Tuan Guru Zainuddin's grandson, through the older Sitti Rauhun, a young scholar named Zainul Majdi (now famous as *Tuan Guru Bajang* or "Young Tuan Guru") was elected as a rival organizational head for NW. Thus, since 1998, two separate factions of the organization recognizing two separate sets of institutional leaders have existed.

The factional split within NW also led to a social split and deep and abiding social conflict. In the central town of the organization—Pancor, the home of the NWDI school—there was fighting on the streets, back-and-forth property damage, and the burning of shops affiliated with either side throughout September 1998. In October 1998, the younger Sitti Raihanun and those who followed her leadership emigrated from Pancor, where the faction supporting her uncle and her sister's son was ascendent, to a village several kilometers away. Eventually in 2000, Sitti Raihanun established a permanent base for the organization under her leadership at the village of Anjani. From 2000 to 2021, the two factions of NW have thus been known by the towns that hosted their main establishments: NW-Anjani has been led by the younger daughter Sitti Raihanun (and later by her son), and NW-Pancor has been led by Zainul Majdi.

The most heated period of violent conflict lasted until 2005. During this period, the move by one faction or the other to claim an Islamic school, prayer group, or local NW asset was frequently the spark that led to recriminations, personal violence, or the destruction of buildings. Qur'anic recitation groups that should have been locations for spiritual guidance instead turned into training vehicles for armed conflict. This split

---

[15] Bianca J. Smith, "Reorienting Female Spiritual Power in Islam: Narrating Conflict between Warriors, Witches and Militias in Lombok," *Indonesia and the Malay World* 40 (2012): 249–71.

communities down the middle, often with different teachers or leaders in the same village taking different sides.[16]

The two decades since the split have also brought some progress to the organization. Both NW-Anjani and NW-Pancor were able to establish new schools, including expanding to more provinces across Indonesia. The most notable success has been NW-Pancor's political ascendance, with Zainul Majdi elected twice as governor of West Nusa Tenggara province (serving 2008–18), and his older sister Sitti Rohmi Djalilah coming into office as Lieutenant Governor in 2018. Individuals from both factions have also served in the legislatures at the national, provincial, and local levels. The area in which there had not been progress up to 2021 was in reconciliation between Nahdlatul Wathan's two factions.

Efforts at Reconciliation in NW and Why They Failed

For two decades since the split in 1998, there had been efforts toward reconciliation by NW elites, but without any lasting success. From NW's 10th Congress in Praya in 1998 until 2020, the reconciliation process had not seen much meaningful progress. This section will focus on prior attempts at reconciliation and demonstrate how the government failed to play any positive role pushing the sides together.

The hurdles impeding reconciliation between the two factions in NW are multifaceted. They include theological arguments (e.g., women cannot be legitimate spiritual leaders under Islamic law), political concerns (with the domination of NW-Pancor in provincial politics), and cultural elements (such as the tradition of leadership within NW). In light of this, efforts by provincial and national governmental leaders to facilitate reconciliation—to say nothing of initiatives by religious and societal leaders—have never borne fruit. On the contrary, some observers have suggested that the NW conflict has been perpetuated by governmental leaders, most notably by cozying up to one side or the other to seek electoral support, thus increasing the level of conflict between the two factions.[17] At least one leader in the NW-Pancor faction has suspected that the whole organizational split was intentionally designed and caused by the government through the military, which has feared the power of a united NW since the 1990s.[18]

Since the failure of the two NW factions to reconcile after the 10th Congress in 1998, the closest the two sides came to *islah* was in 2010. In that year, the political momentum of a local election in Central Lombok pushed the two sides to negotiate toward reconciliation, especially the NW-Anjani faction. The eldest son of younger sister Sitti Raihanun, Tuan Guru Haji L. Gede Sakti Amir Murni, entered the ring as a candidate for district head of Central Lombok in the 2010 elections. To win this election, he needed the votes of the whole NW community, including those who were affiliated

---

[16] The best source on the split within NW and the ensuing violence is Hamdi, *Nahdlatul Wathan di Era Reformasi*. On the gendered aspects of this, see Bianca J. Smith and Saipul Hamdi, "Between Sufi and Salafi Subjects: Contested Female Leadership, Spiritual Power, and Gender Matters on Lombok," in *Gender and Power in Indonesian Islam: Leaders, Feminists, Sufis, and Pesantren Selves*, ed. Bianca J. Smith and Mark R. Woodward (New York: Routledge, 2014), 25–48.

[17] Fauzan Fuad, Habibuddin, and Muhammad Rafii (lecturers in Hamzanwadi University and Nahdlatul Wathan activists), interview by Saipul Hamdi, October 20, 2010.

[18] Rosiady Sayuti (vice-chairman of NW Pancor), interview by Saipul Hamdi, March 25, 2021.

with NW-Pancor. If the NW bloc was split, it would mean he had very little chance of winning, because NW is not the dominant group in Central Lombok district. The leaders of NW-Anjani agreed to reconcile (*islah*) with NW-Pancor in May 2010 and engaged in joint campaigning. The sisters Sitti Rauhun and Sitti Raihanun met in person for the first time in ten years, at the grave of their father—an act of great spiritual importance for the NW community. This meeting was also attended by their children, including the two prominent political sons of Sitti Rauhun: Governor M. Zainul Majdi and district head of East Lombok Syamsul Lutfi. Besides showing up to campaign for TGH. Sakti in Central Lombok, the two sides also had several meetings toward consolidation. The NW-Anjani group for the first time attended the anniversary celebrations of the school NWDI in Pancor that year.[19]

The *islah* in 2010 created controversy among society, because they thought it reeked of politics. This NW *islah* was seen by some of society as a pseudo-*islah*, not a pure effort from a selfless (Indonesian and Arabic: *ikhlas*) desire by each faction to unite. In spite of this, the *islah* in Praya in 2010 had a positive effect to reduce the tensions and accusations between the factions, particularly at the grassroots level. The reconciliation at Praya also helped TGH. Sakti win a plurality (but not majority) the first round of the election. However, in the second round (where only the top two candidate teams participate), Sakti lost badly, winning only 40.7% (to his opponent's 59.3%).[20] This loss shook the reputation of NW, which had been on the rise after winning the governorship of West Nusa Tenggara and the district head position in East Lombok (both held by sons of Sitti Rauhun). This loss also killed the reconciliation process within NW, in particular the discussions of the format of the leadership of NW and the integration of the two leadership boards into one umbrella organization.

The loss of Sakti in the second round of the Central Lombok district head election in 2010 killed the great plans for an NW reconciliation, and the two sides blamed each other in connection with that failure. The NW-Anjani faction accused NW-Pancor of not making serious efforts to help them in the lead-up to the run-off. According to NW-Anjani leaders, the momentum of reconciliation was just used by NW-Pancor to get sympathy from the public. According to this narrative, the NW-Pancor faction wanted to show the public that they were the ones who had wanted reconciliation all along. On the other side, NW-Pancor thought that the failure of Sakti was because they were no longer being involved by the NW-Anjani side in the second round during the political campaign. According to this narrative, NW-Anjani became overly proud after winning the first round, even though they had spent billions of rupiah to support Sakti's success, according to Muhammad Suruji, the Secretary-General of NW-Pancor.[21] In the first round, both sides were very active campaigning and the reconciliation was a force to unite the votes of NW followers. However, in the second round, the two sides each went their own way and notes of reconciliation were no longer heard during the campaigns, nor were they seen together. In the end, the results of the 2010 election for the district head

---

[19] For more on this, see Kevin W. Fogg and Muhammad Saleh Ending, "One Islamic Community, Two Rival Sisters," *Inside Indonesia* 103 (Jan 2011).

[20] Hamdi, "Politik Islah," 1–14; "KPU Tetapkan Maiq Meres Pemenang Pilkada Lombok Tengah," *Antara News*, September 28, 2021, https://mataram.antaranews.com/berita/12538/kpu-tetapkan-maiq-meres-pemenang-pilkada-lombok-tengah .

[21] Muhammad Suruji (secretary-general of NW-Pancor), interview with Saipul Hamdi, October 12, 2010.

of Central Lombok ended the reconciliation process in NW for the moment. Amid that failure, NW-Anjani argued that it had never been an organizational reconciliation—just a reconciliation within the family.[22]

After the failure in the 2010 Central Lombok election, the relationship between NW-Anjani and NW-Pancor deteriorated again. Both sides sniped at each other, claiming that their own faction was the legitimate one recognized by the government. This conflict reached a peak in the 2013 regional elections because NW-Anjani put forward one of its cadres, Muhyi Abidin, the son-in-law of Sitti Raihanun, as a Lieutenant Governor candidate, against the incumbent ticket that had NW-Pancor's Zainul Majdi at the head. Zainul Majdi won a clear victory, beating the ticket with an NW-Anjani figure and another ticket put forward by the Islamist party PKS.[23] This phenomenon showed that the conflict within NW cannot be separated from political interests and is played out directly on the political field at the time of elections.

The examples above show that the conflict in NW was not only caused by internal factors, but also external factors. This article argues that political interests of the government—particularly the provincial-level government—toward the NW conflict increased the intensity of the conflict between these two factions. The intervention of the government to take the side of or cooperate with one faction or the other on the political field created new spaces for the NW conflict to grow. This intervention also prevented the reconciliation of NW's factions.

That is not to say that the government was the only hurdle to reconciliation—far from it! Internal personal conflicts, economic interests, saving face, and the weakness of the culture of dialogue were also contributing factors. Perhaps the most interesting (and most discussed) issue contributing to the failure of reconciliation was a written legacy—almost a prophecy—from the founder of the organization himself. Tuan Guru Zainuddin wrote a book (called *Wasiat Renunang Masa*), published in several editions since the 1970s, that is filled with his daily experiences in politics, economics, spirituality, and even social relations in society—written in the form of poetic quatrains. In this book, he predicts future events, such as natural disasters that will happen in Indonesia and around the world. Besides that, he also has prophecies about the path forward for NW in the future, including a prophecy about conflict and division in NW. Tuan Guru Zainuddin in his book predicted a split and conflict in NW would happen for a fifth of a century, or twenty years. The text runs as follows:

> Seperlima abad anakku berpisah, selama itu timbullah fitnah.
>
> Di sana-sini anakku berbantah, bersama saudara di dalam *nahdlah*.
>
> Wahai anakku mari kembali, kepada NW karya sendiri.
>
> Tak usah lari kesana kemari, agar bersama sepanjang hari.
>
> Aku melihat banyaknya fitnah, karena anakda berpisah-pisah.
>
> Tidak seturut pada ayahanda, *masya'allah wa innalillah*.

---

[22] Ustaz. Jaelani, Tuan Guru Hajji Anas Hasri, Hayyi Nu'man, and Mugni SN (NW-Anjani figures), interview with Saipul Hamdi, November 20, 2010.

[23] Sutarno, "Pilkada NTB: Gubernur Incumbent Menang 45% Suara," *Kabar24*, May 14, 2013, https://kabar24.bisnis.com/read/20130514/15/138869/pilkada-ntb-gubernur-incumbent-menang-45-suara .

For a fifth of a century my children will be divided, during that time there will rise slander.

My children will quarrel everywhere, with their siblings in the revival [referencing the organization's name, Revival of the Nation].

Oh my children, come home, to the NW that is your own work.

It is no use to run hither and thither, to be together all day long.

I see so much slander arising, because my children are divided.

They do not obey their father, Lord have mercy.[24]

Counting from the emergence of conflict in NW, i.e., 1998, many NW loyalists believed as a matter of faith that NW would be unified in 2018. As a result, some NW followers (and even NW elites) felt that no matter how strong the efforts at reconciliation were, they would not come to fruition before their time, just as predicted in Tuan Guru Zainuddin's text. The NW community that believes this prophecy felt resigned to the conflict in the organization, and they just waited until the expected reconciliation in 2018—which did not come as predicted.

The Role of Jokowi in Initiating the Reconciliation of NW

After two decades of deadlock, with sporadic (but decreasing) violence and enduring enmity between the two sides, the conflict between the two factions of NW became a focus of national governmental action during the Joko Widodo (Jokowi) administration, and it finally reached a formal resolution in 2021. The reconciliation of NW saw progress under the Jokowi administration after he gave special attention to NW—in particular when he needed the support of large social organizations (and Islamic voices) in the 2019 presidential election. Losing the province of West Nusa Tenggara to his rival in the 2014 election pushed Jokowi to approach the NW organization as the largest Islamic organization on Lombok. Jokowi used his structural relationship with the governor of West Nusa Tenggara, Zainul Majdi, to build political cooperation in the lead-up to the 2019 national election. This effort by Jokowi was fairly successful; he not only won the support of NW-Pancor led by Zainul Majdi, but he also won the support of NW-Anjani under the leadership of Zainuddin Atsani, son and spiritual heir of Sitti Raihanun. This differed from the 2014 presidential election, when NW-Pancor supported the ticket of Prabowo Subianto and Hatta Rajasa, while the NW-Anjani faction supported Joko Widodo and Yusuf Kalla.

Jokowi's cooperation with Zainul Majdi was built starting in 2016, after Zainul Majdi gave a speech before national governmental figures clearly and forcefully criticizing the government's policy to import rice and corn. That event also raised the profile of Zainul Majdi on the national level, because of his boldness in criticizing the president.[25] From

---

[24] Kyai Hamzanwadi Pancor [an honorific for Muhammad Zainuddin Abdul Madjid], *Wasiat Renungan Masa Pengalaman Baru* (Pancor, Lombok Timur: Yayasan Pendidikan Hamzanwadi, n.d.), 89–91. These three quatrains are numbered 8, 9, and 10 in the "new" book of poetry, authored in 1970. There are many invocations of "my children" throughout the whole book of poetry that are clearly not about his genetic daughters but rather about his spiritual sons—but these quatrains have most often been interpreted as about familial descendants.

[25] Novy Lumanauw, "Di Depan Jokowi, Gubernur NTB Kritik Bulog soal Impor Beras dan Jagung," *Berita Satu*, February 9, 2016, https://www.beritasatu.com/ekonomi/348153/di-depan -jokowi-gubernur-ntb-kritik-bulog-soal-impor-beras-dan-jagung.

that point onward, Jokowi frequently visited Lombok to strengthen his relationship with the people of West Nusa Tenggara generally and the NW community specifically. On November 9, 2017, Jokowi awarded the title of National Hero to the founder of NW, Tuan Guru Zainuddin Abdul Madjid.[26] Jokowi also visited both headquarters of NW-Anjani and NW-Pancor on November 23, 2017, as part of his giving congratulations to the family of the new national hero.[27] Jokowi's initiative to visit both NW Islamic schools marked a historic occasion and also indirectly formed part of the strategy to unite the NW organization that was still in a time of conflict and division. The interesting thing in the visit to NW-Anjani was the participation of Zainul Majdi (head of NW-Pancor and also governor at the time), accompanying the president and meeting with the NW-Anjani leadership that had been in conflict with him for so long.

Coming into the 2019 presidential election, the Jokowi camp had built ties with both NW factions. This was especially true with NW-Pancor, where its leader Zainul Majdi emerged on several short-lists for vice-presidential candidates to run with Jokowi for his reelection.[28] The eventual vice-presidential running mate chosen by Jokowi was another Islamic leader, K. H. Ma'ruf Amin, who also visited both the NW-Anjani Islamic school and the NW-Pancor Islamic school on October 26, 2018, during the campaign.[29]

Jokowi succeeded in getting support from both factions of NW in the 2019 presidential election, but despite this he still lost the province in the 2019 presidential election, with only 35% of the vote on Lombok. At the very least, Jokowi's portion of the vote was preserved, and it even improved a little on his performance in the 2014 presidential election. The same support from the two factions of NW did not mean they could campaign together; on the contrary, they went out separately, which prevented Jokowi from getting the maximum turnout he could have had.

Running simultaneous with this political courtship, the NW conflict was being fought in courts of law. This all began when NW-Pancor re-registered Nahdlatul Wathan as an organization under the Ministry of Law and Human Rights in 2014; this registration brought a lawsuit from NW-Anjani. NW-Pancor had registered the organization on the ministry's online portal because Nahdlatul Wathan had not yet appeared in that database. NW-Pancor took advantage of that opportunity to go into the system and register the leadership according to their faction. According to Rosiady Sayuti, at the beginning the faction of Zainul Majdi wanted to register the NW organization so that they would be recognized by the government under the name of NW-Pancor because the name "Nahdlatul Wathan" had already been registered by NW-Anjani with the Ministry

---

[26] On this, see Kevin W. Fogg, "Making an Indonesian National Hero for Lombok: The Shifting Category of *Pahlawan Nasional*," *Indonesia and the Malay World* 46, no. 137 (2019): 1–22.

[27] Debbie Sutrisno, "Jokowi Kunjuni Ponpes NW Anjani di Lombok Timur," *Republika*, November 23, 2017, https://republika.co.id/berita/nasional/umum/17/11/23/ozv00v440-jokowi-kunjungi-ponpes-nw-anjani-di-lombok-timur.

[28] Friski Riana, "Poros Pemuda Nusantara Dukung TGB Zainul Majdi di Pilpres 2019," *Tempo*, May 2, 2018, https://nasional.tempo.co/read/1085035/poros-pemuda-nusantara-dukung-tgb-zainul-majdi-di-pilpres-2019/ ; Rayful Mudassir, "Pendukung TGB Yakin Zainul Majdi Dipilih Jokowi Jadi Cawapres, Ini Alasannya," *Bisnis.com*, August 8, 2018, https://kabar24.bisnis.com/read/20180808/15/825978/pendukung-tgb-yakin-zainul-majdi-dipilih-jokowi-jadi-cawapres-ini-alasannya.

[29] "Kiai Ma'ruf Amin Silaturahmi ke Ponpes NW," *Radar Lombok*, October 27, 2018, https://radarlombok.co.id/kiai-maruf-amin-silaturahmi-ke-ponpes-nw.html . From field data, NW-Anjani also had a personal, familial connection with K. H. Ma'ruf Amin, through the wife of Zainuddin Atsani.

of Home Affairs.[30] A new regulation from the ministry of Law and Human rights gave a window to the NW-Pancor faction to gain recognition by the Ministry of Law and Human Rights. After registering NW as an organization and the leadership according to their faction, the Ministry of Law and Human Rights immediately accepted the data and recognized them in a letter dated July 11, 2014.[31]

The re-registration of NW in 2014 and the recognition by the Ministry of Law and Human Rights caused renewed polemics and brought the two sides to court. NW-Anjani took umbrage with the leadership of NW-Pancor that made a new legal body, even though NW had been established in 1953 and formally registered with the government since 1960.[32] The younger sister Sitti Raihanun, on behalf of NW-Anjani, formally sued in 2014 over the letter of the Ministry of Law and Human Rights, as issued to NW-Pancor. NW-Anjani won in this lawsuit.[33] The impact of this lawsuit was the issuance of letters of cancellation by the Ministry of Law and Human Rights in 2016 on its letter of recognition from 2014. This cancellation simultaneously changed the recognized leadership of Nahdlatul Wathan in the ministry to be the leadership headed by Sitti Raihanun (i.e., NW-Anjani).

NW-Pancor's loss after the cancellation of the 2014 ministry letter by the courts was not the end of the matter. NW-Pancor tried to appeal, but the appeal was rejected. A second attempt at appeal was considered by the Supreme Court, which was accepted, and NW-Pancor won the appeal in 2019. This appeal decision created yet another letter of recognition by the Ministry of Law and Human Rights.[34] This letter recognized NW-Pancor under the leadership of Zainul Majdi as the legitimate "Nahdlatul Wathan," which caused fury and frustration among the supporters of NW-Anjani. They held huge public demonstrations demanding that the Ministry of Law and Human Rights withdraw the 2019 letter recognizing NW-Pancor and return to the decision of the Supreme Court that recognized Sitti Raihanun's leadership. This demonstration was led by Zainuddin Atsani, who had just been seated as the new head of NW (in the Anjani version) as a result of the 15th organizational congress in 2019 held in Mataram, replacing his mother who had been the organizational leader for two decades since 1998.

The followers of NW-Anjani demonstrated in front of the provincial office of the Ministry of Law and Human Rights in West Nusa Tenggara on September 18, 2019, attended by some five thousand people from many different villages and towns. They came from morning until almost the sunset prayers, expressing their demands. Push and pull between the NW community and the police force, throwing of stones and destroying the front gate of the ministry's provincial office raised the tension level in the city. The demonstrators put forward four demands, namely that (1) the Minister of Law and Human Rights uphold the law and justice for Nahdlatul Wathan; (2) the Minister of Law and Human Rights void the 2019 letter (which had recognized NW-Pancor as the legitimate Nahdlatul Wathan); (3) the Minister of Law and Human Rights apologize publicly to the NW community for his mistake that was offensive and violated the law;

[30] Rosiady Sayuti (vice-chairman of NW-Pancor), interview by Saipul Hamdi, March 25, 2021.
[31] Surat Keputusan Menkumham No. AHU-00297.60.10.2014.
[32] Nu'man, *Maulanasysyaikh*, 10.
[33] Putusan PTUN Jakarta Nomor 203/G/2014/PTUN.JKT. jo. 186/B/2015/PT.TUN.JKT. jo. 37 K/TUN/2016.
[34] Surat Keputusan Menkumham No. AHU-0000810.AH.01.08 tertanggal, September 10, 2019.

Figure 1: Supporters of NW-Anjani demonstrated on September 17, 2020, at the provincial office of the Ministry of Law and Human Rights. Photo by Hayatun Sofian of Radio Republik Indonesia, used with permission.

and (4) the Ministry cancel the license of notary public Hamzan Wahyudi, because he was accused of being the source of this tension and violating the notary's code of ethics.[35]

This demonstration drew the attention of both the regional and national governments because it was held for two days straight, causing unbelievable traffic jams. NW elites gave speeches on a rolling basis, criticizing the policies of the Ministry of Law and Human Rights, while the crowd recited Sufi prayers of the organization continuously and waited for the fulfillment of their demands. The crowds later dispersed before sunset prayers, and some of the elites were received by the local Ministry office to discuss next steps in solving the conflict within NW.

The two factions of NW were called by the Minister of Law and Human Rights in Jakarta to discuss a path toward reconciliation as a resolution to the conflict within

[35] "Dinilai Provokator, 5 Ribu Massa NW Segel Kantor Kemenkumham," *Suara Rinjani News*, September 17, 2019, https://suararinjaninews.co.id/?p=7135; "Ribuan Massa NW Anjani Gedor Kantor Kemenkumham NTB," *Arki Radio Online*, September 18, 2019, https://arkifm.com/7016-ribuan-massa-nw-anjani-gedor-kantor-kemenkumham-ntb.html.

Figure 2: Delegations from NW-Pancor (led by Muhammad Zainul Majdi, in the coat and open-collar shirt) and NW-Anjani (led by Zainuddin Atsani, immediately to the left of Zainul Majdi) met in Jakarta for a reconciliation meeting convened by the Ministry of Law and Human Rights, January 11, 2020. Photo by Mohammad Azhar of Suara NTB, used with permission.

NW—seemingly at the urging of President Jokowi, who was pushing for a solution. This closed meeting was held at the Ministry offices on January 11, 2020, attended by NW elites from both factions.[36] This meeting did not result in any consensus, but it opened the door to communication and clarification between the two sides that had not met formally in two decades. Even though the two factions argued with each other and disagreed on the roots of the conflict, the two sides restrained themselves and were able to embrace at the end of the discussions.

This meeting to open the door to reconciliation could not relieve the tension and conflict between members in society. The two factions continued to disagree and to claim their own side as the righteous and true organization recognized by the

---

[36] From NW-Anjani the delegation was Muhammad Zainuddin Atsani, Prof. Dr. Fahrurrozi, Tuan Guru Anas Hasri, L. Gede Samsul Mujahidin, Prof. Dr. Agil al-Idrus, Nur Kholis, and Dr. L. Muhyi Abidin, while from the NW-Pancor side the delegation consisted of Dr. Zainul Majdi, Tuan Guru Hasanain Juani, Tuan Guru Yusuf Ma'mun, Dr. Rosiady Sayuti, Dr. Najmul Akhyar, Dr. Iswandi, and Irzani. See "Kedua Kubu NW Bertemu di Kantor Kemenkumham. Ternyata Ini yang Dibicarakan," *Koran Merah*, January 10, 2020, https://www.koranmerah .com/2020/01/10/kedua-kubu-nw-bertemu-di-kantor-kemenkumham-ternyata-ini-yang-dibicarakan/.

government, with their respective letters from the Ministry of Law and Human Rights. The government then froze (again) the 2019 letter recognizing NW-Pancor, and the national administration asked the two sides to come together in a joint organizational congress (Muktamar). Not only from the government in Jakarta, but the provincial government of West Nusa Tenggara through the head of the Office of National and Political Unity (Kesbangpol) tried to facilitate the two sides by inviting them to discuss a few offers. These ideas included a joint congress that would draw together both leaderships into one board, respective congresses for each faction and registering the Nahdlatul Wathan organizational name with a new and different one, or the formation of a day-to-day leadership that would rotate. Amid this time when the fate of NW was unclear, NW-Anjani also continued the judicial process against the 2019 decision by the Ministry of Law and Human Rights that had recognized NW-Pancor, asking for judicial reconsideration of the previous judgement. In the judicial reconsideration the court accepted and endorsed the leadership of NW-Anjani, which caused the Ministry of Law and Human Rights to issue yet another Letter of Recognition.[37]

The issuance of this letter to NW-Anjani by the Ministry of Law and Human Rights in 2020 was welcomed happily by the NW-Anjani leadership, after they had felt quite pressured by the letter in favor of NW-Pancor in 2019. This letter of recognition was used to the hilt as a weapon to regulate activities under the name of NW, including reporting any activities of NW-Pancor as illegal if they happened without the blessing of the head of NW-Anjani. NW-Anjani put out notices and warnings not to use the logo or flag of NW in any context without their blessing, because NW-Anjani owned the rights to these symbols.[38] The Anjani faction also viewed the 2020 letter as voiding the 2019 letter that preceded it, and thus their leadership was seen as the only one recognized by the state. An instruction from the headquarters of NW-Anjani that prohibited the use of NW symbols gave rise to a controversy among the public. Some activities of NW run by the Pancor faction were reported to the police because they were seen as violating the law on mass organizations. The activities that were reported to the police were, for example, the installation of the leadership of NW-Pancor branches and the installation of the leadership for the auxiliary organization NW Youth in West Lombok, which was attended by the Lieutenant Governor of the province and the district head of West Lombok. Besides that, the branch congress of NW-Pancor that took place at the Darul Muttaqien NW Perian Islamic boarding School, East Lombok, on Tuesday, January 18, 2021, was also reported. Syamsu Rizal, a member of the leadership of NW-Anjani, said that the police reports happened because of the misuse of the logo and symbols of NW, which were deployed without permission, even though the Ministry of Law and Human Rights letter of recognition in 2020 had recognized NW-Anjani and voided the letter for NW-Pancor.[39] The individuals who were reported to the police by NW-Anjani were called into the station to explain themselves.

---

[37] Surat Keputusan Menkumham No. AHU-0001269.AH.01.08 tertanggal, 30 November 2020.

[38] "Laporan Peggunaan Lambang dan Logo NW Berbuntut Panang," *Suara Nusra*, March 18, 2021, https:// nusramedia.com/hukum-kriminal/laporan-penggunaan-lambang-dan-logo-nw-berbuntut-panjang-25992. html.

[39] Syamsu Rizal (NW-Anjani activist), interview by Saipul Hamdi, March 27, 2021.

The violations of the use of NW symbols and logos brought a reaction from broader society, especially those who supported NW-Pancor. They felt that the actions of NW-Anjani broke with the vision and mission of the founder of NW, Tuan Guru Zainuddin, who instructed them to spread the NW flag and logo to every corner of the archipelago and even the world. Bickering and arguments were seen on social media like WhatsApp and Facebook. Rahmat (fifty years old), a follower of NW-Pancor, strongly criticized the leadership of NW-Anjani in a video on Facebook, saying they prohibited the use of the logo and symbols of NW even though they were still young. In his view, the founder of NW, Tuan Guru Zainuddin, never prohibited the use of the logo, so it made no sense that the young generation would do that now. Rahmat also invited anyone who disagreed with him on the question of the NW logo to fight him.[40]

NW-Pancor leader and former governor Zainul Majdi also publicly discussed the prohibition on using the NW logo, and he found it to diverge sharply from the teachings of NW. In his view, the logo and symbol of NW were not a commercial product that could be bought or sold. The symbol of NW was the intellectual property of the NW founder Tuan Guru Zainuddin, and after he passed away the copyright passed down with all the other inheritance, including to Zainul Majdi's mother Sitti Rauhun, as Tuan Guru Zainuddin's oldest daughter. As an heir himself, Zainul Majdi told all the followers of NW that there was no prohibition on using the NW logo—and, to the contrary, he asked the NW community to keep spreading the NW logo. He also emphasized that Islamic schools could not be hindered from using the NW logo, but rather should be encouraged. Organizations should not pressure Islamic schools because the schools were not the property of the organization; the role and position of organizational leaders was to serve the schools. Majdi expressed his gratitude that organizational followers and communities had built up Islamic schools, and that through these schools the logo and symbol of NW could shine and be spread to all corners of the world.[41]

In anticipation of physical clashes within the NW community, Zainul Majdi sent a letter to the Ministry of Law and Human Rights to clarify the question of the new letter of recognition that was issued for NW-Anjani, even though one year earlier the Ministry had issued a letter for NW-Pancor. Because he did not get a response, Zainul Majdi wrote a letter to the president to facilitate and mediate the NW conflict. The president then ordered the Ministry of Law and Human Rights to solve the NW conflict without recourse to the courts. The Director General of the Law Administration Directorate of the ministry came himself to Lombok on March 22, 2021, to meet the two sides and discuss a format for reconciliation of NW, and the two sides were invited to attend and sign an agreement in the Lombok Astoria Hotel on March 23, 2021.[42]

---

[40] This viral Facebook video was posted by user madi.harlan23, "Jamaah Wirid NW Bersuara Terkait Penggunaan Logo NW," February 10, 2021, https://www.facebook.com/madi.harlan23/posts/722903541919959.

[41] "Penjelasan Lugas TGB Dr. TGKH M. Zainul Majdi, MA Tentang Organisasi dan Lambang Organisasi NW," KM Channel on *YouTube.com*, March 11, 2021, https://www.youtube.com/watch?v=YowZcvwRREM.

[42] Rosiady Sayuti (vice-chairman of NW-Pancor), interview by Saipul Hamdi, March 25, 2021. See also Hayatun Sofian, "Berselisih 23 Tahun, Dua Ormas NW Didamaikan Kemenkum HAM," *Radio Republik Indonesia*, March 23, 2021, https://rri.co.id/mataram/daerah/1004762/berselisih-23-tahun-dua-ormas-nw-didamaikan-kemenkum-ham.

NWDI as the Compromise

The meeting at the Lombok Astoria Hotel on March 23, 2021, was a historic and monumental meeting for the two factions of NW, because they reached agreement on the details of a reconciliation. The prophecy of Tuan Guru Zainuddin that anticipated "for a fifth of a century my children will be split" was proved true with the signing of the reconciliation document, ending the dualism of leadership in the body of NW. This meeting was attended by the security apparatus of the province, including the head of the provincial police, the regional commander of the military, and the Director-General of Law Administration at the Ministry of Law and Human Rights. This meeting was broadcast live through both print and electronic media.[43] The leaders and respected elders of the two factions of NW also attended, and the meeting included the heads of each faction: Zainul Majdi for NW-Pancor and Zainuddin Atsani for NW-Anjani. This meeting had an atmosphere that was full of a spirit of brotherhood, peace, and harmony. Of course, this differed from the condition on the street, where the two factions criticized and argued with each other about who was right and who was wrong.

In this reconciliation meeting, there were seven points in the peace settlement that were signed by the leaders of the two factions of NW, Zainul Majdi and Zainuddin Atsani. These points were:

1. RTGB Lalu Gede Muhammad Zainuddin Atsani will continue to carry forward NW as founded by Tuan Guru Kyai Haji Muhammad Zainuddin Abdul Majid, based in Mataram, West Nusa Tenggara province.

2. At the same time, TGB Muhammad Zainul Majdi will found a new group named Nahdlatul Wathan Diniyah Islamiyah (or NWDI), based in Pancor, East Lombok.

3. The two parties are equal in their efforts to continue the struggle in the fields of education, social work, and propagation that had been done by Nahdlatul Wathan.

4. RTGB Lalu Gede Muhammad Zainuddin Atsani has the right to use the symbol and flag of Nahdlatul Wathan, while TGB M. Zainul Majdi will use a different symbol and flag.

5. Both parties must preserve good relations, mutual respect, and recognize the legality and legitimacy of the other in realizing the goals of Tuan Guru Kyai Haji Muhammad Zainuddin Abdul Majid, the founder of the collective Nahdlatul Wathan.

6. Both parties also agree to avoid disputes or quarrels and to withdraw criminal reports, lawsuits, and/or bureaucratic complaints and to cease and desist in any actions of discrimination, insults, bullying, and persecution in any form.

7. Regarding schools, Islamic schools, and institutions for social work or propagation such as orphanages, family centers, and study groups under educational foundations that are formed by cadres, students, or the

---

[43] "Momen Momen Pertemuan Islah NW Pancor dan NW Anjani," *Radar Lombok*, March 24, 2021, https://www.youtube.com/watch?v=oRnan9Ufa-Q.

community of Nahdlatul Wathan, each is given the full rights to choose freely which organizational leadership to align with, led by the first party or by the second party, without any intimidation or compulsion.[44]

The second point in this document established a new organization, Nahdlatul Wathan Diniyah Islamiyah (NWDI), led by Zainul Majdi, while the organization known as NW was surrendered to Zainuddin Atsani. According to Rosiady Sayuti, on the afternoon the day before the reconciliation, the leaders of NW-Pancor had a meeting and agreed to use the name "NW-Pancor" for their organization. However, on the morning of the reconciliation, Zainul Majdi received a "divine insight" (*ilham*) to use the name NWDI for his new organization, to avoid drawing out the polemics in society about the status of NW.[45] If they used the name "NW-Pancor," they could later be accused of establishing a new NW, which would be labeled as a false NW, according to Rosiady. The term NWDI was chosen because it was created by the founder of NW Tuan Guru Zainuddin as the name of his first Islamic school and the kernel for the organization NW. In other words, NW and NWDI were both the intellectual property of Tuan Guru Zainuddin that have been made eternal and developed by the NW community. NWDI would just experience a small shift in status: from previously being the name of the Islamic school, now NWDI would be a mass organization on equal footing with NW.

It was still unclear whether this move would be accepted by society or would simply give rise to new issues among the NW community. The decision of Zainul Majdi to let go of the term NW entirely in the structural context and to use the term NWDI as the new mass organization did manage to bring to a close the conflict and polemics that existed. Even though they were of the same general idea and ideological lineage, they would still be two different, separate units on an institutional level, with equal status. There was no reason for the old proponents of NW-Anjani, for example, to insult and tear down NWDI, because it would be outside the structure of NW. NWDI was a middle road to end the conflict within NW and the associated, drawn-out conflict. Although it elicited a varied response from the NW community, still the emergence of the organization NWDI made that group more independent to undertake activities and develop the teachings of Tuan Guru Zainuddin. This prevented fighting for seats in the leadership of NW, which had become a factor preventing reconciliation internally because individuals were angry and acrimonious toward each other.

The fifth and sixth points were no less important in securing stable relations between the two factions of NW. Both factions agreed to respect each other and to stop all forms of derision, insults, police reports, and to recognize each other's legality. Throughout the NW conflict, both factions continually tore down the other and attacked them verbally in sermons from the pulpit. NW-Anjani, for example, produced a discourse about itself as the group that was most faithful to the instructions of Tuan Guru Zainuddin, preserving religious traditions such as *melontar*—throwing of coins or paper money up during NW sermons and study groups, so this could be donated to charity—and claimed itself as the descendants who were given a mandate to lead NW. The most popular expression of

[44] Rosiady Sayuti (vice-chairman of NW-Pancor), interview by Saipul Hamdi, March 25, 2021; Syamsu Rizal (activist with NW-Anjani), interview by Saipul Hamdi, March 27, 2021. See also "7 Butir Nota Kesepakatan NW Anjani dan Pancor," *Lombok TV News*, March 27, 2021, https://lomboktvnews.com/7-butir-nota-kesepakatan-nw-anjani-dan-pancor.

[45] Rosiady Sayuti (vice-chairman of NW-Pancor), interview by Saipul Hamdi, March 25, 2021.

Tuan Guru Zainuddin was "ine Zainuddin Atsani gentik Zainuddin sak tokol," meaning Zainuddin Atsani is the replacement for Zainuddin who was sitting before you. (The name "Zainuddin Atsani" is the Indonesianized version of the Arabic for "Zainuddin the Second"—he was anointed as a successor very early on.) The NW-Anjani discourse was constructed, reproduced, and capitalized on continually to augment the legality and the recognition of their leadership in the NW community. They also accused NW-Pancor of being a group that was not faithful to Tuan Guru Zainuddin, always going against his ideas, and trying to erase the NW traditions that had been built up by Tuan Guru Zainuddin.

The discourse built up by the NW-Pancor side in the public eye was different from what came out of Anjani. NW-Pancor strived to avoid words of conflict and division in their leaders' speeches and on the contrary continued to speak of unity and reconciliation. This strategy was very effective to win sympathy from the NW community, especially those who had not yet chosen an affiliation or who were still confused. In fact, there were many in the community and several Islamic schools who moved their affiliation to NW-Pancor, where they had previously been aligned with NW-Anjani. The public saw that NW-Pancor was more polite, well-mannered, and not coarse in addressing the issue. Zainul Majdi as a representative of NW who held the position of head focused in every speech on rationality in organizational life, for example going to the substance rather than the symbols of NW, which had become part of the indoctrination and cult of personality for certain other figures. Zainul Majdi defined NW as a tool for the struggle in support of the religion of Islam, not something sacral that had to be deified. When asked whether one could or could not practice a Sufi order besides the NW's own order (*Hizib Nadhlatul Wathan*), he told people they could. This different discourse that developed in the elites and cadres of NW-Pancor pointed to the inconsistencies of the NW-Anjani faction in following the Shafi'i school of Islamic jurisprudence, because they elevated a woman to be the head of NW (Sitti Raihanun). According to them, there was not a single Islamic mass organization in Indonesia that was led by a woman, other than NW-Anjani.

The seventh point was crucial to both sides and has given rise to polemics until the time of this writing, regarding the affiliation status of institutions like Islamic schools, study circles, and orphanages. According to Anjani, this point was removed (or at least not agreed to) on the day before the document was signed, however the point reemerged at the signing because it was pushed by NW-Pancor. According to Syamsu Rizal, NW-Anjani claimed that Islamic schools and branches of NW had to retain affiliation to their faction, not to Pancor whose NWDI organization was new and did not have any connection at all with the old NW.[46] On the other hand, in the agreement the institutions are given freedom to choose their affiliations with no compulsion or intimidation from any side. One must note that fighting over Islamic schools' affiliations was one source of conflict and violence within the body of NW, where one faction wanted to fight for and control Islamic schools and the other side wanted to defend them. If there were teachers who favored both Anjani and Pancor inside one school, that guaranteed that tension and conflict would arise between the teachers.

As much as the solution of creating separate "NW" and "NWDI" organizations was a compromise between the two factions, it was also a moment of resolution pushed

---

[46] Syamsu Rizal (activist with NW-Anjani), interview by Saipul Hamdi, March 27, 2021.

by the government. The meeting was convened by officials from the Ministry of Law and Human Rights, and the presence of the province's entire security apparatus demonstrated how the most powerful regional players were on board. The president himself was on the record calling for and promoting reconciliation between the two factions. Since 2014, the organizations had primarily used government institutions (recognition letters from the national ministries, court rulings in Jakarta, interventions with national political leadership) as the venue for their struggle, rather than primarily on the streets of East Lombok. Thus, it made sense that the resolution in 2021 was also mediated by figures connected to the central government.

Conclusion: What Does This Say About the Government and Social Conflict in Indonesia?

The resolution of the internal conflict in Nahdlatul Wathan, hailed as *islah* or reconciliation between the two sides, represents a new day for society on Lombok, but also a shift in how governmentality works in Indonesia. This is a case of *Reformasi*-era social conflict where the government was actually crucial in bringing both sides to the table, mediating between conflicting elites, and using its authority to strengthen the terms of reconciliation. Furthermore, this is a case where the government's authority was recognized (and sometimes even weaponized) by the conflicting sides—a far cry from the early years of *Reformasi* when government authority was very weak.

There are several reasons why government influence might be particularly strong in this kind of conflict between mass organizations. First, both of the groups in question were heavily involved in local and provincial government, vying constantly for and frequently winning elected leadership positions. This makes them likely to recognize institutions of state as bases of power. Equally important, though, might be the negative example of how the Indonesian central government has censured social organizations (most notably mass Islamic organizations) that do not comply with government directives. This has been most notable in the Jokowi administration's ban of Hizbut Tahrir Indonesia (HTI) in 2017, followed by the ban on the Front Pembela Islam (FPI) in 2020.[47] In both cases, the Jokowi administration used a legal tool (at first a Regulation in Lieu of Law [Perppu], which then became a part of the Law on Mass Organizations [UU Ormas]), but outside observers remain skeptical of this method as providing actual resolution to the appeal of Islamist groups.[48] Greg Fealy has even framed this increased control of civil society by the government as "repressive pluralism."[49] Thus, it is easy to understand why other mass Islamic organizations in 2021—even staunchly nationalist

---

[47] Masdar Hilmy, "The Rise and Fall of 'Transnational' Islam in Indonesia: The Future of Hizbut Tahrir Indonesia (HTI)," in *Rising Islamic Conservatism in Indonesia: Islamic Groups and Identity Politics*, ed. Leonard C. Sebastian, Syafiq Hasyim, and Alexander R. Arifianto (London: Routledge, 2020), 133–45; Masdar Hilmy, "The Rise and Fall of 'Transnational' Islam in Indonesia: The Future of Hizbut Tahrir Indonesia (HTI)," in *Rising Islamic Conservatism in Indonesia: Islamic Groups and Identity Politics*, ed. Leonard C. Sebastian, Syafiq Hasyim, and Alexander R. Arifianto (London: Routledge, 2020), 133–45; the-indonesian-governments-crackdown-on-islamists/.

[48] Usman Hamid and Liam Gammon, "Jokowi Forges a Tool of Repression," *New Mandala*, July 13, 2017, https://www.newmandala.org/jokowi-forges-tool-repression/; Hilmy, "Rise and Fall."

[49] Greg Fealy, "Jokowi in the Covid-19 Era: Repressive Pluralism, Dynasticism and the Overbearing State," *Bulletin of Indonesian Economic Studies* 56, no. 3 (2020): 301–23.

groups like Nahdlatul Wathan—would fall in line with the administration's push for reconciliation, rather than risk "securitization" of their social conflict.[50]

In the case of Lombok, specifically, the end to the longstanding power struggle over NW and among the descendants of Tuan Guru Zainuddin will cause some to celebrate. However, there remain also reasons for skepticism and concern. At a local level, the *islah* mediated by the government has not actually ended recriminations between the two sides, particularly from NW (formerly NW-Anjani) against NWDI (formerly NW-Pancor). These have largely taken the form of internet memes and sharp sermons about how Nahdlatul Wathan is a genuine creation of Tuan Guru Zainuddin from decades ago, whereas the NWDI organization is merely months old and was founded by Islamic scholars of much less prestige.[51] It seems that creating separate organizations has not eliminated the personal acrimony from elites, at least on one side.

On a broader level, the strong role of the government in conflict resolution may feed the idea (a recurring theme in the recent volume by Thomas Power and Eve Warburton)[52] that Indonesia is trending toward greater authoritarianism. Following the framework suggested by Tajima's exhaustive study,[53] societal groups may be reverting to the New Order model of expecting resolution from above (i.e., the state).

---

[50] See also Ayu Rikza, "The Securitization of Hizbut Tahrir Indonesia," *Politik Indonesia: Indonesian Political Science Review* 5, no. 2 (2020): 172–91.

[51] For example, see the Facebook post of Junaid Al Bagdadi, "Gagal Faham . . .!!" July 13, 2021, https://www.facebook.com/permalink.php?story_fbid=1226815451123582&id=100013854167404.

[52] Thomas Power and Eve Warburton (ed.), *Democracy in Indonesia: From Stagnation to Regression?* (Singapore: ISEAS, 2020).

[53] Tajima, *Institutional Origins*.

"This Is What Happens to Enemies of the RI"

The East Timor Torture Photographs within the New Order's History of Sexual and Gender-Based Violence

Hannah Loney and Annie Pohlman

In late 1997, a collection of approximately 260 torture photographs were smuggled out of Indonesian-occupied East Timor.[1] The photographs show the aftermath of an array of violent acts: dead and injured East Timorese men and women, bodily remains, shallow graves, and Indonesian soldiers posing with decapitated heads. The majority of the photographs, however, show acts of torture in progress. We infer that these shots were deliberately staged by the soldiers to capture the violence being perpetrated on

Dr Hannah Loney is a Visiting Assistant Professor in Gender Studies at the Central European University, Austria.
Annie Pohlman teaches Indonesian at the University of Queensland, Australia.

[1] The images examined are disturbing and not available to the public; we reproduce none that show acts of torture in this article. A copy of this collection of photographs is contained within the papers of the late human rights campaigner Dr Andrew McNaughton, held at the Mitchell Library, State Library of New South Wales. The authors were granted permission to view the collection by his estate on July 4, 2018 and were granted permission to copy these photographs for research purposes on March 19, 2019. We have examined this collection in terms of their circulation as trophies in another piece, see Hannah Loney and Annie Pohlman, "The Sexual and Visual Dynamics of Torture: Analysing Atrocity Photographs from Indonesian-Occupied East Timor," in *Gender, Violence and Power: Indonesia Across Time and Space*, ed. Katharine McGregor, Ana Dragojlovic, and Hannah Loney (Abingdon: Routledge, 2020), 84–100.

the bodies of their victims. These photographs were not the first to be smuggled out of the territory during the Indonesian occupation, but they were distinct in the particularly brutal and graphic nature of their content, as well as the gendered violence being depicted. Of the 262 photographs in the collection under examination, some 200 show acts of torture, of which around 130 depict scores of male victims. The remaining seventy photographs feature what appear to be five women and teenage girl victims.[2]

This article focuses on the seventy photographs that show acts of torture being perpetrated against women and girls, and on the sexual and gendered violence contained within them. We situate the acts shown in these photographs, taken during the Indonesian occupation of East Timor (1975–99), within a continuum of similar forms of gendered violence and display under the New Order military regime in Indonesia (1966–98). We compare the acts of sexual and gendered violence shown in the East Timor photographs with similar acts of violence perpetrated by Indonesian security services during two other periods under the New Order: the mass violence against suspected Communists (1965–66) and during the conflict between the Free Aceh Movement (Gerakan Aceh Merdeka, GAM) and the Government of Indonesia (particularly during the heightened military "DOM" period, 1989–98). We argue that this comparison of similar acts of sexual and gendered violence across the breadth of the New Order reveals, in part, the dynamics of how the regime dealt with those identified as "internal enemies" of the state. More specifically, this comparison uncovers how the security services used gendered forms of violence to harm, humiliate, and destroy those enemies.

In the first part of the article, we focus on this collection of photographs showing women and girl victims from occupied East Timor. We describe the acts of torture that they depict with reference to how these images reveal the sexual and gendered nature of this violence. Specifically, we reconstruct the sequence in which the photographs were taken, outlining the torture of each of the five women, and observe that it was the same group of six (maybe seven) male perpetrators who created this series of photographs within a very short time frame. In the second part of the article, we turn to the history of similar acts of gendered violence and their display during other periods of mass violence under the New Order. Drawing on human rights reports and testimony provided by survivors and witnesses, we highlight the gendered forms of harm perpetrated against women and girls. To that end, we connect the regime's practices of sexual and gendered violence with the identification of "internal enemies" more broadly. We argue that these technologies of gendered harm were deliberate forms of attack used against those deemed to be internal enemies of the New Order state: suspected Communists in 1965, and GPK (Gerombolan Pengacau Keamanan, "Bands of Security Disruptors") in East Timor and in Aceh. By identifying the victims as internal enemies and thus an existential threat to the New Order state, the gendered and sexual forms of violence used to harm, humiliate, and destroy these women were seen as necessary and justified. As crudely written in black pen across the top of one woman's left thigh in a series of the East Timor photographs showing her naked and injured body, "This is what happens to enemies of the RI."

---

[2] In the Andrew McNaughton collection, there are multiple doubles of some photographs, and so here we are estimating the number of original non-duplicates. The faces of the female victims are obscured with black hoods and pieces of cloth, and so it is difficult to determine how many individuals are shown. In the quote at the start of this article from A Paz é Possível em Timor-Leste, they estimate seven female victims; our estimate is five (the CAVR also estimates five).

The East Timor Torture Photographs

The East Timor torture photographs are infamous within human rights and solidarity networks connected to East Timor and Indonesia. The photographs were initially acquired in November 1997 by an Australia-based organization that supported self-determination for East Timor, the East Timor International Support Centre (ETISC), and were rapidly circulated internationally among activist and human rights networks.[3] We believe that the photographs were created by Indonesian military personnel in early to mid-1997.[4] This determination has been made on the basis of temporal markers contained within the photographs, including references to the 1996 Nobel Peace Prize, as well as broader patterns in military violence in East Timor: specifically, an escalation in detentions and torture of suspected clandestine members in Dili and Baucau around the time of the 1997 Indonesian national election. We suspect that some of the photographs were taken at the "Red House" (Rumah Merah), a much feared detention and interrogation compound that was operated by KOPASSUS (Komando Pasukan Khusus, Army Special Forces Command) in Baucau.[5] In their infamy, these photographs have subsequently been reproduced, repurposed, and reused many times, becoming part of the internet's visual imaginary of torture and abuse.[6]

Atrocity images, despite their currency in campaigns for the recognition of human rights violations in many parts of the world, are an imperfect and incomplete medium for the visual evidentiary claims often placed on them.[7] Incomplete though the East Timor photographs are as artifacts to bear witness to the atrocities that they depict, in this article we look carefully at these images: at the people in them, what they are doing or having done to them, the places where they are staged, and the objects captured in those places. We examine and describe these photographs not to eroticize the suffering depicted, nor to reproduce that suffering. Rather, our objective here is to try to understand better "the histories, the politics, the *world* that gave birth to [them]."[8]

---

[3] For instance, some of the images were circulated by a Taiwanese NGO soon after May 1998 with claims that they were of ethnic Chinese women who had been raped and killed in Jakarta. For more detail, see Monika Swasti Winarnita, "The Politics of Commemorating the May 1998 Mass Rapes," *Review of Indonesian and Malaysian Affairs* 45, no. 1/2 (2011): 133–64. In another publication in development, we discuss the production, circulation, and consumption of these photographs.

[4] We would like to thank our anonymous reviewer for pointing us in this direction. On patterns of military violence in East Timor, see CAVR, *Chega*, 552–53 and 1613–17.

[5] This is information given in a video that was presented by José Ramos-Horta to the United Nations' Special Rapporteur on extra-judicial, summary, or arbitrary executions, Bacre Waly Ndiaye, in April 1997. See ETAN (East Timor and Indonesia Action Network), "Latest East Timor Torture Photos," *ETAN*, undated, accessed March 2, 2019, http://etan.org/etanphoto/imtort03.htm. On the Red House and other places of torture used by the Indonesian security services, see George J. Aditjondro, "Ninjas, Nanggalas, Monuments, and Mossad Manuals: An Anthropology of Indonesian State Terror in East Timor," in *Death Squad: The Anthropology of State Terror*, ed. Jeffrey A. Sluka (Philadelphia: University of Pennsylvania Press, 2000), 158–88.

[6] On the cultural and social imaginary of the internet, see Majid Yar, *The Cultural Imaginary of the Internet: Virtual Utopias and Dystopias* (New York: Palgrave Macmillan, 2014).

[7] See Barbie Zelizer, *Remembering to Forget: Holocaust Memory through the Camera's Eye* (Chicago: University of Chicago Press, 1998). For critiques on the use of atrocity images in human rights' projects, see, for example, Jane Lydon, "Introduction: Visualising Human Rights," in *Visualising Human Rights*, ed. Jane Lydon (Crawley: University of Western Australia Publishing, 2018), 1–26; and Joel R. Pruce, *The Mass Appeal of Human Rights* (Cham: Palgrave Macmillan, 2019), 77–111.

[8] Susie Linfield, *The Cruel Radiance: Photography and Political Violence* (Chicago: University of Chicago Press, 2010), xvii.

Christophe Busch, in his consideration of photographs taken by Waffen-SS members and others in the Nazi concentration camps during the Second World War, explains that such photographs "help us in understanding how the perpetrators reflected upon the world, how they positioned themselves in it and how it shaped their respective behavior."[9] By looking at the people, objects, and places shown in this series of photographs created by the Indonesian soldiers capturing their violence against their women and teenage girl victims, we hope to understand better the institutional structures and norms that gave rise to, permitted, or indeed encouraged and nurtured the perpetration of such violence. To invoke Megan MacKenzie's helpful proposal, analyzing visual patterns and signals within soldier-produced illicit images can shed new light on aspects of internal military "band of brother" culture.[10] We take this approach one step further by situating our analysis of these photographs alongside testimonial accounts from survivors, in an attempt to demonstrate that these practices were not only normalized within the culture of the Indonesian army, but also that sexual and gendered forms of violence were central features of New Order state discourse and practice.

It is difficult to discern how many female victims are shown in the seventy photographs. In re-circulations of these images, some sources cite seven female victims, others cite five.[11] Unlike the photographs of the male torture victims, which are mostly single shots for each man, those featuring female victims are clearly multiple shots of each woman. Unlike many of the male victims, the female victims' faces are obscured with either a black hood or a piece of black cloth tied around their heads. Furthermore, unlike in the photographs showing male victims, in the female victim images the male perpetrators all wear balaclavas to cover their own features. After looking carefully through the collection, we believe there are five young women depicted in these seventy photographs. We base this assessment on the women's clothing, their physical features (such as their hair, where visible), the similarity of the environs (the same room or background, the same objects in the background or on their bodies), and the injuries to the women's bodies. Accordingly, we identified twenty-eight photographs of the first woman, seventeen of the second, twenty of the third and fourth women together, and five of the fifth woman.[12] We spent some time grouping together the images of each woman and organizing them in the order in which we believe they were taken, based primarily on the progression of forced clothing removal and injury accumulation on the victims' bodies. This sequencing was essential because it revealed not only the sexual nature of the torture inflicted and the scopophilic intent of the photographer/s, but also how the five women were tortured within a relatively short timeframe by the same group of perpetrators, which we explain further below.

Here, we describe each woman in turn, before discussing the group of perpetrators who created, and who are shown in, these seventy photographs. We do not describe each photograph, but rather focus on what we are able to observe or interpret from each

[9] Christophe Busch, "Bonding Images: Photography and Film as Acts of Perpetration," *Genocide Studies and Prevention* 12, no. 2 (2018): 56.

[10] Megan MacKenzie, "Why Do Soldiers Swap Illicit Pictures? How a Visual Discourse Analysis Illuminates Military Band of Brother Culture," *Security Dialogue* 51, no. 4 (2020): 340–57.

[11] For example, seven in A Paz é Possível em Timor-Leste (1996, 31); but five in the East Timor International Support Centre (ETISC) materials (1997, 4).

[12] See note 7.

series of photographs. The individual images capture single moments of violence, while each series reveals a broader narrative of how such moments of violence were enacted. Certainly, we make these observations highly subjectively, and our interpretation is one that frames these images as purposefully created exploitative trophies meant to capture and commemorate the perpetrators' violence against, humiliation of, and domination over their female victims. Yet, as Elissa Mailänder explains in her analysis of a photograph showing a rape by German soldiers in the Second World War, "Once we engage with the gaze of the photographer, it becomes clear that the depicted scene follows a completely different logic," a logic that may even "convey the impression of fun."[13] It is these different logics at play, by those who made these photographs, that we attempt to uncover by reconstructing and interpreting the sequence of these images.[14]

Five Young East Timorese Women

While we cannot be certain of their exact ages, we believe the five female victims were young women or teenage girls, with three of them shown wearing the light blue skirt of the Indonesian national high school (Sekolah Menengah Atas, SMA) uniform in some photographs. As we reconstructed the sequence in which the photographs were taken, all five women are shown to be partially or fully clothed at the beginning of their torture. The first woman was dressed in a black-and-white checked skirt and floral blouse, the second woman in the white blouse and blue skirt of the SMA uniform, with black shoes and colored socks. The third and fourth women were always photographed together, as they were tied back-to-back against a tree, and both were already half naked at the beginning of the sequence: the third woman had on a pair of jeans, while the fourth had on a blue SMA skirt. The fifth woman, who features in the smallest number of photographs, is shown only in her blue SMA skirt: we believe she is already deceased in these images, the last of which is a blurry photograph of her body dumped in a shallow grave, with one of the perpetrators covering her with sticks and other debris.

One of the first apparent "logics" of these violent moments consciously captured by the perpetrators was their intent to document the forced removal of their female victims' clothing. The planned nature of these photographs is immediately apparent in the sequence of how the perpetrators forcibly strip their victims, deliberately staging their sexual violence with the ostensible intent of creating mementos of this violence. In the sequence of images of the first, second, third and fourth woman, all have their clothing gradually taken from them by various perpetrators. This sequencing, and the attention paid to the women's bodies, is markedly different from those in the collection featuring male victims: there is no attempt to document the men's forced removal of clothing, nor are there repeated shots of naked men from various angles. Several of the images of the women are focused closely on the perpetrators removing items of clothing, and they have posed for the photographer so that the torso of the female victim and the forced

---

[13] Elissa Mailänder, "Making Sense of a Rape Photograph: Sexual Violence as Social Performance on the Eastern Front, 1939–1944," *Journal of the History of Sexuality* 26, no. 3 (2017): 494.

[14] On how images demand multiple interpretations beyond those that created them in the context of World War Two photography, see, for example, Elizabeth Harvey and Maiken Umbach, "Introduction: Photography and Twentieth-Century German History," *Central European History* 48, no. 3 (2015): 287–99.

removal take up the majority of the frame; the rest of the frame is filled with the hands of the perpetrator/s pulling off the item of clothing.

Another logic to these forced clothing-removal sequences plainly mimics pornographic scripts meant to titillate through the sexual objectification of each woman's body; this is a script that these men are observably taking pleasure in reenacting.[15] Nearly half of the photographs of the first, second, third, and fourth woman were taken in deliberate order to document the men removing their victims' clothing, item by item, in what appears to be a social, even jocular, performance. The men's movements and poses—and how they position their victims—are strongly conscious of where the photographer is at all times. While the images are composed mainly of their victims' bodies (the focus is more often than not the naked or partially naked torso of the victim, particularly the chest and pubic region), with the male perpetrators on the periphery, there are photographs within each series that betray the seemingly playful interactions between individual perpetrators and the photographer. Such interactions are clear, for example, in a photograph where one perpetrator looks back over his shoulder at the camera, his eyes crinkled through the gap in his balaclava in what is likely a smile. He uses one hand to gesture toward the photographer, beckoning him closer, with his other fist punching into the fourth woman's naked abdomen.

The twenty-eight photographs of the first woman, wearing the black-and-white checked skirt, are the most detailed and methodical of the entire collection. She was photographed inside a dark room with a dirty cement floor and cement block walls; the only light in the room seems to come from the camera's flash. She appears to be alive, dressed, and standing at the beginning of the series, though blood appears across the back of her floral shirt. As the series progresses, she is forced to the floor, stripped of her clothes, and her torturers inflict numerous burning, blunt, and penetrating injuries; some with a plank of wood, some with the long nails that are also seen scattered on the floor, with a lit cigarette, and with their fists and booted feet. In some photographs, her hands and feet have been tied together with a long green cord. It is difficult to discern whether she was unconscious or deceased by the end of the series; the last few photographs show her prone body in one corner of the room, and there seems to be blood on the cement floor under her black-hooded head.

After stripping off the first woman's clothing, the perpetrators used a black marker pen to write a series of messages and images on her body, with eleven of the twenty-eight photographs showing them writing and drawing on her front and back. First, one man writes on her chest above her breasts, *Inilah jagoan Timor begini wa—ny-*[unclear] *kalau anti-RI* ("This is the champion of Timor, this is the [unclear] when [you are] anti-RI [Republic of Indonesia]"; or, roughly, "This is what happens to enemies of the RI"). The next shots show a cross has been drawn on her stomach and *Jagoan bodoh* ("Stupid champion" or "Stupid hero") written on the front of her upper left thigh. The group of

---

[15] Our point is only to highlight that there are prevalent "scripts" within pornography that consumers can learn from and reenact (see Ana J. Bridges, Chyung F. Sun, Matthew B. Ezzell, and Jennifer Johnson, "Sexual Scripts and the Sexual Behavior of Men and Women Who Use Pornography," *Sexualization, Media, & Society* 2, no. 4 [2016]: 1–14), not that there is a positive association between pornography and violence against women. See, for example, Neil M. Malamuth, Tamara Addison, and Mary Koss, "Pornography and Sexual Aggression: Are there Reliable Effects and Can We Understand Them?" *Annual Review of Sex Research* 11 (2000): 26–91.

perpetrators then turned the first woman onto her front, and the dust from the cement floor cakes her back and thighs, so much so that she must have been pushed into the floor in order for the dust to coat the entire back of her body. The next few photographs show one of the perpetrators writing on her upper back, *Begini supaya kamu rasa-kan akibatnya* ("This is so you feel the consequences") and then *Jagoan ta'i kucing mati seperti tikus* ("Cat shit hero, dead like a rat") on the back of her upper right thigh and buttock. The following photographs are close-ups and show clearly the writing on her naked body, as well as her multiple injuries, the nails on the floor, and the blood spatter. The perpetrators then turned the first woman onto her back again (the dust now caking her front) and added further messages, such as *Ini dia* ("This is the one" or "This is her") on the front of her right upper thigh and other writing (not legible) under the cross drawn on her stomach. Lastly, there are two photographs in which two perpetrators lean over the first woman's naked body to hold up a sign in front of her black-hooded face; the sign is written on a piece of white card and reads, *Hidup hadia Nobel* ("Long live the Nobel [Peace] Prize [winner]").

We believe the second woman was tortured in the same dark cement room very shortly after the perpetrators had finished torturing the first. As far as we can discern in the photographs, the floor and walls are the same; as are the items in the room, such as the blood spatter patterns, old newspapers and long nails on the floor, and the long green cord used to tie up the first woman.[16] Moreover, the same white Nobel Prize sign is placed on the second woman's face by the perpetrators in the last two photographs of the first sequence. Here, the second woman is lying naked and prone on the floor on her back, with her clothing dumped in a pile on her abdomen, the boots of the group of perpetrators visible around her, two of them shown standing on her legs. The sequence of seventeen photographs showing the second woman is similar to the first, insomuch as she is alive, hooded, standing, and fully dressed in her high school uniform at the start; then she is gradually stripped, forced to the floor, and progressively injured by the perpetrators. In this series of photographs of the second woman, however, the perpetrators do not write or draw on her body. The photographer also takes greater care to capture the infliction of injuries to the second woman's body than in the series of the first woman: in one image, for example, the men stand aside so the photographer can capture a dagger being pushed into her upper back; in another, one of the men lies on top of the woman to either simulate or document a sexual assault.

We believe the twenty photographs featuring the torture of the third and fourth woman were taken shortly after those showing the first two. As we discuss below, we believe the same group of perpetrators was involved; further, the men's clothing is so similar that the torture of the third and fourth women probably happened within hours of the first two. The location, however, is different: all twenty of these photographs were taken outside, in what seems to be a sparsely wooded forest. Although these photographs were taken at night (the flash provides the limited light), we think it likely that this forest is also the location for the final five photographs showing the fifth woman (who seems deceased and is buried in a shallow grave).

The third and fourth woman are tied back-to-back around a tree with what seems to be the same long green cord used on the first two women. This series of photographs

---

[16] Specifically, there are particular blood spatter patterns that emerge in the series as the first woman was tortured, and we believe that these are the same patterns visible on the floor under the second woman.

involves a circling action by the soldiers and photographer: for example, one shot focuses on the third woman having her jeans stripped from her, the next moves to the fourth woman, whose blue SMA skirt is pulled off; the next returns to the third woman. In their torture of these two women, the perpetrators show themselves using their fists on both, but their focus is less on capturing the injuries that they inflict and more on documenting their sexual assaults. In this series, there are many more consciously positioned or staged poses, whereby two or three of the perpetrators position themselves around their victim (with her at the center), each using their hands to punch, hit or pinch the woman's breasts, pubic area, or lower abdomen, while sometimes the men's heads turn back toward the camera. As in the previous series of photographs of the first two women, the perpetrators wear balaclavas to cover their faces and there are black cloths tied over the women's faces (though their hair is still visible).

The final series of photographs comprises five photographs of a fifth young woman and only one of the male perpetrators during daylight, in what appears to be the same forest depicted in the series of the third and fourth women. Naked except for a black hood over her head, the green cord tied around her wrists, and her blue SMA uniform skirt, this fifth young woman could be one of the previous four female victims. However, we believe that she is a separate victim, based on her hair (visible in two of the photographs) and the injuries on her back and around her ribcage and breasts (which does not appear to match the injuries visible on the other women). As stated, we also believe that she is unconscious or deceased: the first image shows the perpetrator dragging her limp body, holding her by the neck and under one arm, and the last photograph shows her remains in a shallow grave in the forest. The remaining photographs show this same perpetrator standing over her body, which is slumped forward on the forest floor among the leaves, while he leans over to punch his right fist into her ribcage.

A Small Group of Male Perpetrators

We believe there were six (possibly seven) male perpetrators who took part in the torture and photographing of the five young women. Allowing for the camera to have been passed between men, there is one photograph at the start of the sequence of the second woman that shows five perpetrators.[17] We are able to discern that it is the same group of men who created these seventy images in much the same way that we identified the five women victims, which is their physical appearance. As we reconstructed the series of photographs, each perpetrator was identifiable mainly through their clothing, but also their stature: perpetrator 1 has on military fatigues, a dark balaclava, black boots, and a beret that is either faded red or orange[18]; perpetrator 2 also wears fatigues, a pale balaclava, a pair of blue flip-flops, and sometimes a black cowboy hat; perpetrator 3 is similar to the first and wears fatigues, boots, and a black balaclava; perpetrator 4 wears black and white camouflage pants, black boots, and a black balaclava with white horizontal stripes; and lastly, perpetrator 5 is not in uniform, he has on a pair of dark

[17] Given the angle of many shots and the clear movement from one shot to the next, we do not believe that a tripod was used; thus, one person must have been holding the camera during all photographs.

[18] The camera flash makes it difficult to determine the color: a red beret would indicate a member of Kopassus (Army Special Forces Command), while an orange one would likely indicate a member of Paskhas (Korps Pasukan Khas, Special Forces Corp), both Indonesian Army units. At the time, the Paskhas regiment were known as Kopasgat (Komando Pasukan Gerak Cepat, Quick Reaction Force Command).

pants, a light-colored jacket, a dark balaclava, and a pair of white sneakers. Aside from the photographer, a probable seventh perpetrator appears briefly in the series of the third and fourth women. This man wears fatigues but with the same black balaclava with white stripes as the fourth perpetrator; these men appear together in one photograph, however, confirming that they are separate figures.

In the seventy photographs of the women victims, this small group of perpetrators are clearly interested in documenting not only the ways in which they terrify, injure, and debase their victims, but also their own creative, social efforts. By "creative" and "social," we mean the behaviors and actions of this group that they carry out as integral to their own homosocial performance and bonding (for one another), and that are also a seemingly conscious effort to create trophies or mementos of their violence (for themselves and potentially for others).[19] Their tactics for brutalizing their victims, and how they use their victims' bodies as objects on which to perform these social acts, change over the course of the four sequences. All show deeply dehumanizing forms of sexual violence, but their "logics" in taking these photographs of their violence seem to move from triumphal scorn over their victims, to voyeuristic indulgence, to extreme objectification and fetishization of their victims' bodies.

The homosocial interactions between this small group of perpetrators are evident in many of the seventy photographs. While the center of the images is almost always a woman's torso, the men on the periphery are clearly interacting with one another (including the photographer), with the woman's body an object on which they stage their actions. Some of these images capture clear moments of positive emotions and interactions between the men. One example is the communication and almost palpable felicity between three perpetrators as they stand around the second young woman, forcibly removing her clothing; their heads are turned toward one another, their focus on the other men, not the girl. In the sequence showing the third and fourth women, there are multiple shots of two or three of the men together sexually assaulting one of the women with their hands, but the women themselves seem almost interchangeable. Again, their focus is on their own performance, their stances for the camera, and on one another. Others include photographs in which the men pose for the camera around their victim's body, in obvious triumphal stances. As Peggy Reeves Sanday, a researcher of homosocial bonding through gang rape, remarks, "One might well ask why the woman is even necessary for the sexual acts these men stage for one another."[20]

Aside from capturing their performance for one another, taking these photographs allowed the men to create mementos of their violence; perhaps to relive their acts later on, perhaps to create tools for intimidating other detainees, or perhaps to make commodities

[19] In a previous chapter, we examine the homosocial bonding and trophy-making elements in more detail. See Loney and Pohlman, "The Sexual and Visual Dynamics of Torture," 84–100. On homosocial bonding by groups of men through enacting group assailant sexual assaults, see, for example, Peggy Reeves Sanday, *Fraternity Gang Rape: Sex, Brotherhood, and Privilege on Campus* (New York: New York University Press, 1990); Karen Franklin, "Enacting Masculinity: Antigay Violence and Group Rape as Participatory Theater," *Sexuality Research and Social Policy* 10, no. 3 (2004): 25–40. On trophy-taking behaviors during violence, see, on individual offenders, Robert R. Hazelwood and Janet I. Warren, "The Sexually Violent Offender: Impulsive or Ritualistic?" *Aggression and Violence Behaviour* 5, no. 3 (2000): 267–79; and during mass violence, Simon Harrison, "Skull Trophies of the Pacific War: Transgressive Objects of Remembrance," *The Journal of the Royal Anthropological Institute* 12, no. 4 (2006): 817–36.

[20] Sanday, *Fraternity Gang Rape*, 12.

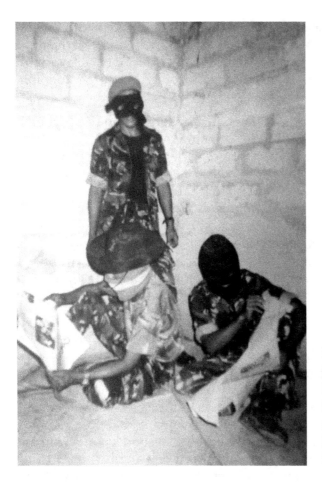

Figure 1: Perpetrators posing for the camera: Perpetrator 1 standing, Perpetrator 2 (Left), and 3 (Right) sitting. Source: Dr Andrew McNaughtan collection, Mitchell Library, State Library of New South Wales, MLMSS 7714, Px23–Px27.

to exchange with their peers.[21] Further evidence that these photographs were made for themselves is Figure 1 (below), the only image in this series with no woman victim in the frame, one perhaps intended to capture their prowess or comradery. In this one highly contrived shot, three of the men pose nonchalantly for the photographer in the cement room where the first two women were tortured: two sit on the floor reading newspapers, the third stands behind them looking toward the camera. This image may have been taken before they tortured these women, and certainly the casualness of their poses—men simply reading the newspaper—is artifice meant to be juxtaposed against what they are wearing, the room in which they sit, and their activities in the rest of the photographs. They are wearing their same balaclavas and face masks, and they are reading newspapers that may be those seen on the floor later in the series under their bloodied victims. Under one of the men is a plank of wood, likely the one they used when torturing the first woman.

The meticulous staging and documentation of the violence against, and writing on, the first woman's body most clearly shows the fetishization by the perpetrators

---

[21] Despoina Mantziari, "Sadistic Scophophilia in Contemporary Rape Culture: *I Spit on Your Grave* (2012) and the Practice of 'Media Rape,'" *Feminist Media Studies* 18, no. 3 (2018): 397–410.

of their female victims. Certainly, the sequencing of the photographs displaying the men performing sexual violence against the second, third, and fourth young woman demonstrates their desire to document their sexual assaults, but it is the first woman whose body very literally becomes a signifier and a stage for their violence and their creative expression.

In this sense, the treatment of the first woman shows in the most obvious way how these women were transformed into artifacts by their captors. As anthropologist Allen Feldman explains, the violence done to victims during periods of mass violence disconnects the body from the self and transforms it into a political commodity and signifier.[22] While the women and girls in the photographs are not named,[23] what is clear is that who they are or were as individuals has been displaced by what they have been made into. They are no longer young women who may or may not have been involved in the popular youth resistance movement of the 1990s in the territory, they have been made into artifacts for the East Timorese civilian resistance.[24] This is because, just as the violence against these young women separates the individual from the body to create a commodity, it is also deterministic; the violence invests the body with meaning that both rationalizes and creates the reason for its perpetration. For Feldman, this is a process of false motives, of "how the ritualized and the symbolic provide the foundations for the rationalization of power and thus the fictionalization of its violence."[25] The fact that these young women have been captured and tortured by these men means that they must be members of the East Timorese resistance, because their capture and torture prove it so. All five women are also made artifacts in the sense that they are depersonalized and anonymized: their faces are obscured with black cloth, to hide the main part of their bodies that could identify them as individuals. Yet they are also anatomized, so that their individual body parts—specifically those parts that identify them as female—are the focus of the men's violence and the photographing of that violence.

The men's treatment of the first young woman, in which her body is used as a prop for their own staged movements, shows most clearly their motivation to capture their own creative and social efforts. The men pay detailed attention to the injuries they inflict and the words they inscribe on her body, each message clearly having significance for themselves and for any intended future use of their photographic mementos. The young woman in the photographs is not the intended recipient of these messages; rather, she has been made into the object on which to scrawl these messages for others. The demonstrative communicative intent behind these images includes messages that might be interpreted as clear intimidation to those who might be tempted to take part in the resistance ("This is what happens so that you feel the consequences"), and threats against them ("This is what happens to enemies of the Republic of Indonesia"), to derision of

[22] Allen Feldman, *Formations of Violence: The Narrative of the Body and Political Terror in Northern Ireland* (Chicago: University of Chicago Press, 1991), 63–64.

[23] We have also made a conscious decision *not* to seek to identify them—nor to reproduce any of the photographs in this article to avoid the potential re-traumatization that this act may engender for the victims and their families.

[24] On youth involvement in the resistance, see Hannah Loney, *In Women's Words: Violence and Everyday Life during the Indonesian Occupation of East Timor, 1975–1999* (Abingdon: Sussex Academic Press, 2018), 115–41; Clinton Fernandes, *The Independence of East Timor: Multi-Dimensional Perspectives—Occupation, Resistance, and International Political Activism* (Eastbourne: Sussex Academic Press, 2011), 125–44.

[25] Feldman, *Formations of Violence*, 114–15.

East Timor's 1996 Nobel Peace Prize winners, José Ramos-Horta and Bishop Carlos Filipe Ximenes Belo ("Long live the Nobel [Peace] Prize [winner]"). This last message can be read as one of a handful meant to mock the Catholic-aligned popular resistance; other purposefully placed signs include a poster depicting the ascension of Jesus stuck to one wall in the cement room and the cross drawn on the first woman's stomach. The use of the cross—a powerful Catholic symbol of sacrifice, suffering, repentance, and solidarity for the East Timorese resistance—emphasizes and reinforces the targeted nature of these violent acts.

The performance of creating these messages is one that exploits and manipulates all objects in the cement room, drawing in the items that the men use to torture this woman, including their hands and boots, her body, and the injuries they inflict on it. The writing that they capture so carefully is simply another, though certainly more explicit, dimension of the highly symbolic fabric of their performance. Yet, as these men draw in and manipulate all objects in the room, they also manipulate their own bodies for their violent performance. Aside from how they position their bodies for the camera, and how they use their hands and feet as props in their own staging, they also write on their own bodies. In two of the close-up photographs where one of the perpetrators (we think perpetrator 2, because of the light color of his wristwatch) is using his left hand to grope the first woman's breast and his right to write on her naked chest, we can see writing on the inside of his own right forearm. Written in the same black marker pen, the message is much simpler: "AntiGPK," the "GPK" standing for "Gerakan Pengacau Keamanan," or "Security Disruptors Movement," the term used by the Indonesian authorities to refer to internal enemies of the New Order state, in this setting meaning members of the local resistance in occupied East Timor.[26] Writing and drawing on the woman's body and their own enables these men to create special framing for their messages that brings a new level of crude materiality to their performance. If it were not clear enough that these soldiers had made these women into signifiers for the civilian resistance, they reinforce this message by remaking their own bodies into signifiers of the occupation. "This is what happens to enemies of Republic of Indonesia," and they, the "AntiGPK," are those to inflict the violence that these enemies deserve.

Visual Echoes of State-Sanctioned Violence

The photographs smuggled out of East Timor in 1997 reveal types of violence that were part of a longer genealogy of similar acts perpetrated by Indonesia's security services throughout the New Order (and beyond). Created at the end of that regime, we might understand the photographs as a product of a range of factors, including the individual desire on the part of these soldiers to stage and make these photographs; the technology available to them, that is, the photographic film and cameras ubiquitous in the 1990s; and, most importantly, the institutional environment in which these images were created.[27] In our discussion here, we are most concerned with the institutional

[26] See Geoffrey Robinson, "*Rawan* Is as *Rawan* Does: The Origins of Disorder in New Order Aceh," *Indonesia* 66 (October 1998): 127.

[27] Indonesia's security forces, as documented in the Final Report of the Commission for Reception, Truth and Reconciliation in East Timor (Comissão de Acolhimento, Verdade e Reconciliação de Timor-Leste, CAVR), were known to photograph their victims of torture and extrajudicial killings in the territory. See CAVR, *Chega! The Final Report of the Timor-Leste Commission for Reception, Truth and Reconciliation*, vol. 1 (Jakarta:

environment; that is, the culture and norms of the New Order's military and its auxiliaries that were deployed to attack, control, and terrorize civilians. These factors are common in enabling "atrocity environments," as Martha Huggins, Mika Haritos-Fatouros, and Philip Zimbardo found in their study of Brazil's state torturers. Such factors—the state's paranoia and drive to eliminate internal enemies; small, loosely supervised security units that undertake violence with the approval of superiors; a structure of impunity with little oversight[28]—were those that enabled the creation of places like Baucau's Red House, the torture of the five young women, and the actions of this small group of soldiers. As Richard Tanter has convincingly argued, atrocities like those perpetrated in the Red House were a product of three political processes that were fundamental to the New Order regime's institutions and the institutionalization of violent means within them: militarization, surveillance, and terror.[29] It was this wider institution environment, we argue, that allowed, facilitated, and encouraged this violence and the creation of such images.

The images described above are among the handful of similar photographs produced by Indonesian soldiers during the occupation of East Timor.[30] Critically, they show some of the types of violence that had been reported by survivors from the territory over the previous two decades. These survivor accounts gave details of the massacres, as well as the disappearances and the killings of East Timorese resistance fighters and civilians by the Indonesian armed forces.[31] Further, the photographs show—purposefully captured in their performance—the forms of violence used systematically by the Indonesian security services to interrogate and torture their detainees. For the purposes of our analysis, the photographs reveal how these forms of violence often contained a pronounced sexual dimension, particularly when used against women and girls.[32] In this sense, the East Timor torture photographs gave proximate visual form to

---

KPG and STP-CAVR, 2013), 805, 963, 1546, 1565, 2007, 2015–17. Indonesian Special Forces also sometimes video-recorded their planning and interrogations. See, for example, the video of Xanana Gusmão's capture and interrogation from 1992, featured in Mark Davis, "The Capture of Xanana Gusmao," *SBS Dateline*, May 22, 2011, YouTube video, 16:55, https://youtu.be/7CTp1X47QHQ.

[28] For a summary of these main findings, see Martha K. Huggins, Mika Haritos-Fatouros, and Philip G. Zimbardo, *Violence Workers: Police Torturers and Murderers Reconstruct Brazilian Atrocities* (Berkeley: University of California Press, 2002), xx.

[29] Richard Tanter, "Intelligence Agencies and Third World Militarization: A Case Study of Indonesia, 1966–1989, with Special Reference to South Korea, 1961–1989" (PhD dissertation, Monash University, 1991). See also Geoffrey Robinson, *"If You Leave Us Here, We Will Die": How Genocide was Stopped in East Timor* (Princeton: Princeton University Press, 2010), 41–46.

[30] For a collection of other photographs, see A Paz é Possível em Timor-Leste, *Photos of East Timor*. Many survivors of detention from Timor-Leste have spoken about being photographed by their interrogators or having photographs shown to them. See, for example, the testimonies by "Ms X" and João Maria dos Reis in *"I Am Timorese": Testimonies from East Timor* (London: Catholic Institute for International Relations, 1990), 6–9, 34–36; CAVR, *Chega!*, 2015–17.

[31] See, for example, Carmel Budiardjo and Liem Soei Liong, *The War Against East Timor* (London: Zed Books, 1984), 127–38; Amnesty International, *Indonesia and East Timor, Power and Impunity: Human Rights under the New Order*, ASA 21/17/94, September 1994; Amnesty International, *Women in Indonesia and East Timor*, AI Index ASA 25/51/1995 (London: Amnesty International, 1995).

[32] On some of the accounts of women's experiences of sexual and gender-based violence, see Loney, *In Women's Words*; Michelle Turner, *"Telling" East Timor Personal Testimonies 1942–1992* (Sydney: New South Wales University Press, 1992); Rebecca Winters, ed., *Buibere: Voice of East Timorese Women* (Darwin: East Timor International Support Center, 1999); and Jude Conway, ed. *Step by Step: Women of East Timor, Stories of Resistance and Survival* (Darwin: Darwin University Press, 2010). Contemporaneous stories about sexualized torture being used against women detainees include "Testimony of Two Victimized Women from Alas,"

the descriptions of this violence that had been heard in the oral and written testimonies by survivors and eyewitnesses circulated in the 1990s and long before. When the 1997 photograph collection was published by East Timor solidarity groups, they made this link explicit: these photographs, which in their entirety showed scores of victims, were purposely positioned as irrefutable visual evidence for the atrocities against many thousands of others in the territory over the previous decades of occupation. Framed thus, the photographs proved, beyond any doubt, that survivors had been telling the truth.

Beyond the immediate context of East Timor, the photographs also provided a visual echo for similar forms of the New Order's violence in other places and at other times. While disconnected from the women and girls who were abused and photographed in 1997, the photograph collection examined in this article is a resonant visual reference for the violence of the regime against many other women and girls in other parts of the archipelago and in other contexts. Indeed, we argue that these photographs provided visual echoes of the stories told by survivors from earlier and contemporaneous mass atrocities perpetrated by the New Order regime. These images, therefore, somehow remediated the violence of the regime in the long durée: not because they were able to convey the suffering of those five women and girls fully nor meaningfully, but rather, because their images resonated with the suffering of so many (unseen) others. That resonance is grounded in the similarities between what happened to these East Timorese women and girls with what had happened to many others, revealing the magnitude of the New Order's systematic atrocities against women and girls.[33]

First and foremost, the photos gave visual form to the perpetration of such atrocities in East Timor. During the Indonesian occupation, sexual and gendered violence was deployed by Indonesian security forces and their auxiliaries against East Timorese civilians from the initial days of the invasion and throughout the twenty-four-year military occupation of the territory. Sexual violence, and the threat of sexual violence, were at the center of the atmosphere of fear and intimidation that characterized the occupation. Indonesian security forces used sexual and gendered violence to terrify and humiliate individual women, but women were also implicated as victims of proxy violence—the hurt of which was sometimes aimed at husbands, fathers, or sons who were part of the armed resistance movement.[34] The threat of sexual violence was sometimes used to extract a confession or to obtain information during interrogation sessions. There were also opportunistic features to this violence; it was often perpetrated at places where victims were most vulnerable and the military imposed absolute control, such as during interrogation or detention sessions, in military or police custody, or during medical treatment in hospitals. In other cases, it was perpetrated in people's homes, in cars, in prisons, and during military operations.[35]

---

email message originally from Yayasan Hak, Dili, East Timor, December 1, 1998, http://etan.org/et/1998/december/1-7/05alasw.htm.

[33] On the visual resonance of images—particularly iconic atrocity images—and their power to stand in for, or become resonant referents of, other events, see Robert Hariman and John Louis Lucaites, *No Caption Needed: Iconic Photographs, Public Culture, and Liberal Democracy* (Chicago: University of Chicago Press, 2007).

[34] Loney, *In Women's Words*, 73–74.

[35] Loney, *In Women's Words*, 74.

Torture that occurred within the context of detention or interrogation sessions often had pronounced sexual and gendered dimensions, as was so clearly demonstrated in the photographs of the torture of the five young women discussed in this article. Rape and sexual assault were a common part of torture against female detainees. In testimonies given by survivors, they recount, for example, that cigarettes were butted out by Indonesian soldiers on the bodies of women, including on their breasts and vaginas, and women were sexually abused with bottles and other objects.[36] After participating in a public protest, for example, "Sintadewe" was among a group of young people who were captured, interrogated, and beaten by Indonesian security forces in Dili in 1998: "They beat, they kicked, they poked me very hard here and there with their fingers. They touched my body as if I was a worthless woman. They touched my breasts. They did things like they do to prostitutes. They touched my face, they could do what they liked. This was all part of their interrogations."[37]

Our emphasis here is that the seventy photographs that feature women and girl victims from 1997—as with the testimonies by women survivors like Sintadewe and many others from the occupation period—echoes the stories of so many other women survivors of mass violence under the New Order regime. The use and forms of sexual and gendered violence in occupied East Timor, we argue, must be understood as a product or extension of similar forms of violence used by Indonesia's security service personnel in other contexts and times across the span of the regime. Accordingly, we argue that the testimonies of survivors and eyewitnesses to this violence from these other contexts echo those from East Timor. The stories from across these contexts share a symmetry in the forms of violence they recount, suggesting that they belong to the same semiotic family of gendered harm deployed against women and girls by the New Order state.

Here, we identify two of these other contexts: one that predates the occupation of East Timor and that occurred at the start of the New Order regime; the other running parallel to the occupation's (and the regime's) final decade. The first is the mass killing and detention of suspected communists in the mid-to-late 1960s, and the second is the 1989–98 period of heightened military operations (known as the "DOM" period, for Daerah Operasi Militer) in the conflict in Aceh between GAM and the government of Indonesia. The contexts for these two cases and East Timor were divergent, yet the militarized response to all three was constructed through New Order rhetoric as campaigns to eradicate internal enemies. As Richard Tanter and others have shown, these campaigns were built on the institutionalization of terror tactics to deal with these internal threats (constructed as "GPK" or "PKI").[38] We emphasize that these terror functions were fundamentally gendered in their deployment of sexual and gendered violence, particularly in the forms of attacks against women and girls. Further, we emphasize that the military's terror tactics were also gendering, in the sense that they constructed these internal enemies in specifically gendered ways.

---

[36] Loney, *In Women's Words*, 69.

[37] Sintadewe, *Buibere, Voice of East Timorese Women, Volume 1*, comp. Rebecca Winters (Darwin: East Timor International Support Centre, 1999), 12.

[38] Tanter, "Intelligence Agencies"; see also Michael van Langenberg, "The New Order State: Language, Ideology, Hegemony," in *State and Civil Society in Indonesia*, ed. Arief Budiman (Clayton, Victoria: Monash Papers on South East Asia, No. 22, 1990), 121–50.

The 1965–66 Anti-Communist Violence

The 1965–66 anti-Communist mass killings were the foundational event of the Indonesian New Order regime.[39] It was through the eradication of suspected Communists, depicted as betrayers of the nation who had to be eradicated in order to save the country, that the Indonesian military was able to take over the state.[40] The army leadership, under General Suharto, blamed the September 30, 1965 attempted coup on the Indonesian Communist Party (Partai Komunis Indonesia, PKI) and then mobilized the armed forces and civilian proxies to kill an estimated 500,000 "suspected Communists," most of these deaths occurring between October 1965 and March 1966.[41] The PKI and its associated organizations were depicted in widespread Army propaganda as dangerous, internal enemies of the state who had to be eliminated. Communist women, in particular, were demonized for their alleged role in the attempted coup.[42] In addition to those killed, approximately one million others were rounded up between 1965 and 1970 and held in political detention. There, many people were tortured, starved, and had to perform forced labor.[43] From research conducted with those who survived the detention centers (including by one of the authors), the majority were interrogated and, of those, many experienced torture during the interrogation sessions.[44]

Sexual and gendered violence was an integral part of these state-led purges against the Indonesian Left. This violence was perpetrated by security service personnel and their coopted militias during the massacres, in the detention centers, and in the homes and communities of suspected Communists. The primary victims of sexual and gendered violence were women and older teenage girls who were deemed Communists, either through their membership or affiliation with the party or through their familial ties

[39] On how these killings should be understood as genocidal, see Jess Melvin and Annie Pohlman, "A Case for Genocide: Indonesia, 1965–1966," in *The Indonesian Genocide of 1965: Causes, Dynamics and Legacies*, ed. Katharine McGregor, Jess Melvin, and Annie Pohlman (Cham: Palgrave Macmillan, 2018), 27–47. On their role in establishing the New Order, see Michael van Langenberg, "Gestapu and State Power in Indonesia," in *The Indonesian Killings of 1965–1966: Studies from Java and Bali*, ed. Robert Cribb (Clayton, Victoria: Centre of Southeast Asian Studies, Monash University, 1990), 45–62. The killings were also foundational in the Derridean sense, in that they served as a kind of self-creating authorization for the regime and each subsequent violent repression carried out by that regime, see Jacques Derrida, "Force of Law: The 'Mystical Foundation of Authority,'" trans. Mary Quaintance, *Cardozo Law Review* 11, nos. 5–6 (1990): 920–1045.

[40] See Jess Melvin, *The Army and the Indonesian Genocide: Mechanics of Mass Murder* (New York: Routledge, 2018).

[41] For estimates on the number killed, see Robert Cribb, "Introduction: Problems in the Historiography of the Killings in Indonesia," in *The Indonesian Killings of 1965–1966: Studies from Java and Bali*, ed. Robert Cribb (Clayton, Victoria: Centre of Southeast Asian Studies, Monash University, 1990), 11–14.

[42] On the propaganda campaign, see Steven Drakeley, "Lubang Buaya: Myth, Misogyny and Massacre," *Nebula* 4, no. 4 (2007): 11–35; Annie Pohlman, "Incitement to Genocide against a Political Group: The Anti-Communist Killings in Indonesia," *Portal: Journal of Multidisciplinary International Studies* 11, no. 1 (2014): 1–22.

[43] On the conditions of those camps, see Amnesty International, *Indonesia: An Amnesty International Report* (London: Amnesty International, 1977); Carmel Budiardjo, "Political Imprisonment in Indonesia," *Bulletin of Concerned Asian Scholars* 6, no. 2 (1974): 20–23; TAPOL, *Indonesia: The Prison State* (London: TAPOL, 1976).

[44] See John Roosa, "The Truths of Torture: Victims' Memories and State Histories in Indonesia," *Indonesia* 85 (April 2008): 32. See also, Annie Pohlman, "Torture Camps in Indonesia, 1965–70," in *Detention Camps in Asia: The Conditions of Confinement in Modern Asian History*, ed. Robert Cribb, Sandra Wilson, and Christina Twomey (Leiden: Brill, 2022), 137–55.

to members.[45] The forms of this violence ranged from rape and numerous other forms of sexual assaults, through to longer-term forms of sexual violence, similar to those perpetrated during the occupation of East Timor, such as coercive sexual relationships and forced marriage.[46]

For those women and girls rounded up and held within the vast network of detention centers, the torture that they experienced frequently involved sexual and gendered forms of violence. Stories by survivors attest that the forms of this violence ranged widely and included rapes, gang rapes, and sexual assaults, as well as many forms of sexualized humiliation meant to shame and intimidate by the soldiers, police, and sometimes civilian militia who tortured them. Some more common forms of gendered humiliation included forced nakedness, hair-shaving, and being forced to perform sexual and other demeaning acts. This abuse often accompanied the physical torture with purposeful sexualized intent, particularly rape (by the penis or hands of the perpetrator, or by the insertion of other objects) and the physical injuries inflicted on the genital region or breasts of women victims (such as burning, cutting, or electric shocks).[47]

The DOM Period in Aceh, 1989–98

The stories by women survivors of sexualized forms of torture at the hands of security service personnel at the start of the New Order are resonant of similar stories from occupied East Timor and of the photographs analyzed within this article. They also echo the stories of those captured and interrogated during the secessionist conflict in Aceh. As Catherine Smith and others have shown, the conflict in Aceh is understood by survivors as part of a longer history of violence, suffering, and resistance, but that rapidly escalated and became particularly violent in the early 1990s. The Indonesian government designated Aceh a Military Operations Area (Daerah Operasi Militer, DOM) in 1989, beginning what was to become the first in a series of particularly brutal military operations. During the DOM period (1989–98), Acehnese people suffered high levels of violence, intensified poverty, and the militarization of everyday life.[48] Human Rights organizations such as Amnesty International have demonstrated that gender-specific violations, such as rape and other

---

[45] See Annie Pohlman, *Women, Sexual Violence, and the Indonesian Killings of 1965–1966* (London: Routledge, 2015), 23–46.

[46] On some of the longer-term forms in the late 1960s, see Annie Pohlman, "Sexual Slavery, Enforced Prostitution, and Forced Marriage as Crimes against Humanity during the Indonesian Killings of 1965–1966," in *The International People's Tribunal for 1965 and the Indonesian Genocide*, ed. Saskia E. Wieringa, Jess Melvin, and Annie Pohlman (London: Routledge, 2019), 96–114. The Indonesian army personnel perpetrated similar forms of longer-term sexual abuse of women in East Timor, such as through the taking of "TNI [Indonesian Army] wives," see Lia Kent, "Narratives of Suffering and Endurance: Coercive Sexual Relationships, Truth Commissions and Possibilities for Gender Justice in Timor-Leste," *The International Journal of Transitional Justice* 8 (2014): 289–313.

[47] For a summary of the forms of sexual violence used as part of torture, see Annie Pohlman, "Sexual Violence as Torture: Crimes against Humanity during the 1965–66 Killings in Indonesia," *Journal of Genocide Research* 19, no. 4 (2017): 580–82. For a broader analysis of the types of torture used in 1965, see Galuh Wandita, Indria Fernida, and Karen Campbell-Nelson, "Mass Torture in 1965–66: A Continuing Legacy," in *The International People's Tribunal for 1965 and the Indonesian Genocide*, ed. Saskia E. Wieringa, Jess Melvin, and Annie Pohlman (London: Routledge, 2019), 60–79.

[48] Catherine Smith, *Resilience and the Localisation of Trauma in Aceh, Indonesia* (Singapore: NUS Press, 2018), 2–5.

forms of sexual abuse of women and girls, were carried out by the Indonesian security forces as a form of intimidation and as punishment for actual and suspected support for GAM, either on the part of the woman concerned or her family members.[49]

There are numerous stories by women who experienced sexualized forms of torture at the hands of the Indonesian security forces during the DOM period in Aceh. One collection, for example, contains accounts by survivors of the notorious "Rumoh Geudong" interrogation center; Rumoh Geudong was a private house in Pidie district, located in the north of the province, that was taken over by the Indonesian Special Forces Command (Kopassus) and used as an interrogation and detention center during the 1990s.[50] In this collection, survivors recount experiences of repeated rape, forced nakedness, and the infliction of injuries to their genitals, abdomen, and breasts through electric shocks, cigarette burns, and beatings.[51] Women detainees also reported that they were repeatedly raped and subjected to other forms of reproductive and sexual violence, including the forced consumption of birth control pills.[52] The statement-taking work currently being undertaken with thousands of survivors by the Aceh Truth and Reconciliation Commission (Komisi Kebenaran dan Rekonsiliasi Aceh, KKR-Aceh) is further revealing the patterns of torture meted out by the Indonesian security forces in Aceh. These findings include strong patterns of sexual and gender-based violence, particularly against women and girls perceived to be "GPK" supporters, which, in this setting, meant GAM (and that we discuss in more detail below).[53]

Several researchers, such as Douglas Kammen and Geoffrey Robinson, have observed the similarities between the military campaigns in 1965, East Timor, and Aceh.[54] The similarities in the terror tactics used by the security services—particularly the special forces, like Kopassus—during these three campaigns have also been noted by many. Indeed, the similarities have been highlighted far beyond these cases, to other incidents and campaigns under the New Order, such as the *Petrus* ("mysterious killings") executions of alleged criminals in the 1980s and the ongoing atrocities perpetrated in

---

[49] Amnesty International, "Indonesia: The Impact of Impunity on Women in Aceh," November 23, 2000, Index number: ASA 21/060/2000.

[50] The collection is Dyah Rahmany P, *Rumoh Geudong: The Scar of the Acehnese* (Banda Aceh: Cordova Institute for Social Empowerment, 2004). Rumoh Geudong was a focus of the Independent Commission for the Investigation of Acts of Violence in Aceh in 1999, a team commissioned by then President Abdurraman Wahid (*Laporan: Komisi Independen Pengusutan Tindak Kekerasan Di Aceh*). On the report, see Elizabeth Drexler, "History and Liability in Aceh, Indonesia: Single Bad Guys and Convergent Narratives," *American Ethnologist* 33, no. 3 (2006): 313–26.

[51] See, for example, the testimonies by Cut Sari, Rosmiati and M. Ran, in Rahmany P, *Rumoh Geudong*, 75–84.

[52] M. Ran, in Rahmany P, *Rumoh Geudong*, 85. For a comparative discussion on the violation of women's reproductive and sexual rights in occupied East Timor, see Miranda Sissons, *From One Day to Another, Violations of Women's Reproductive and Sexual Rights in East Timor* (Fitzroy: East Timor Human Rights Centre, 1997).

[53] On this work, see Muhamad Daud Berueh, Faisal Hadi and Annie Pohlman, "The KKR-Aceh's Mapping of Torture Practices," in *The Aceh Truth and Reconciliation Commission in a Culture of Impunity*, ed. Jess Melvin, Sri Lestari Wahyuningroem, and Annie Pohlman (forthcoming).

[54] On the military's command structure under the New Order, and the terror tactics that particular units and battalions used in East Timor and Aceh, see, for example, Douglas Kammen, "Notes on the Transformation of the East Timor Military Command and Its Implications for Indonesia," *Indonesia* 67 (1999): 61–76. On the continuation of tactics, particularly military intelligence planning and their cooption of civilian militias in violence from 1965 onwards to East Timor and Aceh, see, for example, Geoffrey Robinson, "People's War: Militias in East Timor and Indonesia," *South East Asia Research* 9, no. 3 (2001): 271–318.

West Papua.[55] Based on extensive interviews with survivors across Indonesia and East Timor, Galuh Wandita, Indria Fernida, and Karen Campbell-Nelson have shown frequent strong similarities in their research on forms of torture used against "suspected Communists" in the late 1960s and "GPK" in occupied East Timor and Aceh.[56] In the authors' own separate research based on interviews with women survivors in Timor-Leste (Loney) and Indonesia (Pohlman, on the 1965 anti-Communist killings), we have also heard many similar stories from many women who recounted their treatment at the hands of New Order security service personnel and their auxiliaries.[57]

We argue that there is a reason for these similarities in the forms of violence used by the New Order's torturers in 1965, East Timor and Aceh, particularly the forms of sexual and gender-based violence used against mainly women and girls. In all three cases, survivors consistently recount how they were targeted because of their alleged support for, or ties to, individuals or groups that were defined by those who persecuted them as enemies of the New Order state. In 1965, in East Timor and in Aceh, the threat that such groups—"suspected Communists" or, from the 1970s onwards, the "GPK"—posed was constructed by the Indonesian military in their campaigns as insidious, internal enemies.[58] In the next section, we show that the ways in which the New Order perceived its internal enemies necessitated the use of sexual and gender-based violence against them.

Internal Enemies

Driven by the New Order's security intelligence complex, the paranoia over the spread and influence of these ever-present and seemingly undefeatable enemies necessitated the militarization of civilian life (particularly in places such as Aceh and East Timor), intermittent terror tactics, and vast surveillance networks.[59] As Richard Tanter explains, the "fundamental requirement for terror to take hold, to become a form of rule is the diffusion of suspicion of The Other as a normal state."[60] The uncertainty over who these internal enemies of the New Order were—and how far their networks spread—meant that the military needed to use these tactics to fight their most serious enemies, the "Communists," the "GPK," or (particularly in the late 1990s) the "Organisasi Tanpa Bentuk" (OTB, or "Organisations Without Form").[61]

[55] See, for example, Robinson, "*Rawan* Is as *Rawan* Does," 141–43, 146–53; Budi Hernawan, "Confronting Politics of Death in Papua," in *Routledge Handbook of Public Criminologies*, ed. Kathryn Henne and Rita Shah (New York: Routledge, 2020), 213–27; Muhamad Daud Berueh, "Practice of Torture during Soeharto's Regime," *Article 2* 12, no. 2 (2013): 23–30.

[56] This work has been undertaken by Asia Justice and Rights (AJAR) as part of their extensive support programs for victims of violence. See, for example, Wandita, Fernida and Campbell-Nelson, "Mass Torture," 63–64, 68–70.

[57] See Loney, *In Women's Words*; and Pohlman, *Women, Sexual Violence and the Indonesian Killings*.

[58] The term "GPK" emerges in the 1970s; see Dave McRae, "A Discourse on Separatists," *Indonesia* 74 (October 2002): 41.

[59] This point is one made about various military regimes and their "counterinsurgency" campaigns. See, for example, J. Patrice McSherry, *Predatory States: Operation Condor and Covert War in Latin America* (Lanham: Rowman and Littlefield, 2005).

[60] Tanter, "Intelligence Agencies," 102.

[61] See, for example, John Roosa, "Violence and the Suharto Regime's Wonderland," *Critical Asian Studies* 35, no. 2 (2003): 315–23. On the New Order state's (struggles with) naming its perceived enemies, see James T. Siegel, *A New Criminal Type in Jakarta: Counter Revolution Today* (Durham: Duke University Press, 1998).

These processes of constructing, identifying, and destroying "the enemy within" was a central feature of New Order state discourse and violence. From its inception and consolidation in 1965–66, the regime's power—and the central role of the military within it—was justified by the notion that the military had "saved" the population from an attempted takeover by the Communists. Within this narrative, as scholars such as Katharine McGregor have demonstrated, the military was seen to have played a central role in safeguarding Indonesian sovereignty and the spirit of the Indonesian nation, as well as protecting the official national ideology, *Pancasila*.[62] This premise both legitimized the central role that the military played within the political and administrative structures of the New Order state, as well as produced a deep fear of "internal enemies"—groups that were often referred to by the authorities as "GPK"—from which the integrity of the state and the national community more broadly required protection.[63] GPK were depicted within New Order state propaganda as irrational troublemakers and criminals but, critically, they were never seen to pose a significant threat to the legitimacy of, nor a viable alternative to, the state. As James Siegal has argued, such groups were seen to be "on the edge of Indonesian society but never outside it, never the foreigner."[64] This discourse was explicitly mobilized in areas where the state faced significant demands for greater autonomy or independence by armed political groups, such as Aceh and East Timor. In these areas, which were designated by the authorities as "trouble spots" (*daerah rawan*), the state deployed massive resources and successive military operations in an attempt to suppress perceived threats to national security.[65]

Alongside the use of military force, terror was institutionalized within military doctrine and strategy, in an attempt to facilitate the implementation of the goal of integrating these "subversive" populations into the republic. Military and police authorities were permitted, as Amnesty International observed in the case of Aceh, to use "virtually any means deemed necessary" to destroy suspected threats and to coerce the population into submission.[66] As such, the targets of these processes of coercion and control extended beyond the violent suppression of armed political movements: they also involved a systematic campaign to terrorize civilians, the cultivation of a broader atmosphere of fear, and the forced recruitment of civilians to participate in intelligence or security operations to "crush the GPK."[67] In an interview that the Regional Military Commander in Aceh, Major General H. R. Pramono, gave to *Tempo* in 1990, for example, he stated: "I have told the community, if you find a terrorist, kill him. There's no need to investigate him. Don't let people be the victims. If they don't do as you order them, shoot them on the spot, or butcher them. I tell members of the community to carry sharp

[62] See Katharine McGregor, *History in Uniform: Military Ideology and the Construction of Indonesia's Past* (Singapore: NUS Press, 2007).

[63] Robinson, "*Rawan* Is as *Rawan* Does," 127. Comparing the construction of these internal enemies between Aceh, East Timor, and Papua, see also McRae, "A Discourse on Separatists," 37–58.

[64] Siegel, *A New Criminal Type*, 3.

[65] Robinson, "*Rawan* is as *Rawan* Does," 127. On how the Army interpreted the spread and influence of the "GPK" in East Timor, based on their own documentation, see Samuel Moore, "The Indonesian Military's Last Years in East Timor: An Analysis of its Secret Documents," *Indonesia* 72 (2001): 9–44.

[66] Amnesty International, *"Shock Therapy": Restoring Order in Aceh, 1989–1993* (London: Amnesty International, 1993), 11.

[67] Amnesty International, *"Shock Therapy,"* 13.

weapons, a machine or whatever. If you meet a terrorist, kill him."[68] This statement goes some way to explaining the attempt by the military to normalize and conventionalize the use of state-sanctioned violence against suspected GPK. The repetition of "death words" within this statement—kill, shoot, butcher, destroy—also reveals the aim of completely exterminating opposition forces, including their families, at any cost. As George Aditjondro has observed, the "enemy" is treated within such military discourse "as if they were a pest which needs to be eradicated, to prevent the body from future possible infestation."[69] This mentality, Aditjondro suggests, is captured by the Javanese expression *tumpas kelor* ("eradicate to the roots").[70]

In all three contexts—1965, East Timor, and Aceh—this eliminationist rhetoric was invoked in the language used by the security services to describe their own campaigns. Security forces aimed to destroy these internal enemies "down to their roots," or to eliminate "seven generations" of descendants. In 1965, military and militia leaders frequently used this language in their incitement against suspected Communists, and survivors spoke of their attackers using this language against them.[71] A commonly cited threat within interrogation sessions in the East Timor context, for example, was that opponents would be killed "down to their seventh generation": as the East Timorese clandestine member Constâncio Pinto later recalled in his memoir, following the infamous 1991 Santa Cruz demonstration in Dili, Indonesian security forces "said that they would kill any protestors . . . and then kill their families 'to the seventh generation.'"[72] In Aceh too, researchers of the conflict have noted the "savage and dehumanizing language" used by the Army to describe their enemies and the necessity of their methods, that of GAM and their supporters being "'traitors' who had to be 'eradicated.'"[73]

In these eliminationist aims, the campaigns in 1965, in East Timor, and Aceh were akin to other "root-and-branch" extermination campaigns in other contexts, including the Holocaust. This is a phrase, Adam Jones writes, that refers to mass killings against all sectors of the target population: "female and male, old and young, able and disabled."[74] While this is a useful conceptualization that highlights the inherent gendering of some extermination campaigns, we suggest that in the Indonesian context, the phrase holds a particular and distinctive meaning. In all three cases, the New Order's labels attached

---

[68] Interview with Major General H. R. Pramono, *Tempo*, November 17, 1990 (cited in Amnesty International, "Shock Therapy," 14). On the criminal construction of the "GPK" in Aceh, see Elizabeth F. Drexler, "The Social Life of Conflict Narratives: Violent Antagonists, Imagined Histories, and Foreclosed Futures in Aceh, Indonesia," *Anthropological Quarterly* 80, no. 4 (2007): 961–95.

[69] George Aditjondro, "Ninjas, Nanggalas, Monuments, and Mossad Manuals: An Anthropology of Indonesian State Terror in East Timor," in *Death Squad. The Anthropology of State Terror*, ed. Jeffrey A. Sluka (Philadelphia: University of Philadelphia Press, 2000), 166.

[70] Aditjondro, "Ninjas, Nanggalas, Monuments, and Mossad Manuals," 166.

[71] For some examples, see Melvin, *The Army and the Indonesian Genocide*, 41–43, 110–37; Geoffrey Robinson, "'Down to the Very Roots': The Indonesian Army's Role in the Mass Killings of 1965–66," *Journal of Genocide Research* 19, no. 4 (2017): 475–76. See, for example, Pohlman, *Women, Sexual Violence*, 31–32.

[72] Constâncio Pinto and Matthew Jardine, *East Timor's Unfinished Struggle: Inside the East Timorese Resistance* (Toronto: Canadian Cataloguing in Publication Data, 1997), xvi.

[73] For example, Matthew Davies, *Indonesia's War over Aceh: Last Stand on Mecca's Porch* (London: Routledge, 2006), 106.

[74] Adam Jones, "Why Gendercide? Why Root-and-Branch? A Comparison of Vendée Uprising of 1793–94 and the Bosnian War of the 1990s," *Journal of Genocide Research* 8, no. 1 (2006): 9–10. Jones compares "root-and-branch" with other mass killings in which mostly adult men are the primary targets.

to internal enemies had a sticky, infective nature; the targets of state-sanctioned violence to eradicate these enemies extended beyond individual (and often male) members of armed political movements, to include the mothers, wives, children, and communities of those individuals. It was therefore not enough to target the members of these internal enemy networks; indeed, those close to them were also seen as a threat. Thus, in all three contexts, survivors of the violence attest to how the security services and their auxiliaries targeted the family members and communities of suspected Communists or GPK.[75]

The eliminationist rhetoric and violence of the "root-and-branch" campaigns in all three contexts also had generational dimensions. The familial infection was one that could be passed on or inherited. In the two-and-a-half generations born since 1965, certainly, the "infection" of Communism has survived the regime and the original victims, contaminating the children, grandchildren, and great-grandchildren of former (or suspected) Communists.[76] Thus the New Order's need to eradicate its internal enemies, root and branch, required not just the destruction of GPK members and their infected family members, but also their descendants. The elimination of these enemies therefore had explicitly gendered dimensions: it meant that women's bodies were a specific target site and that their reproductive functions, in particular, often bore the brunt of violent acts.

The type of violence used against the five young women in 1997 and depicted in the East Timor torture photographs—as with many other women in East Timor, Aceh, and beyond—was therefore key to both the depersonalization and identification of them as internal enemies and to their eradication.[77] The forms that this violence took were crucial: the material practices of sexual and gender-based violence against women's and girls' bodies were frequently those forms that could eliminate the spread of internal enemies. Indeed, these forms were part of what Elisa von Joeden-Forgey has called "life force atrocities," meaning those acts that showed "a ritualized pattern of violence that targets the life force of a group."[78] Enacted in periods of mass violence, particularly as part of the eradication of whole groups and genocidal campaigns, these life force atrocities are directed at destroying all members of the target group—men and women, young and old—but often the forms that this violence takes involve direct and targeted attacks against the women of the group. For von Joeden-Forgey, these atrocities

---

[75] On the targeting of family members in Aceh, see Kirsten E. Schulze, "Insurgency and Counter-Insurgency: Strategy and the Aceh Conflict, October 1976–May 2004," in *Verandah of Violence: Aceh's Contested Place in Indonesia*, ed. Anthony Reid (Singapore: Singapore University Press, 2006), 252–53. For experiences of this persecution of wives and other family members, see Jacuqeline Aquino Siapno, *Gender, Islam, Nationalism and the State in Aceh* (London: Routledge, 2002), 28–29, 38–43. On the targeting of family members in 1965, see Pohlman, *Women, Sexual Violence*, 30–35; and in East Timor, see Loney, *In Women's Words*, 73–77.

[76] On the infection of Communism through generations, see Martha Stroud, "Ripples, Echoes, and Reverberations: 1965 and Now in Indonesia" (PhD diss., University of California, Berkeley, 2015), 57–61. On intergenerational "PKI" associations, see Andrew Conroe, "Generating History: Violence and the Risks of Remembering for Families of Former Political Prisoners in Post-New Order Indonesia"(PhD diss., University of Michigan, 2012).

[77] This argument builds on the work of researchers on the identificationist functions of violence, see Arjun Appadurai, "Dead Certainty: Ethnic Violence in the Era of Globalization," *Development and Change* 29, no. 4 (1998): 905–25; Feldman, *Formations of Violence*; and Liisa H. Malkki, *Purity and Exile: Violence, Memory, and National Cosmology among Hutu Refugees in Tanzania* (Chicago: University of Chicago Press, 1995).

[78] Elisa von Joeden-Forgey, "The Devil in the Details: 'Life Force Atrocities' and the Assault on the Family in Times of Conflict," *Genocide Studies and Prevention* 5, no. 1 (2010): 2.

commonly comprise attacks, often in ways that are deeply culturally significant, on the relationships within the target group (such as forcing a family member to participate in the rape or murder of a loved one), or through specific violence against the "symbols of group reproduction."[79] These atrocities are, therefore, those necessary to *eliminate* both the cultural and biological reproduction of the target group. Such violence is effective in achieving these aims because of the ways that it undermines the group's social and biological bonds in long-lasting ways.[80]

These atrocities are those so frequently recounted by women survivors of the New Order's campaigns in 1965, East Timor, and Aceh. They include the widespread rape and sexual violence, the acts of sexualized torture that fetishized women's bodies, the acts of violence against women's reproductive functions, among so many forms of violence that targeted not only the lives and bodies of victims, but also those ties that bind human communities together. The transgressions of this violence are as deliberate as they are necessary to eradicate those targeted—the burning, cutting into, and mutilating the parts of the flesh that identify women as women, the numerous forms of cruelty with deeply symbolic meaning aimed at the inversion of social and familial relations—because these acts are "not just of killing people, but of killing the very life force responsible for their existence."[81] The New Order's terror tactics employed these gendered forms of violence against their insidious, internal enemies because such tactics were the most effective way to eradicate them. More to the point, as enemies, they deserved them.

Conclusion

The seventy photographs we examined at the beginning of this article, distributed near the end of both the Indonesian occupation of East Timor and the New Order military regime, reveal in graphic form the highly gendered elements of torture and sexual violence practiced routinely and systematically by Indonesian security services throughout the New Order period. These photographs were created by a small group of Indonesian soldiers and showed their acts of torture against five young women and girls, likely taken in 1997 in East Timor. By looking carefully at the structures and forms of violence depicted within these images, we attempted to understand better the institutional structures that had enabled their creation. Those institutional structures, we argue, were grounded in the culture of violence within the New Order's security services. These structures were built on the institutionalization of violence—and here, we recall Tanter's framework of militarization, surveillance, and terror—to achieve the military's ends, particularly in their campaigns against those seen as internal enemies of the New Order state. The photographs illustrated how these means were deployed against the bodies of five young women in East Timor, but the institutional environment that enabled their production harmed so many more. Thus, in this article, we have

---

[79] von Joeden-Forgey, "The Devil in the Details," 2.

[80] On the use of violence that undermines biological and cultural reproduction of group within the context of genocide, see Damien Short, *Redefining Genocide: Settler Colonialism, Social Death and Ecocide* (London: Zed Books, 2016); Lindsey Kingston, "The Destruction of Identity: Cultural Genocide and Indigenous Peoples," *Journal of Human Rights* 14, no. 1 (2015): 63–83.

[81] von Joeden-Forgey, "The Devil in the Details," 5. Or men as men; sexualized and gendered violence was also used against men by the Indonesian security services during the New Order. On some men's experiences of this in 1965 see, for example, Pohlman, "Sexual Violence as Torture," 583–86.

connected the photographs showing the violence against the few with the unseen violence against the many. In particular, we have compared survivors' accounts of similar forms of sexualized and gendered harm deployed mostly against women and girls in occupied East Timor with that perpetrated by the New Order's security services and their auxiliaries during the anti-Communist purges of the late 1960s and during the DOM period in Aceh.

The violence used in these three contexts showed two common threads. First, that the violence was deterministic, by which we mean that it involved "the use of the body to establish the parameters of this otherness, taking the body apart, so to speak, to divine the enemy within."[82] In this sense, the violence transformed individual victims into artifacts for the targeted internal enemy group, be they supposed members of the PKI or GPK. Second, the forms of violence used in these three contexts showed that the sexual and gendered violence perpetrated by the regime's security services were not just commonalities: they were essential methods of destroying these internal enemies. The forms of this violence, the pervasive use of rape and sexual violence in the torture, and other types of harm—particularly against women—were justified by an eliminationist logic that required the destruction of not just these enemies, but their families and any potential descendants. The atrocities shown in the photographs and told in the accounts by many, many more survivors from East Timor and Indonesia had a self-rationalizing and self-perpetuating logic; the fact that victims were assumed to be members of the PKI, or GAM or GPK, was seen to justify their treatment. As "internal enemies," they were seen as an infectious influence that, unless cleansed, would pose a continuing danger to the stability and security of the New Order state. Extreme violence against such enemies was not simply what they deserved: it was necessary.

---

[82] Appadurai, "Dead Certainty," 233–34.

The Politics of the Fatwa

Islamic Legal Authority in Modern Indonesia

Jeremy Menchik

I. Introduction

On December 2, 2016, the National Movement to Safeguard the Fatwa of the Indonesian Council of Ulama (Gerakan Nasional Pengawal Fatwa Majelis Ulama Indonesia, GNPF-MUI) staged the largest rally in Indonesian history. Over 750,000 people filled the plaza around the National Monument in Central Jakarta for the rally led by Indonesia's leading Islamist organizations, who were demanding action against Jakarta's Chinese Christian governor for alleged blasphemy against Islam. The event was attended not just by Islamists, but also by president Joko Widodo and members of more moderate Muslim organizations. The event was a triumph for the power of Islamists in setting the political agenda for Indonesian politics. At the epicenter of that triumph was a fatwa from the MUI.

Since 2005, fatwas from MUI have shaped public debates and state policies concerning blasphemy, religious pluralism, minority rights, vaccinations, pornography, smoking, and interfaith relations, among other issues. Internationally, fatwas from prominent clerics like Ayatollah Khomeini of Iran have engendered heated debates about

Jeremy Menchik is Associate Professor in the Pardee School of Global Studies at Boston University. He is author of *Islam and Democracy in Indonesia: Tolerance without Liberalism* (Cambridge University press, 2016), and is currently working on a book manuscript about the missionary impulse in world politics.

their influence. Yet, scholars lack a political theory of the fatwa and therefore follow Max Weber (1947) in assuming that a fatwa's influence is a function of charisma or state corporatism. This paper contends classical theories of Islamic law, Weber's typology, and ethical theories of the fatwa cannot explain MUI's growing power.

MUI is now one of the most powerful actors in Indonesia. And yet, looking back at the writings and research on MUI since it was created in 1975, it appears that no one anticipated its rise. The seminal text on Islamic law and society in Indonesia, Daniel Lev's *Islamic Courts in Indonesia: A Study in the Political Bases of Legal Institutions* (1972), was written prior to MUI's creation. There are only two English-language scholarly books devoted to MUI, both of them researched prior to democratization in 1998 and the rise of MUI (Porter 2002; Mudzhar 1993). Since 2005 there has been an uptick in journal articles devoted to MUI, but due to space constraints these writings address only narrow aspects of MUI, usually in the form of descriptive analysis of the content of its fatwas or normative laments about its challenge to liberal pluralism (Ali 2002; Hasyim 2011; 2015; Hosen 2004; Ichwan 2005; Sirry 2013; Nasir 2014). While there are a few more comprehensive accounts (Ichwan 2002, 2005; ICG 2008, 8-10; Olle 2009; Saat 2017), missing from the literature is a synthetic account of how MUI came to occupy a position of such power.

This paper attempts to address both gaps by explaining the power of MUI's fatwas over time as a function of the forms and degrees of authority that MUI itself has accrued. In the 1960s, Daniel S. Lev (1972) noted that the relatively minor influence of Islamic courts in Indonesia was related to the minor influence of Islamic political movements. No one would make such a claim today. MUI is a usually creative and innovative Islamic organization, unshackled by formal constitutional constraints or the ideological limitations of secularism. Rather than delegating religious affairs to the private sphere, MUI has fought against the differentiation of religion from other social spheres. MUI has created new regulatory bodies for oversight of Islamic banking and food certification. MUI has asserted and achieved authority over social spheres once controlled by Suharto's New Order regime and Islamic civil society, such as media oversight, expert authority, mass mobilization, and more.

To explain this evolution, the paper distinguishes three periods in the history of MUI and demonstrates that in each era, fatwas from MUI exerted authority through distinct mechanisms, and these forms of authority accumulated over time. In the first period, from 1975 to 1990, MUI relied on a combination of charismatic authority and expert authority derived from its status as a quasi-state body. MUI was essentially a model of *state corporatism*, created by Suharto in order to control ulama in the same way that the Islam-based Unity and Development Party (Partai Persatuan Pembanguan, PPP) provided a vehicle to control Muslim political parties. In this period, the Weberian framework is effective for explaining Islamic legal authority.

In the second period, from 1990 to 2005, MUI became a regulatory body with state-backed coercive power over Islamic banking and halal food certification. This was a period of institutional innovation. Key to MUI's new power was the overlap between MUI officials and the architects of the Association of Indonesian Muslim Intellectuals (Ikatan Cendekiawan Muslim Se-Indonesia, ICMI). In period II, MUI became not just "quasi-state" but a formal state institution. Paradoxically, however, after democratization

MUI also began to gain autonomy from the state as a result of substantive disagreements with then-presidents Abdurrahman Wahid and Megawati Sukarnoputri, as well as financial autonomy as a result of its lucrative Islamic banking and halal food certification programs.

In the final period, from 2005 to the present, MUI extended its authority even further and began to reap the benefits of innovation. It continued to receive funding from the state and to appoint charismatic leaders, as in period I. It also continued to exert regulatory control over Islamic banking and food certification and in fact has expanded its reach to overseas markets. It expanded its influence over media through close relationships with two other regulatory agencies, the Film Censorship Board (Lembaga Sensor Film, LSF) and the Indonesian Broadcasting Commission (Komisi Penyiaran Indonesia, KPI). Period III is distinct, however, in that MUI aligned with mass movements in order to put pressure on the state. This alliance was implicit in the late 1990s and 2000s, but in the late 2010s became overt, with leaders of radical Islamic mass movements on MUI's central board, including Maman Abdurrahman of Persatuan Islam, the Salafi Muhammad Zaitun Rasmin, and the organizer of the GNPF-MUI, Bachtiar Nasir. Additionally, in 2007 MUI gained access to the president on a regular basis, as well as access to the heads of other government ministries when Ma'ruf Amin was appointed to Susilo Bambang Yudhoyono's Presidential Advisory Council (Dewan Pertimbangan Presiden). In sum, in period III MUI expanded its regulatory capacity while adding lobbying, mass mobilization, and coercive authority through vigilante organizations like FPI to gain leverage over other state institutions, thereby gaining the power of a social movement. In this period, MUI began setting the agenda for Indonesian politics.

This periodization demonstrates the limitations of existing accounts of fatwas and their authority for explaining the case of MUI. Traditional theories of Islamic legal authority depict fatwas as a form of "non-binding" opinion, which accurately describes MUI's fatwas only in period I and then only partially, due to MUI's affiliation with the state. Likewise, state-corporatism theories fall short given MUI's autonomy; MUI's fatwas do not become binding state law like those of gazetted fatwas in Malaysia.

Ethical theories of the fatwa are similarly unhelpful in this case. Drawing on two years of ethnographic observation of the fatwa council of al-Azhar, the most esteemed center of Sunni learning in the Muslim world, Hussein Agrama (2010) convincingly demonstrates that fatwas can be a way for the mufti and Muslims to jointly find an ethical path to the ideal Muslim self. Yet an ethical theory of the fatwa cannot explain the authority of MUI, which operates nothing like the affable ulama of al-Azhar. MUI's fatwas are issued to great media attention. They are drafted following testimony by experts in state law, Islamic law, economic development, and security. They are crafted collectively and issued on MUI letterhead with the MUI stamp of approval and the signatures of the head of MUI's fatwa committee and his assistant. They are issued from MUI's glossy new building, with the fatwa office on the highest floor. Insofar as MUI is advising individuals, it is on paper and under the auspices of expertise, rather than through gentle counsel and ethical imploring of Muslims to be their best selves.

In light of the changing nature of MUI's power and the concomitantly changing authority of its fatwas, the paper argues that contemporary fatwas contain no innate authority, nor do they have any inherent effects. Instead, the authority of a fatwa is tied to the authority and capacity of the organization issuing the fatwa. Scholars seeking to understand the politics of fatwas would do well to start with organizations, rather than state-corporatism (Porter 2002), charisma (Kingsley 2014), or ethics (Agrama 2010). This endeavor requires mapping the organizational position and capacities of a specific actor, at a specific time, in response to a specific set of events.

Such endeavors are valuable beyond Indonesia. Clerics like Ayatollah Khamenei, Supreme Leader of Iran, and Sheikh Muhammad Sayyid Tantawi of al-Azhar in Cairo are central to contemporary politics, yet their mechanisms for influence are poorly understood. By focusing on their organizational vehicles and the attendant forms of authority, scholars can cut through the confusion that too often accompanies debates about Islam and politics.

The remainder of this paper elaborates these arguments. Section II outlines the state of the literature on fatwas, Islamic legal authority, and MUI in order to pinpoint gaps. Section III argues that MUI's fatwas are emblematic of modern Islamic legal authority and its diverse mechanisms of influence. It extends the theory to show how an organizational approach to the fatwa can shed light on the politics of Islamic authority in the Middle East and Southeast Asia. Section IV is divided into the three periods outlined above. Section V discusses the market forces and patronage politics that limit MUI's authority and outlines the implications of MUI's power for Indonesian democracy.

II. Existing Explanations for Islamic Legal Authority

In Islamic legal theory, a fatwa is a statement of nonbinding opinion from a scholar of Islamic law, usually a mufti. Historically, scholars regulated their own activities and delineated professional standards for their behavior, meaning that all that was required for a person to give a fatwa was religious knowledge and piety (*taqwā*). Fatwas were not binding on the person who received them or the person who gave them. Yet, they were not arbitrary or lacking in importance. Some jurists have historically been reluctant to serve as fatwa givers because the issuer of a fatwa has tremendous responsibility to God and is exposed to the possibility of (divinely punished) error (Masud, Messick, and Powers 1996, 4, 16).

Observers who interpret fatwas as positive law often poorly understand this responsibility. The ethical nature of the fatwa was most recently captured in Agrama's (2010) erudite work on Islamic law and society. He pushes back against the idea that fatwas are a tool of doctrinal reform, bridging the divide between a classical tradition and the modern world, by showing that the Islamic tradition has always been adaptive rather than static. Instead, Agrama suggests that muftis issue fatwas in order to guide Muslims toward the ideal self.

The idea that fatwas are ethical in nature provides a useful, albeit insufficient, departure from the commonly-used Weberian typology of political authority. Weber defines authority as that which is accepted as legitimate by those subjected to it. He identifies three forms (Weber 1947, 328–86). Charismatic authority, represented by the Prophet, is the purest form in that it claims the right to supersede existing normative orders and reveal new ones. Customary rulers, such as monarchs, are representative of traditional authority. And rational-legal authority is represented by government officials who hold office on the basis of specific rules and procedures that define and limit their rights and responsibilities.

While Weber's typology proved useful for mapping patterns of authority in 18th-century Europe, it is less helpful for mapping varieties of authority among modern Muslim communities. In the past twenty years, scholars of Islamic law and society have made major advances in understanding the similarities and differences between the traditional shari'a as it was practiced prior to the nineteenth century and as it is understood and envisioned by modern states. Wael Hallah's (2009) influential text, *Sharī'a: Theory, Practice, Transformations*, maps the radical disjuncture between the premodern shari'a and contemporary "Islamic law": the former was grounded in ethics, customary norms, and local customary practices that created and maintained a "well ordered society," while the latter is uniform and implemented by the state. In Iza Husain's (2016) careful analysis, premodern shari'a was flattened to accord with the static, uniform version of law envisioned by colonial administrators and postcolonial state-builders. It was also narrowed; rather than including administrative or commercial law, its jurisdiction has been limited to family law, gender, and religious observance. It is for this reason that Hussin describes the East India Company and Muslim state-builders in India as implementing "Anglo-Muslim law" rather than shari'a (Hussin 2016, 85).

Malaysia is a key case for this literature; Hussin uses it to demonstrate how key features of the shari'a were cast aside or unintentionally subverted by colonial state builders and Muslim elites. The Malaysia example is instructive for the present study as well, since it has served as something of an unachieved normative ideal for MUI (Saat 2017). Tamir Mustafi (2014) demonstrates how the Malaysian state, by making fatwas binding, paradoxically subverts the classical notion of fatwas as nonbinding legal opinions (162). Fatwas from the Islamic Religious Council, State Mufti, and Islamic Legal Consultative Committee can carry the force of state law with no effective oversight from legislative institutions such as the Parliament (Moustafa 2018, 44).

Another useful comparative case is Brunei. Only the State Mufti has the authority to issue "legal" fatwas (Müller 2015; 2017). Fatwas in Brunei are now binding state law, deployed by state religious institutions in order to coopt opposition, promote piety, and authorize a particular version of orthodoxy. The cases of Malaysia and Brunei are helpful for comparative and theoretical purposes, as well as helping to explain where MUI's ideas originate; there is evidence that institutional norms have diffused from Malaysia and Brunei to Indonesia through regular meetings of their respective Ministries of Religion (*Pelita* 1991a; 1991b). This surprising pathway for norm diffusion runs counter to that assumed by the scholarship on transnational Islamic influence, whereby norms diffuse from the Middle East—usually Saudi Arabia, Egypt, or Iran—to the Muslim "periphery."

The new literature on the state cooptation of Islamic law as a form of modern political authority provides a crucial starting point for explaining MUI's power and the authority of the fatwa. Yet, like Weber's rational-legal authority, this research relies on a conception of authority that is grounded in state sovereignty, the rule of law, and control of religion. Such a conception of the authority of the fatwa is less helpful once we depart from "bureaucratized Islam" (Müller and Steiner 2018). Rather than being bureaucratized by the state, MUI has increasingly contested state hegemony by lobbying from above and using mass mobilization and the threat of violence from below (for parallels with al-Azhar, see Moustafa 2000).

Beyond ethical and legal-rational authority, there are two common explanations for MUI's growing power. The first and most common explanation centers on the changing ideology of the Indonesian public. In this view, MUI's growing authority reflects public opinion, which has purportedly evolved from supporting democracy to theocracy (Arifianto 2018).

This explanation has some merit. Indicators from the World Values Survey (WVS) suggest that Indonesians may not favor the differentiation of religion and state as much as they did in the past and thus may favor more religious rather than secular political authority. In a 2001 survey, 90 percent of respondents agree or strongly agree with the statement "Religious leaders should not influence government"; this number drops precipitously to 54 percent in the 2006 survey (WVS 2018). Indonesian religious authorities may also be more conservative now than in the 1980s, when Muslim moderates like Syafi'i Maarif, Abdurrahman Wahid, and Nurcholish Madjid set the public agenda. The loudest intellectuals in contemporary Indonesia are sometimes conservative, which is why Martin van Bruinessen (2013) described Indonesian Islam as having taken a "conservative turn."

Yet this explanation leaves as many questions as it provides answers. On a different WVS indicator of differentiation, there is far less change, with 86 percent of respondents in 2001, then 74 percent in 2006 agreeing that "Religious leaders should not influence how people vote." And the most recently elected leaders of NU and Muhammadiyah, Yahya Staquf and Haedar Nashir, are prominent moderates. In 2020, MUI elected a moderate chair, Kyai Miftachul Akhyar, alongside progressives like Masdar Masudi, Dadang Kahmas, and Sudarnoto Abdul Hakim. Meanwhile prominent conservatives who were influential in the campaign against former Jakarta governor Basuki Tjahaja Purnama (Ahok)—Din Syamsuddin, Tengku Zulkarnain, Bachtiar Nasir, and Yusuf Muhammad Martak—were removed from the central board. If ideology is expected to explain organizational behavior, then one could describe Indonesian Islam as having taken a "moderate turn" during Jokowi's second term.

A second line of explanation focuses less on the changing ideology of the public than on the behavior of elites. Thomas B. Pinsky, R. William Liddle, and Saiful Mujani (2018) contend that religious piety is a poor predictor of political preferences and that the "conservative turn" is a function of strategies of mobilization. Likewise, in a prescient early analysis of MUI's rise, the International Crisis Group noted that MUI has skillfully mobilized radicals in civil society in order to pressure the government, with its greatest success with President Yudhyono, who in 2005 and 2007 gave MUI his support to play a prominent role in policymaking (ICG 2008, 8–10; see also ICG 2001, 2, 16). And Jeremy Menchik's (2014) research on the history of intolerance toward heterodox groups demonstrates that elites have long drawn on intolerance as a productive aspect of Indonesian nationalism.

This second explanation is consistent with the argument pursued in this paper. Yet, the existing literature falls short in several key respects. First, these explanations fail to explain how, when, and why conservatives have been able to set the agenda. They take for granted the authority of the conservatives rather than explicate its origins. Second, these explanations emphasize only the opportunities and innovations of MUI in the post-Suharto period, ignoring the pivotal moves by MUI to developing its economic, media, and links to radicals in the 1990s, long before *reformasi*. Third and finally, these explanations ignore the changing organizational capacity and authority of Islamic organizations; to understand the power of MUI fatwas, it is important to contrast MUI's modes of authority in the three periods, as well as with more traditional Islamic organizations like Muhammadiyah, NU, and al-Azhar.

III. Argument: Modern Islamic Legal Authority

MUI came to be a leading religious and legal authority in Indonesia by aggregating influence through organizational expansion, innovation, and alliance. While discussions of MUI's influence invariably describe its fatwas as "nonbinding" and its institutional position as "quasi-state," these descriptions rely on outdated assumptions. MUI has grown in power by using modern forms of authority familiar to scholars of comparative politics and international relations, such as regulatory authority, expert authority, agenda-setting authority, lobbying, mass mobilization, and coercive authority (Keck and Sikkink 1998).

In that respect, MUI's authority is illustrative of the possibilities presented by the fragmented and decentralized nature of Islamic authority in the modern world. Mass education and the expansion of state control over society has destabilized traditional religious authority (Eickelman 1992; Hefner 1998). While secularization theorists believed that such destabilization would lead to the decline of religion, more recent work suggests that pluralism, competition, and contestation are the result (Meuleman 2011; Eickelman 1998). MUI is a prime example of successful competition. Over time MUI has successfully expanded its authority over issues by aggregating modern forms of social control.

Specifically, since 1990 MUI has expanded its mandate, gaining regulatory power over shari'a banking and food certification through its National Sharia Board (Dewan Syariah Nasional, DSN MUI) and its Institute for Food, Drugs and Cosmetic Assessment (Lembaga Pengkajian Pangan, Obat-Obatan dan Kosmetika, LPPOM MUI), both of which are recognized by parliamentary legislation. Likewise, MUI has built close alliances with the regulatory bodies for media and by doing so has demarcated the limits of acceptable discourse in film and TV. MUI has meanwhile sought to distance itself from the government by shifting its institutional program from the position of a subordinate coopted by the state to that of an autonomous entity that lobbies the state, including as a member on high-level commissions and advisory boards. This innovation has also taken more concrete forms, such as MUI's move out of the national mosque into a separate building that gives it greater autonomy. Around 2010, MUI moved its office from a back hallway of the government-built and -owned Istiqlal Mosque to an independent, modern, luxurious space where MUI could issue decrees from on high.[1] Finally, MUI has meticulously aligned with mass movements in society, directing their

---

[1] The office of the Freedom Institute, now closed, was once located a few doors away from the MUI building. These real estate changes are a potent metaphor, since liberal Islam has fared poorly in the face of MUI's rise.

mobilization in order to lobby for policies from below through the appearance of mass support as well as the threat of violence.

MUI's fatwas thus embody a diverse array of types of authority, all of which are thoroughly modern rather than being solely a function of charismatic authority, state corporatism, legal-rational authority, traditional authority, or ethical authority. To understand MUI's growing power, it is necessary to look beyond these traditional modes of Islamic legal authority to modern organizational forms and their attendant strategies for exerting social control.

MUI is trying to make its fatwas binding like the fatwas of modern Malaysian and Bruneian muftis in the employ of the state, and it has been partially successful (Saat 2017). Where MUI departs from those cases, however, is in its mechanisms for doing so. In period II, select MUI fatwas became binding though regulatory means. In period III, a broader array of MUI fatwas became binding through formal lobbying from above (directed specifically toward the Ministry of Religion, President, Constitutional Court, and Legislature) and through informal lobbying from below using alliances with mass movements and the threat of violence. In other words, MUI has created Islamic law through other means than Malaysian and Bruneian ulama, but with similar effects.

More theoretically, this aggregation of religious-political authority suggests that the key to understanding MUI's influence is recognizing that it uses a broad and creative array of strategies of influence. Like the Malaysian Islamic Development Department (Jabatan Kemajuan Islam Malaysia, JAKIM), MUI relies on its regulatory authority over mundane issues like food certification and Islamic banking to compel everyday Muslims into compliance. Akin to the Egyptian Muslim Brotherhood, MUI deploys mass mobilization, filling the streets and compelling the state into conformity with its policy preferences. Like the European Council for Fatwa and Research, MUI brings together prominent Muslim scholars in order to unify their jurisprudence and issue joint fatwas that represent the expertise of the collective, which in turn shape public behavior through ethical appeals. Similar to Saudi Arabia's leading religious family, the Al ash-Sheikh, MUI partners with government leaders in order to gain influence in return. In comparative theoretical perspective, MUI's fatwas are emblematic of modern religious authority and its creative, diverse mechanisms for social influence (Hoesterey 2015).

This aggregation is innovative for an Indonesian religious organization but should be unsurprising to scholars of law and society. MUI is simply adapting strategies of social control developed by others; Suharto created new institutions to control social forces, liberal activists use NGOs to generate allies in civil society, and Islamists use mass mobilization to put pressure on the state. MUI is playing by the rules of the game. As Michael Peletz (2015) remarks in reference to Islamic court judges in Malaysia, "there is only one game in town, and that game defines both the field of play and the rules governing how to play" (drawing on Bourdieu and Wacquant 1992). Looking beyond religion, then, MUI is both innovative and derivative. In the modern age, the authority of a fatwa reflects the dominant logic of political authority in society.

Beyond MUI, this argument suggests that mapping the political authority of fatwas should begin with organizational capacity. For example, in 2010 Muhammadiyah issued a controversial fatwa saying that smoking was prohibited (*haram*). Responses ranged from strong support by health organizations, to strong opposition from the Ministry of Religious

Affairs, unsurprising given that tax revenue from tobacco makes up a large portion of the ministry's budget. Public commentators said the "nonbinding" fatwa would have no impact. Yet Muhammadiyah runs thousands of schools and hundreds of hospitals and health clinics, and smoking was banned at all of those sites. I witnessed firsthand the power of Muhammadiyah's fatwa at its 2010 meeting when I asked one Muhammadiyah leader to undertake a survey. He agreed to do so, but then turned his back to me in order to get his glasses out of his front pocket without revealing the packet of cigarettes hidden there. Other smokers could be found hiding behind buildings, in the corner of empty rooms, or off the grounds (Personal observation, July 5, 2010, Yogyakarta). Elsewhere in Indonesia's public sphere, smoking was omnipresent. Muhammadiyah's fatwa was authoritative because it became policy in thousands of locations.

JAKIM provides a nice illustration of the virtues of this approach beyond Indonesia. JAKIM fatwas are published by official state organs, viewable online and also distributed among all government offices and public institutions such as mosques and schools. Rather than being emblematic of ethical or pedagogical authority, they are the quintessential example of coercive state authority, so much so that the failure to obey gazetted fatwas can result in a fine or imprisonment (Tayeb 2017, 6, 16n1). Rather than reflecting solely premodern Islamic law, e-syariah and e-fatwa systems reflect modern forms of legal reasoning and the agglomeration of norms from Japan and Britain (Moustafa 2018, 38; Peletz 2013)

Iran provides another illustration of this approach. Ayatollah Khomeini's famous fatwa against chemical, biological, and nuclear weapons has been the source of much debate and confusion. Advocates of international diplomacy have pointed to the fatwa as evidence of the Iranian government's commitment to nonviolent methods of dispute resolution, while skeptics have mined Shiite theology to suggest that the fatwa is not important due to dissimulation (Shuster 2012). Missing from the debate is the more banal conclusion that Khomeini's fatwa should be read as neither transcendent nor irrelevant, but as a policy. Policies are important drivers of state behavior and also subject to change given shifts in political, economic, or military conditions. Indeed, fatwas from the Supreme Leader have been reversed, repealed, and revised in the past, and there is no reason to believe that theological opinions about nuclear weapons are not subject to similar revision (Khalaji 2011, 19).

An organizational approach to the authority of the fatwa is also useful beyond the confines of the state. In 2004, when the Jordanian government was battling militants, King Abdullah wrote to twenty-four of the world's most senior Islamic scholars in order to gather their views on who is a Muslim, under what conditions it is possible to declare someone an apostate (*takfir*), and what qualifications are necessary to issue a fatwa. Based on the fatwas crafted in response, including from Yusuf al-Qaradawi, Mohamed Sayed Tantawi of al-Azhar, and Iraq's Grand Ayatollah Ali al-Sistani, Abdullah convened a conference of two hundred scholars from fifty countries, who issued a declaration called "The Amman Message" to emphasize Islam's values of tolerance and opposition to the practice of *takfir*.

How should scholars interpret these fatwas, or their being bundled into a larger statement? This paper suggests is it less productive to view them as emblematic of ethical, charismatic, or legal-rational authority than as characteristic of the soft international law typical of international agreements between state and non-state actors. On issues of trade, environmental protection, and human rights, such non-binding agreements help build normative order without constraining state sovereignty (Abbott and Snidel 2000). In that respect, The Amman Message should be understood as yet another way in which fatwas are being reimagined and deployed by modern Islamic authorities.

IV. Three Periods of MUI

Period I (1975–89): State Corporatism

In 1975, President Suharto created MUI as a hierarchical series of consultative councils. At the outset, MUI had "little impact on the Islamic community" and the wider public (McVey 1983, 209). Two years earlier Suharto had forced all Islamic political parties into PPP, which helped him to consolidate power and neutralize opposition; MUI was intended to similarly neutralize ulama from a broad range of religious backgrounds, including traditionalists, modernists, and Salafists. It was designed as a mechanism to "co-opt, fragment, and neutralize Islam as an autonomous political force, regulate associational life, and ensure mass turnouts for [the political party] Golkar at election time" (Porter 2002, 76). Figure 1 provides visual representation of this point, depicting MUI members waiting to be received by Suharto.

MUI was also the Indonesian government's formal face abroad in bodies like the Organization of Islamic Countries (OIC). In April 1974 the OIC urged Muslim governments to declare Ahmadiyah, a small religious sect often perceived as heterodox by Sunni Muslims, to be a non-Muslim minority (Friedmann 1989, 44). The statement led to anti-Ahmadi resolutions in Jordan, Mauritania, and Mecca and exacerbated ongoing conflict in Pakistan. MUI issued its own fatwa against Ahmadiyah in 1984, decrying the group as a heretical sect.

The 1984 fatwa against Ahmadiyah had little effect. The Suharto government was more concerned with development than heterodoxy, and MUI fatwas that opposed state policy were largely ignored, or in some cases opposed by Suharto, such as the fatwa on Muslims not attending Christmas celebrations, which led to the MUI chair's resignation (Nasir 2014, 494). The 1984 fatwa on Ahmadiyah was ignored; the few newspaper articles mentioning the fatwa focused on the dispute between the Ministry of Religion, which like MUI sought to ban Ahmadiyah, and the Ministry of Justice, which had given Ahmadiyah legal recognition (*Pelita* 1984).

MUI's authority in this period was a product of its charismatic religious scholars (*ulama* or *kiyai* in the common Indonesian form)—in this period, the famous Muhammadiyah leader Hamka (1977–81), then Syukri Ghozali (1981–84), then another Muhamadiyah leader, Hasan Basri (1984–90)—as well as of MUI's corporatist association with the state. It was seen as the umbrella for Indonesian Islam. Yet, its authority was also contested, with Abdurrahman Wahid launching the earliest critiques in 1981 (Sirry 2013, 106). Without more muscular sources of authority, MUI's influence was limited.

By focusing on the organizational reasons for MUI's authority, this paper seeks to counter more ideological accounts of its influence. That said, it is worth closing this

Figure 1: A line of MUI members wait to be received by their superior, Suharto. With Suharto is Datuk Palimo Kayo, MUI Provincial Chair for West Sumatra (*Pelita* 1985).

section with a brief account of MUI's mission in 1975, since it changed so drastically in subsequent periods. MUI was tasked with serving as the "translator of the concepts and activities of national or local development for the people," being a council that "gives advice and opinions to the government concerning religious life," and being the "mediator between the government and the *'ulamā*" (Ichwan 2005, 48). MUI's authority stemmed from the charisma of its ulama and its closeness to the state, which led to influence around the margins of the state and fatwas that amplified state policy, weakly resisted state corporatism, or were simply ignored.

Period II (1990–2005): Institutional Innovation

Period II was a time of institutional innovation and expansion under the leadership of two prominent NU scholars, Ali Yafie (1990–99) and Sahal Mahfudh (1999–2014). The Institute for Food, Drugs and Cosmetic Assessment was created in January 1989, then issued its first halal certificate in 1994 (Ichwan 2013, 71). Halal certification is a labeling system that assures consumers that a product complies with rules about ritual cleanliness and slaughtering. Islamic banking began in May 1992 with the Bank

Muamalat Indonesia (BMI), an MUI project with support from government officials including Suharto (Ichwan 2006, 205). Both programs began small, and MUI continued to be a resource-poor organization for most of the 1990s. Hosen reports that MUI would frequently give board members only a day's notice about meetings and an honorarium of 50,000 rupiah ($22 USD), which would not even cover their transport to Istiqlal mosque. Many members did not have access to a library to prepare for meetings (Hosen 2004, 177). Not surprisingly, many scholars have commented on the relatively shallow quality of MUI's arguments in this decade; Ahmad Sukardja argues that MUI in the early 1990s was a low-capacity organization whose fatwas were prepared hastily (Hosen 2004, 177).

Growing financial independence, however, led to program development. At its 1995 congress, MUI laid out an ambitious program that included the promotion of Islamic brotherhood, education, Islamic economics, Islamic identity and propagation (da'wa), community development, and the training of ulama (Ichwan 2005, 49). MUI claimed that it was sending two thousand preachers (da'i) to areas where the state's transmigration program was active (Antara 1993). Mocha Nur Ichwan (2006) reports that each da'i received 100,000 rupiah ($44) per month for three years, as well as one bike (202).

The early 1990s was also a period of cooperation between MUI and ICMI. Created in December 1990, ICMI was a Suharto-sponsored association designed to mobilize Muslim supporters against Suharto's opponents (Liddle 1996). It was initially organized by five students from the Universitas Brawijaya in Malang, East Java, but its importance lies more in its backing by B. J. Habibie and Minister for Population and the Environment Emil Salim. Neither was then known as a Muslim leader, but instead as high-ranking officials close to Suharto. Habibie was an engineer and technocrat, Salim a prominent economist. The group they put together included many government officials that were jointly associated with MUI, namely Azwar Anas, then coordinating minister for people's welfare; Lt. Gen. (ret) Achmad Tirtosudiro, head of the critical National Logistics Body, which controlled food distribution; and West Sumatran Governor Hasan Basri. Other Suharto officials with prominent Islamic credentials included Ministry of Manpower official Din Syamsuddin and the agricultural economist Amin Aziz. ICMI also included genuine kiyai like K. H. Ali Yafie and other prominent religious scholars like the legal scholar Jimly Asshidique, Muhammadiyah leader and Gadjah Mada University political scientist Amien Rais, the Shia intellectual Jalaluddin Rahmat, the journalist and historian Syafi'i Anwar, and very senior Islamist figures from the 1950s like Anwar Haryono and Lukman Harun.[2] There were formal ties between MUI and ICMI, such as their joint statement against a state-run lottery program (MUI 1997, 193). The lottery, commonly known as *Pork as* (Forecast), was discontinued less than two weeks later. But the more important relationships were informal. ICMI's architects infused MUI with more power than previously, with Jimly Asshiddique and Amin Aziz at the helm of MUI's emergent halal food certification program and Azwar Anas, Emil Salim, and Ali Yafie at the center of the Islamic banking program (*Pelita* 1993). These ties suggest that the enduring legacy of Suharto's emboldening of political Islam can be found not in ICMI, whose influence has waned, but in the expanded power of MUI.

---

[2] Key sources of names of ICMI leaders include Hefner 2000, Aspinall 2005, and Schwarz 2000. Key sources of names of MUI leaders include MUI 1992, 1997a, 1997b, and 2005. I am grateful to Bob Hefner for suggesting this line of analysis.

During this period and into period III, MUI gained regulatory power as a result of administrative regulations and parliamentary law. DSN MUI oversees the Sharia Supervisory Boards (Dewan Pengawas Syariah, DPS) that are required in all Islamic financial institutions, including banks and Islamic insurance companies (Lindsey 2012, 261). The DSN is currently headed by Miftachul Akhyar and receives funding from the government through the Ministry of Finance and the central bank, as well as payments from DPS in Islamic financial institutions. Scholars estimate that this is a significant source of funding for MUI, given that Islamic banking is estimated to account for 6 percent of the country's $634 billion in financial assets (*Al Jazeera* 2021). Each DPS is required to consult the DSN MUI for guidance on issues of doctrine, which it gives in the form of fatwas. It issued fifty fatwas between 1993 and 2003 related to banking and insurance and maintains active authority in finance (Lindsey 2012, 265).

MUI also received funding and authority from its halal food certification program. The law on Animal Health and Husbandry required that a certifying body endorse all halal meat (Lindsey 2012, 266). Ministry of Agriculture regulations obliged all businesses in foreign countries producing meat for export to Indonesia to have a staff to ensure their products are halal. This staff was to be "controlled and supervised by a Halal Certification Institute recognized by and cooperating with [LP-POM MUI] and the Fatwa Commission of the MUI" (Lindsey 2012, 266–67, citing article 15[1][e]). MUI had sole authority as the inspection agency for halal food until the late 2010s (Lindsey 2012, 267; *Jakarta Globe* 2021).

Given its regulatory authority, the legal scholar Tim Lindsey (2012) describes MUI in this period as a "QUANGO," a quasi-autonomous nongovernmental organization (255). In the British and American traditions, QUANGOS are financed largely by the government, are responsible to their own board of directors, and are located on government property. Examples include research units sponsored by the US Department of Defense and private organizations established by government funding, such as the Rand Corporation. The implications of this change for the authority of MUI's fatwas are striking: "MUI fatwas in Indonesia are no longer always just religious recommendations issued from civil society that lack binding force, as in the past. In the case of the halal certification industry, as for Islamic banking, some MUI fatwas now have legal status as enforceable regulatory instruments of state" (Lindsey 2012, 268).

The result of this increased power is that in period II MUI began contesting state authority. In December 2000, MUI issued a fatwa stating that the Japanese company Ajinomoto's products were haram because the company used *bacto soytone*, which contains a pig enzyme, in the production of its widely used monosodium glutamate (MSG) products (Ichwan 2005, 69–70). As a result, MUI revoked Ajinomoto's halal certification.

Indonesian President Wahid disagreed with MUI's decision and issued a fatwa in support of Ajinomoto. Yet, by this point in his presidency Wahid was plagued by scandal, and MUI proved to be more powerful than him. Loaded Djeni Hasmar of Golkar said that only MUI had the authority to issue such a fatwa. PPP and other Islamist parties followed suit. The chief of police, General Bimantoro, said his officers would follow MUI rather than Wahid (Ichwan 2005, 70–71). MUI was building on its growing authority as well as its other battles with Wahid; in 1999 Wahid had suggested that MUI should be financially independent and have an office outside of Istiqlal, and MUI had opposed Wahid's policies on opening trade with Israel and overturning the 1966 ban on Communism (Ichwan 2005, 62, 70). This fatwa is also a reminder of the limits of explanations grounded in charismatic authority. Wahid was a far more charismatic, famous, and popular ulama compared to Ma'ruf Amin or Mahfudh, yet he proved less powerful than MUI due to its regulatory authority and political alliances.

MUI has also shaped the country's media environment. In 1983, during the production of the film *Sunan Kalijaga*, MUI leaders participated in a discussion about how religious principles could be promoted though film, but MUI had no effect on programming (Hereen 2012, 116). Period II saw greater influence. In 1994, Ali Yafie and Hasan Basri called for the film *True Lies* to be banned on the grounds that it was offensive to Muslims (*Republika* 1994). The film was removed from theaters less than two weeks later. In 1996, Basri protested the films *Jinx dan Jun* and *Si Manis Jembatan Ancol* on the grounds that they presented false religious teachings. His critique did not lead to censorship of these specific films, but two years later the Film Censorship Board was instructed by the Minister of Information to ban films and television series with themes that misrepresent religious teachings (Hereen 2012, 146). And in 2004, MUI signed on to the popular television preacher AA Gym's campaign to get the film *Buruan cium gue!* (Hurry up and kiss me!) banned on the grounds that it promoted premarital sex among teenagers. The film was withdrawn from cinemas (Hereen 2012, 163).

MUI has gained even more power over media through its influence on LSF and the Indonesian Broadcasting Commission and through its partnership with the mass movement FPI. As a result, MUI no longer needs to rely on fatwas or government ministers to have programs censored. The most recent manifestation of influence is an award that KPI presented in 2018 to Ma'ruf Amin for being a major figure in broadcasting (RMOL 2018). In another innovation, MUI itself has handed out media awards since 2001 in order to incentivize television producers to run religious programs during Ramadan (Hereen 2012, 128, 175). The criterion for the awards seems to be the quantity of programming, not the quality (Barkin 2004, 15).

MUI's ally, ICMI, was innovative during this period in its strategies to defeat its opponents, using the claim that they were guilty of "defamation of religion" (*penodaan agama*) in order to have them harassed, prosecuted, and jailed. In March 1995, the ICMI leader and Suharto loyalist Din Syamsuddin launched such a campaign against a critic of Suharto, Permadi Satrio Wiwoho. Syamsuddin used a recording of a speech Permadi had given in April 1994 to allege that Permadi had insulted Suharto, Golkar, and the Prophet Muhammad. This was a repeat of an earlier campaign by Syamsuddin and Golkar to mobilize the Muslim community against Arswendo Atmowiloto, editor of the mass tabloid *Monitor* (Hefner 2000, 175–78). On the same day that Syamsuddin's statement was published, MUI chair Basri called a press conference to denounce Permadi's statements and demand legal action against him. In the end, Permadi was convicted of slander and sentenced to eight months in jail. Shortly thereafter, in 1998, Syamsuddin became Secretary of the MUI Steering Committee (Panitia Pengarah), then General Secretary in 2000 (MUI 1999, 2005). Syamsuddin and MUI again deployed the charge of "defamation" against Ahmadi Muslims in the early 2000s and in 2016 against the Christian governor of Jakarta in order to cripple his reelection campaign.

After the fall of Suharto, MUI's purview expanded horizontally (through tackling more issues and contesting state power) and vertically (by reaching down to society). As it moved out from under the corporatist control of the Ministry of Religion, MUI began acting more like a peer institution, contesting the state's policy prerogatives. This shift is readily apparent in MUI's changing approach to the Compilation of Islamic Law (*Kompilasi Hukum Islam*, KHI). In 1985, MUI was involved in the project of codifying Islamic law to be used by the Islamic court system but was only one of seventeen committee members that drafted the KHI. This was a top-down process, with MUI "simply there to justify KHI" (Ichwan 2006, 128). This is in sharp contrast to MUI's influence by 2004, when a team within the Ministry of Religious Affairs developed a series of reforms to the KHI. After the proposals were made public, MUI and other organizations objected and successfully blocked even a discussion of reforms to the KHI, let alone their enactment (Ichwan 2006, 266–67).

In Islamic legal theory, fatwas are a response to a specific question asked of a specific mufti about an actual situation; they are very rarely hypothetical (Masud, Messick, and Powers 1996). Yet after 2000, MUI began setting the "agenda" for policy in Indonesia, giving fatwas whether requested or not (Nasir 2014, 495; Ichwan 2005, 50). In 2000, MUI's mission reflected its new role, defined as being the *fatwā* giver *(mufti)* "whether requested or not," guide and servant of the Muslim community (*rā'i wa khādim al-ummah,)* pioneer in the reform and the renewal movement (*al- iṣlāḥ wa'l tajdīd*), and upholder of the Quaranic dictate to be a "moral force . . . for social rehabilitation" (Ichwan 2005, 50).

Period III (2005–present): Mass Mobilization

The year 2005 marked the debut of the assertive, agenda-setting MUI, powered by regulatory, charismatic and formal state authority while free from the financial constraints of the state. In this period, MUI has repeatedly crafted fatwas that have been seen as binding. The mission of MUI as articulated in 2005 included the roles listed at the end of the previous section, as well as "upholder of the known good and forbidding the reprehensible" (*al-amr bi al-ma'rūf wa al-nahy 'an al-munkar*). Notice that there is nothing in the mission about being the advisor of the state. MUI in this period often leads the state.

MUI reissued its fatwa against Ahmadiyah in July 2005. The difference in the influence of MUI's fatwas in 1984 and 2005 is instructive in two respects. First, there is a common perception that MUI has grown more conservative since democratization, and indeed it has grown more assertive about its support for shari'a-based legislation (Hasyim 2015; Ichwan 2013). Yet on the Ahmadiyah issue—as with the issues of religious deviance, interreligious marriage, Muslims' attendance at Christmas celebrations, the visual depiction of the Prophet Muhammad, penalties for drug users, alcohol consumption, opposition to transgender persons, and support for family planning—MUI's views are best characterized as static.

Second, what has changed are MUI's mechanisms for influence. The 2005 fatwa against Ahmadiyah was part of a broader campaign launched at a seminar titled "Ahmadiyah: Its Deviation and Danger" at Istiqlal Mosque (then MUI's headquarters) on August 11, 2002. Amin Djamaluddin, the head of the Islamic Research and Study

Institute (Lembaga Penelitian dan Pengkajian Islam, LPPI) and the most persistent proponent of the anti-Ahmadiyah movement, was one of the main presenters (Burhani 2013, 226). Violence followed two months later, with mass mobilization in East Lombok, Kuningan, and Tasikmalaya, then spreading in 2005 to Bogor under the leadership of FPI and Djamaluddin. On July 15, 2005, upwards of ten thousand people attacked the Bogor headquarters of the Ahmadiyah Indonesia Congregation (Jamaah Ahmadiyah Indonesia). Armed with sticks and batons, the attackers broke into the compound and set fire to buildings. Nearly four hundred police officers stood outside the compound as this happened, then shuttled Ahmadis to the Bogor prosecutor's office for "safekeeping" (*Jakarta Post* 2005). Djamaluddin's campaign against Ahmadiyah dates back decades, but only in the 2000s did his research have the authority of the state. In 2005 he was appointed by MUI to be its representative for discussions about heretical sects with a team from the Coordinating Body for the Surveillance of Spiritual Movements in Society (Badan Koordinasi Pengawasan Aliran Kepercayaan Masyarakat, Bakor Pakem) in the Attorney General's Office. When Bakor Pakem recommended to the government that it outlaw and disband Ahmadiyah, the contents of its recommendation strongly resembled the letters that Djamaluddin had sent to the Attorney General's Office in 1994 and 1996 (Burhani 2013, 228–29).

When MUI reissued its fatwa against Ahmadiyah, it did so not from a position of subservience, but with financial autonomy from the state, strong ties to violent movements, and close ties to President Susilo Bambang Yudhoyono (SBY). Rather than focus its energies on getting the Ministry of Justice to repeal recognition of Ahmadis, as in 1984, MUI lobbied SBY directly and partnered with Islamic vigilantes to lobby from below using the threat and enactment of violence. The alliance between FPI and MUI was thus born of shared goals and complementary avenues of influence. Ahmad Najib Burhani notes, "When the government did not give its support, in a number of cases, it was through the muscle of the mob that Islamic orthodoxy could be defended and enforced" (2013, 234). FPI helped MUI establish itself as a more independent actor without losing its status as a quasi-state institution: "FPI uses MUI's fatwa to legitimize violent vigilantism such as its attacks on the Ahmadiyah sect, while MUI uses this violence to justify the need for its fatwa to be followed in order to ensure 'religious harmony'" (Wilson 2008, 205; Schäfer 2019, 240).

Unlike in periods I and II, MUI now runs a lucrative patronage network that benefits vigilante groups. MUI received funding from the Ministry of Religion in the amount of 2 billion rupiah ($144,000) in 2009 and 3 billion rupiah ($216,000) in 2010 and in 2011 (Lindsey 2012, 262). Based on interviews with leaders and MUI reports, Ichwan estimates that MUI received 649 billion rupiah ($46,682,636) from its halal certification activity between 2012 and 2017, or around 108 billion rupiah ($7,780,000) annually (Moch Nur Ichwan, May 9, 2018, email message to author). When Parliament established a legislative committee to review a draft law on pornography and pornographic actions in response to pressure from MUI (Bush 2007, 178), MUI then received "socialization funds" from the Ministry of Religious Affairs, which it distributed to its allies in the street: FPI, the Betawi Brotherhood Forum (Forum Betawi Rempug), the Indonesian Mujahidin Council (Majelis Mujahidin Indonesia), and the Indonesian Liberation Party (Hizb ut Tharir) (Wilson 2008, 204–5). And similar to the national level, MUI has clear connections at the provincial level with radical groups that help it gain leverage with the police and government ministries by using violence to create crises (Ichwan 2012, 170).

The result of this dynamic is that MUI fatwas regarding blasphemy are very often binding, backed by the coercive capacity of the state. Ichwan notes, "Government, police, judges and media have treated the MUI as if it is part of [a] state institution" (Ichwan 2012, 170). On the issue of Ahmadiyah, MUI defined the problem (exercising its agenda setting authority), issued a formal definition of deviancy (expert authority), lobbied the state for support in meetings with the Ministry of the Interior and Ministry of Religion (employing lobbying and regulatory authority), and then used mass mobilization (people power) and explicit or implicit violence (coercive authority) to convince the police to enforce its fatwa. Further, MUI took actions to ensure that the fatwa would be enforced consistently. ICG (2008) reports, ". . . Ma'ruf Amin told the television audience, and later reiterated in an interview, that MUI was putting together a monitoring team to determine whether Ahmadiyah was obeying the decree. The team would be organized by MUI branches at province, district and subdistrict levels, and mass Islamic organizations would be invited to participate" (8). In monitoring Ahmadis for compliance with the fatwa, MUI was simply extending its regulatory power from the realms of food and finance to faith.

MUI has deployed mass mobilization and coercive authority on multiple occasions since 2005. In a 2010 trial on the constitutionality of Indonesia's blasphemy law, mentions of crimes against Ahmadi Muslims led to the vigilantes on the second floor of the courtroom screaming at the witnesses until the lawyer for MUI, Muhammad Luthfi Hakim, signaled for his allies to quiet down (Personal observation, Jakarta, March 10 and 12, 2010). Likewise, former Jakarta governor Basuki Tjahaja Purnama (Ahok) landed in prison in 2017 through a combination of an MUI fatwa, political alliance, and mass mobilization. In this respect, the name of the coalition that organized the mass protests, Gerakan Nasional Pengawal Fatwa MUI (National Movement to Safeguard the Fatwa of the MUI) is misleading: more appropriate would be Gerakan MUI Melakukan Fatwa MUI (MUI Movement to Enforce the Fatwa of the MUI).

V. Conclusion

This article has demonstrated that classical theories of Islamic law, Weber's typology, and ethical theories of fatwas cannot explain MUI's growing power or its modes of authority. MUI has grown powerful by aggregating *modern* forms of authority: agenda-setting, lobbying, expert authority, regulatory authority, mass mobilization, and coercive authority may all underpin the power of a MUI fatwa.

MUI's repertoire of influence raises two immediate questions. First, would MUI be as powerful if it did not issue fatwas, but simply exerted authority through other means? After all, in period III much of MUI's influence has been exercised through lobbying, patronage, violence, and other mechanisms. Yet, MUI appears to believe that its fatwas are not dispensable. Ma'ruf Amin's October 11, 2016, statement about Ahok was titled a "Religious Opinion" (*Pendapat dan Sikap Keagamaan*) and not a fatwa (MUI 2016). But everyone involved elided this distinction, especially the leaders of the GNPF-MUI.

Second, what are the limits of MUI's influence? There remain issues on which MUI's authority is muted. Its 2007 fatwa against "infotainment" had little effect (Hartono 2015, 305–6). Even shows about Islam tend to be folksy rather than pedagogical, leading MUI to accuse producers of making "dakwahtainment" (Sofjan and Hidayati 2013). MUI has influence over such shows through the KPI but does not have a veto. MUI leader Cholis Ridwan recently criticized filmmaker Hanung Bramanyato for his film *Tanda Tanya* (Question mark), but the film was released nonetheless and went on to be nominated for nine awards during the 2011 Indonesian Film Festival (Saat 2016, 562). Similarly, MUI's attempt to have the National Commission on Human Rights (Komisi Nasional Hak Asasi Manusia) disbanded was unsuccessful (*Jakarta Post* 2000). And despite its being widely mocked, each year MUI reissues its fatwa against Muslims saying "Merry Christmas" or participating in Christmas celebrations (Hussain 2012). These examples of truncated impact suggest that MUI has been most influential when it moves into issue-areas that are not already occupied by other powerful actors and when it is not competing against market forces.

MUI is also constrained by the dominant logic of power in Indonesia: patronage (Aspinall 2010). Suharto ruled through coercion and cooptation through patronage distribution. Likewise, in recent years Jokowi has weakened MUI's independence by removing radical figures from the central board while coopting NU figures, including Akhyar and Amin (Saat 2020). In doing so, Jokowi seems to have truncated MUI's oppositional stance, at least until the 2024 presidential election.

Nonetheless, from the standpoint of empirical democratic theory MUI is too powerful and unaccountable an institution. MUI's transformation into the Indonesian version of JAKIM could still accelerate. The result would be national regulations that were once unthinkable, including requirements for Muslims to attend Friday prayers and fast during Ramadan and for all businesses to obtain halal certification. Indeed, mandatory halal certification for large sectors of the market appears likely within the next five years (*Jakarta Globe* 2021). Similar to Malaysia, Indonesia could see mandatory prohibitions on drinking alcohol, gambling, blasphemy, "sexual deviance," interfaith marriage, and conversion out of Islam (Moustafa 2018, 31).

Indonesia is a remarkably resilient democracy, but for democracy to endure, the place and power of MUI must be made consistent with democratic norms and practices (Aspinall 2015). This article concludes with observations on the ways in which MUI's power is in conflict with democracy, as well as potential remedies.

First, MUI has used its "non-state" status to avoid the transparency demanded of public institutions, while simultaneously deploying multiple forms of authority to have its fatwas enacted as if they were state law; this contradiction merits attention. One way to resolve this conflict is to have all MUI funding made contingent on transparency in its contracting and decision-making. Too little is known about MUI's relationship to Parliament and to the Ministry of Religious Affairs, the internal working of MUI committees, the extent of the funding MUI receives and the conditions under which it obtains funding; the mechanisms by which MUI decisions are made, the methods by which it influences the KPI and the LSF, and the mechanisms by which MUI leaders come into power. These are also pressing areas for scholarly research.

Second, MUI's control over halal food regulation and Islamic banking certification incentivizes corruption and gives an unelected, unrepresentative actor power over the public welfare (Kunkler and Stepan 2013). MUI is fulfilling tasks that are outsourced by the state, yet the contracts are not granted based on meritocratic criteria and competition between MUI and other organizations. Obvious options for reform include making food certification and Islamic banking certification private and competitive, or a state responsibility akin to health inspection. At the time of writing it appears that the state is pursuing a hybrid approach. The 2014 Halal Products Law created a new body under MORA, the Halal Assurance Agency (Badan Penyelenggara Jaminan Produk Halal), which is working in tandem with the MUI to develop a mandatory certification regime for personal care products, clothing, headwear, accessories, household equipment, food and beverages packaging, stationery, office supplies, and medical devices (*Jakarta Globe* 2021).

Third and finally, MUI's usurpation of the power of the legislature and the executive contravenes the rule of law (Kunkler and Stepan 2013). Although MUI aspires to have its fatwas seen as binding law by the state and society, similar to those of religious officials in Brunei and Malaysia, that power has not been granted to MUI by Indonesia's democratic institutions. The police, courts, and elected officials need not treat MUI's opinions as more than just that.

References

Abbott, Kenneth, and Duncan Snidal. 2000. "Hard and Soft Law in International Governance." *International Organization* 54 (3): 421–56.

Agrama, Hussein Ali. 2010. "Ethics, Tradition, Authority: Toward an Anthropology of the Fatwa." *American Ethnologist* 37 (1): 2–18.

Ali, Muhammad. 2002. "Fatwas on Interfaith-Marriage in Indonesia." *Studia Islamika* 9 (3): 1–33.

Arifianto, Alexander R. 2018. "Quo Vadis Civil Islam? Explaining Rising Islamism in Post-Reformasi Indonesia." *Kyoto Review of Southeast Asia* 24. https://kyotoreview.org/issue-24/rising-islamism-in-post-reformasi-indonesia/.

Aspinall, Edward. 2005. *Opposing Suharto: Compromise, Resistance, and Regime Change in Indonesia.* Stanford: Stanford University Press.

___. 2010. "The Irony of Success." *Journal of Democracy* 21 (1): 20–34.

___. 2015. "The Surprising Democratic Behemoth: Indonesia in Comparative Asian Perspective." *The Journal of Asian Studies* 74 (4): 889–902.

Bourdieu, Pierre, and Loïc Wacquant. 1992. *An Invitation to Reflexive Sociology.* Chicago: University of Chicago Press.

Burhani, Ahmad Najib. 2013. "When Muslims Are Not Muslims: The Ahmadiyya Community and the Discourse on Heresy in Indonesia." PhD diss., University of California Santa Barbara.

Bush, Robin. 2008. "Regional Sharia Regulations: Anomaly or Symptom?" In *Expressing Islam: Religious Life and Politics in Indonesia*, edited by Greg Fealy and Sally White, 174–91. Singapore: ISEAS Press.

Casanova, José. 1994. *Public Religions in the Modern World.* Berkeley: University of California Press.

Eickelman, Dale F. 1998. "Mass Education and the Religious Imagination in Contemporary Arab Societies." *American Ethnologist* 19 (4): 643–55.

Friedmann, Yohanan. 1989. *Prophecy Continuous: Aspects of Aḥmadī Religious Thought and Its Medieval Background*. Berkeley: University of California Press.

Hallaq, Wael B. 2009. *Sharī'a: Theory, Practice, Transformations*. New York: Cambridge University Press.

Hartono, Savitri Hanny. 2015. "Muslim Mothers and Indonesian Gossip Shows in Everyday Life." *Indonesia and the Malay World* 43 (126): 298–316.

Hasyim, Syafiq. 2011. "The Council of Indonesian Ulama (Majelis Ulama Indonesia, MUI) and Religious Freedom." Irasec's Discussion Papers, no. 12. https://www.irasec.com/documents/fichiers/47.pdf.

___. 2015. "*Majelis Ulama Indonesia* and Pluralism in Indonesia." *Philosophy and Social Criticism* 41 (4–5): 487–95.

Hefner, Robert. 1998. "Multiple Modernities: Christianity, Islam, and Hinduism in a Globalizing Age." *Annual Review of Anthropology* 27: 83–104.

___. 2000. *Civil Islam: Muslims and Democratization in Indonesia*. Princeton: Princeton University Press.

Hereen, Kantinka van. 2012. *Contemporary Indonesian Film: Spirits of Reform and Ghosts from the Past*. Leiden: KITLV Press.

Hoesterey, James Bork. 2015. *Rebranding Islam: Piety, Prosperity, and a Self-help Guru*. Stanford: Stanford University Press.

Hosen, Nadirsyah. 2004. "Behind the Scenes: Fatwas of Majelis Ulama Indonesia (1975–1998)." *Journal of Islamic Studies* 15 (2): 147–79.

Hussain, Zakir. 2012. "AntiChristmas Clerics Rebuffed in Indonesia; Muslims Ignore Order Calling on Them Not to Offer Festive Greetings." *The Straits Times*. December 24, 2012.

Hussin, Iza R. 2016. *The Politics of Islamic Law: Local Elites, Colonial Authority, and the Making of the Muslim State*. Chicago: University of Chicago Press.

Ichwan, Moch Nur. 2005. "Ulamⵡ, State and Politics: Majelis Ulama Indonesia After Suharto." *Islamic Law and Society* 12 (1): 45–72.

___. 2006. "Official Reform of Islam: State Islam and the Ministry of Religious Affairs in Contemporary Indonesia, 1966–2004." PhD diss., University of Tilburg.

___. 2012. "The Local Politics of Orthodoxy: The Majelis Ulama Indonesia in the Post-New Order Banten." *Journal of Indonesian Islam* 6 (1): 167–94.

International Crisis Group (ICG). 2001. "Indonesia: Violence and Radical Muslims." Crisis Group Asia Briefing. October 10, 2001. https://www.crisisgroup.org/asia/south-east-asia/indonesia/indonesia-violence-and-radical-muslims.

___. 2008. "Indonesia: Implications of the Ahmadiyah Decree." Crisis Group Asia Briefing No. 78. July 7, 2008. https://www.crisisgroup.org/asia/south-east-asia/indonesia/indonesia-implications-ahmadiyah-decree.

Keck, Margaret E., and Kathryn Sikkink. 1998. *Activists Beyond Borders: Advocacy Networks in International Politics*. Ithaca: Cornell University Press.

Khalaji, Mehdi. 2011. "Shiite Jurisprudence, Political Expediency, and Nuclear Weapons." In *Nuclear Fatwa: Religion and Politics in Iran's Proliferation Strategy*. The Middle East Institute, Policy Focus #115. https://www.washingtoninstitute.org/media/3344?disposition=inline.

Kingsley, Jeremy. 2014. "Redrawing Lines of Religious Authority in Lombok, Indonesia." *Asian Journal of Social Science* 42: 657–77.

Künkler, Mirjam, and Alfred Stepan. 2013. "Indonesian Democratization in Theoretical Perspective." In *Democracy and Islam in Indonesia*, edited by Mirjam Künkler and Alfred Stepan, 3–24. New York: Columbia University Press.

Lev, Daniel S. 1972. *Islamic Courts in Indonesia: A Study in the Political Bases of Legal Institutions.* Berkeley: University of California Press.

Liddle, R. William. 1996. "The Islamic Turn in Indonesia: A Political Explanation." *The Journal of Asian Studies* 55 (3): 613–34.

Lindsey, Tim. 2012. "Monopolising Islam? The Indonesian Ulama Council and State Regulations of the 'Islamic Economy'" *Bulletin of Indonesian Economic Studies* 48 (2): 253–74.

Majelis Ulama Indonesia (MUI). 1992. *Majelis Ulama Indonesia Keputusan Rapat Kerja Nasional Majelis Ulama Indonesia Th. 1992.* Jakarta: Sekretariat Majelis Ulama Indonesia.

___. 1997a. *Himpunan Fatwa Majelis Ulama Indonesia.* Jakarta: Majelis Ulama Indonesia.

___. 1997b. *Majelis Ulama Indonesia: Resume Garis-Garis Besar Program Kerja dan Ketentuian Tugas Komisi Majelis Ulama Indonesia Periode 1995–2000.* Jakarta: Majelis Ulama Indonesia.

___. 1999. *Kumpulan Hasil-Hasil Kongres Umat Islam Indonesia: Umat Islam Menyongsong Era Indonesia Baru.* Jakarta: Majelis Ulama Indonesia.

___. 2005. *Himpunan Keputusan Musyawarah Nasional VIII Majelis Ulama Indonesia 2005.* Jakarta: Sekretariat Majelis Ulama Indonesia.

___. 2016. "Pendapat dan Sikap Keagamaan Majelis Ulama Indonesia." October 11, 2016.

Masud, Muhammad Khalid, Brinkley Messick, and David S Powers. 1996. "Muftis, Fatwas, and Islamic Legal Interpretation." In *Islamic Legal interpretation: Muftis and Their Fatwas* Muhammad Khalid Masud, Brinkley Messick, and David S. Powers, 3–32. Cambridge, MA: Harvard University Press.

Menchik, Jeremy. 2014. "Productive Intolerance: Godly Nationalism in Indonesia." *Comparative Studies in Society and History* 56 (3): 591–621.

Moustafa, Tamir. 2000. "Conflict and Cooperation Between the State and Religious Institutions in Contemporary Egypt." *International Journal of Middle East Studies* 32: 3–22.

___. 2013. "Judging in God's Name: State Power, Secularism, and the Politics of Islamic Law in Malaysia." *Oxford Journal of Law and Religion* 3 (1): 1–16.

___. 2018. *Constituting Religion: Islam, Liberal Rights, and the Malaysian State.* New York: Cambridge University Press.

Müller, Dominik M. 2015. "Sharia Law and the Politics of 'Faith Control' in Brunei Darussalam: Dynamics of Socio-Legal Change in a Southeast Asian Sultanate." *Internationales Asienforum* 46 (3–4): 313–45.

___. 2017. "The Bureaucratization of Islam and its Socio-Legal Dimensions in Southeast Asia: Conceptual Contours of a Research Project." Working Paper no. 187, Max Planck Institute for Social Anthropology Working Papers, Halle, Germany.

Müller, Dominik M., and Kerstin Steiner (2018). "The Bureaucratisation of Islam in Southeast Asia: Transdisciplinary Perspectives." *Journal of Current Southeast Asian Affairs* 37 (1): 3–26.

Mudzhar, Mohamad Atho. 1993. *Fatwa-Fatwa Majelis Ulama Indonesia* [Fatwas of the MUI]. Jakarta: INIS.

___. 1996. "The Council of the Indonesian Ulama on Muslims' Attendance at Christmas Celebrations." In *Islamic Legal Interpretation: Muftis and Their Fatwas*, edited by M. K. Masud, B. M. Messick, and D. S. Powers. Cambridge, MA: Harvard University Press.

Nasir, Mohamad Abdun. 2014. "The 'Ulamā', Fatāwā and Challenges to Democracy in Contemporary Indonesia." *Islam and Christian–Muslim Relations* 25 (4): 489–505.

Olle, John. 2009. "The Majelis Ulama Indonesia Versus 'Heresy': The Resurgence of Authoritarian Islam." In *State of Authority: The State in Society in Indonesia*, edited by Gerry van Klinken and Joshua Barker, 95–116. Ithaca: Cornell University Press.

Peletz, Michael. 2013. "Malaysia's Syariah Judiciary as Global Assemblage: Islamization, Corporatization, and Other Transformations in Context." *Comparative Studies in Society and History* 55 (3): 603–33.

___. 2014. "A Tale of Two Courts: Judicial Transformation and the Rise of a Corporate Islamic Governmentality in Malaysia." *American Ethnologist* 42 (1): 144–60.

Pepinsky, Thomas B., R. William Liddle, and Saiful Mujani. 2018. *Piety and Public Opinion: Understanding Indonesian Islam*. Oxford: Oxford University Press.

Porter, Donald J. 2002. *Managing Politics and Islam in Indonesia*. New York: RoutledgeCurzon.

Saat, Norshahril. 2016. "Theologians 'Moralizing' Indonesia? The Case of the Post-New Order Ulama Council of Indonesia (MUI)." *Asian Journal of Social Science* 44: 546–70.

___. 2017. *The State, Ulama and Islam in Malaysia and Indonesia*. Amsterdam: Amsterdam University Press.

___. 2020. "The MUI 2020 Congress: Path Towards Moderation?" ISEAS. https://www.iseas.edu.sg/media/commentaries/the-mui-2020-congress-path-towards-moderation/.

Schwarz, Adam. 2000. *A National in Waiting: Indonesia's Search for Stability*. Boulder, CO: Westview Press.

Schäfer, Saskia. 2019. "Democratic Decline in Indonesia: The Role of Religious Authorities." *Pacific Affairs* 92 (2): 235–55.

Sirry, Mun'im. 2013. "Fatwas and Their Controversy: The Case of the Council of Indonesian Ulama (MUI)." *Journal of Southeast Asian Studies* 44 (1): 100–17.

Sofjan, Dicky, and Mega Hidayati. 2013. "Religion and Television in Indonesia: Ethics Surrounding Dakwahtainment." Geneva: Globethics.net.

Tayeb, Azmil. 2017. "State Islamic Orthodoxies and Islamic Education in Malaysia and Indonesia." *Kajian Malaysia* 35 (2): 1–20.

Weber, Max. 1947. *The Theory of Social and Economic Organization*. Translated by A. M. Henderson and Talcot Parsons. Glencoe, IL: The Free Press.

Wilson, Ian Douglas. 2013. "'As Long as It's Halal': Islamic *Preman in* Jakarta." In *Expressing Islam: Religious Life and Politics in Indonesia*, edited by Greg Fealy and Sally White, 192–210. Singapore: Institute of Southeast Asia Publishing.

World Values Survey. Accessed April 25, 2018. http://www.worldvaluessurvey.org/wvs.jsp.

Newspaper Articles

Al Jazeera. 2021. "Indonesia's 'Born-Again' Muslims Quit Banks for Islamic Finance." June 21, 2021. https://www.aljazeera.com/economy/2021/6/21/indonesias-born-again-muslims-quit-banks-for-islamic-finance.

Antara. 1993. "MUI Rencanakan Korim 2,000 Da'i ke Daerah Transmigrasi." July 20, 1993.

Jakarta Globe. 2021. "Indonesia Begins Mandatory Halal Certification on Drugs, Cosmetics." *Jakarta Globe*. October 17, 2021. https://jakartaglobe.id/business/indonesia-begins-mandatory-halal-certification-on-drugs-cosmetics.

Jakarta Post. 2000. "MUI Calls for Rights Body to be Dissolved." January 12, 2000.

___. 2017. "Government Ends MUI's Authority to Issue Halal Certificates." October 13, 2017. http://www.thejakartapost.com/news/2017/10/13/government-ends-muis-authority-to-issue-halal-certificates.html.

Medina, Ayman Falak. 2021. "Indonesia's Omnibus Law: Halal Certification to Impact Businesses." *ASEAN Briefing*. October 8, 2021. https://www.aseanbriefing.com/news/indonesias-omnibus-law-halal-certification-to-impact-businesses/.

Pelita. 1984. "MUI Serukan Pengikut Ahmadiyah Qadiyan Kembali ke Islam yang Benar." May 5, 1984.

___. 1985. "President Soeharto Buka Munas ke-III MUI: Pancasila adalah Pancasila dan Agama adalah Agama." July 22, 1985.

___. 1991a. "Produk Cantumkan Label Hala Agar Bersedia Diperiksa MUI." March 21, 1991.

___. 1991b. "MUI tak Perlu Menunggu UU Pengawasan Makanan." March 22, 1991.

___. 1993. "MUI Bentuk Badan Penggerak Ekonomi Umat." April 13, 1993.

___. 1994. "Kita Wajib Beri Tahu, Apa yang Kita Tahu." *Kompas*. May 3, 1994.

Republika. 1994. "Ali Yafie Persoalkan Pernyataan MUI." September 20, 1994.

RMOL.co. 2018. "Kiai Ma'ruf Amin Tokoh Penyiaran 2018." April 1, 2018. https://politik.rmol.id/read/2018/04/01/333436/kiai-maruf-amin-tokoh-penyiaran-2018.

Sufa, Theresia. 2005. "Thousands Besiege Ahmadiyah Complex." *Jakarta Post*. July 16, 2005.

Current Data on the Indonesian Military Elite

October 2014–December 2021

The Editors

Introduction

The 2014 General Election (*Pemilihan Umum*, Pemilu) was no different from the three consecutive polls since the fall of Suharto's authoritarian regime. The country held legislative elections in April and voted for new national leadership in July 2014, which marked the end of the ten-year tenure of Susilo Bambang Yudhoyono's presidency. Spearheaded by the Indonesian Democratic Party for Struggle (PDIP), Joko "Jokowi" Widodo won 53.15 percent of the popular vote over former general Prabowo Subianto.

Ten years of democratic consolidation during the Yudhoyono era coupled with a peaceful transfer of power in the 2014 presidential election notwithstanding, the centerpiece of Suharto's authoritarian New Order, the Indonesian National Armed Forces (TNI), still remains an important factor in the country's post-authoritarian political life. Prior to the 2014 election and Jokowi's ascendancy, President Yudhoyono had abruptly removed of General Budiman from his position as army chief of staff in July 2014 long before General Budiman's retirement age. At the time, President Yudhoyono had perceived that Budiman had political ambitions and was incapable of maintaining the army's political neutrality during the up-coming election season.[1] In addition, the TNI

---

[1] In July 2014, Budiman's name was mentioned as a potential minister candidate in Jokowi's cabinet and by April 2014 his name had surfaced as a potential vice-president candidate. The case of involvement of TNI's village supervisory non-commissioned officers (Babinsa) in promoting the Prabowo Subianto-Hatta Rajasa

Commander General Moeldoko (2013–15) had also embarked on a substantial personnel rotation stratagem throughout the years 2013 to 2014 with the aim of depoliticizing and professionalizing the military.

That said, President Jokowi had struggled to consolidate his control over the armed forces back in 2014. To support TNI professionalism—or to be more precise, to make the military more subservient to civilian authority—the Jokowi administration needed to maintain its political commitment to increase funding for defense and embark on provisions to improve soldier welfare. Since then, Indonesia had embarked on a target to increase defense spending up to a standing baseline of 1.5 percent of the country's gross domestic product (GDP). However, the president had simultaneously tied his hands by making such a goal dependent on an annual economic growth target of 7 percent. Yet, before such objectives could be attained, the double whammy of a pre-2019 global economic downturn and the SARS-Corona Virus-2 (COVID-19) pandemic reduced these aspirations to a pipe dream.

In addition, President Jokowi's first five-year term had seen changes to several policies related to military reform.[2] The Jokowi Administration had made three amendments to the previous Presidential Regulation (Perpres) on the TNI's organizational structure. However, these three amendments came under criticism as it enlarged the corps of high-ranking military officers.[3] Such policy changes seemed to solidify Jokowi's—who once again defeated Prabowo this time by over 17 million more votes—control over the armed forces in his second five-year term after the 2019 Indonesian general election.[4]

TNI personnel rotation from October 2014 to December 2021 resulted in a total of 101 personnel reshuffles that affected 4,614 officers. The most significant events were the appointments of General Gatot Nurmantyo (July 2015), Air-Chief Marshal Hadi Tjahjanto (December 2017), and General Andika Perkasa (November 2021) as the TNI commander-in-chief (Panglima TNI). In addition, Indonesia also witnessed three rounds of key leadership changes within army, navy, and air force headquarters between 2014 and 2021.

Against this backdrop, this paper provides an analysis of Indonesia's military developments from October 2014 to December 2021. It carries over from the previous edition of *Current Data on the Indonesian Military Elite* that examined the transition of leadership from the alumni of the classes of 1976–78 to a younger batch of officers from the 1980s cohort. The previous Current Data article in October 2014 also concluded that

---

pair had also undermined Budiman's credibility. See Selamet Ginting, "Manuver Jelang Lengser," *Republika*, August 25, 2014, https://www.republika.co.id/berita/koran/teraju/14/08/25/naunuh-manuver-jelang -lengser; Tempo, "Babinsa Partisan Dipenjarakan TNI AD," *Tempo.co*, June 8, 2014, https://pemilu.tempo .co/read/583381/babinsa-partisan-dipenjarakan-tni-ad.

[2] For an example, Jokowi ratified Presidential Regulation (Perpres) no. 37/2019 on Functional Positions within TNI, which allows TNI officers to occupy more positions at civilian institutions. Jokowi also accommodated the formation of the Special Operation Command (Koopsus) and reestablished the appointment of Deputy Commander-in-Chief, respectively, through Perpres no. 42/2019 and 66/2019.

[3] See, "Keputusan Jokowi Lahirkan Ratusan Jenderal Baru," *Republika*, September 11, 2020, https://www .republika.co.id/berita/qggub1484/keputusan-jokowi-lahirkan-ratusan-jenderal-baru.

[4] See, "KPU Names Jokowi Winner of Election," *The Jakarta Post*, May 21, 2019, https://www.thejakartapost .com/news/2019/05/21/kpu-names-jokowi-winner-of-election.html.

there was a growing commitment to military professionalism among the new military officer generations.[5]

The paper continues to observe TNI organizational developments by focusing on five interconnected themes relating to the ebb and flow of TNI dynamics under the Widodo presidency to provide a more comprehensive analysis: the nomination for Indonesian military leadership positions, appointments related to the TNI main commands (Komando Utama, Kotama TNI) and executive agencies (Badan Pelaksana Pusat, Balakpus TNI), the major reorganization of the Indonesian military, Jokowi's political engagement with retired military officers, and last, the Indonesian military involvement in the nationwide COVID-19 pandemic management.

This article begins the discussion by highlighting general trends of military personnel reshuffles from 2014 to 2021. The second section examines the appointments of new military leadership and personnel reshuffles (*mutasi*) relating to key positions. The next part scrutinizes the placement of military officers in the Kotama and Balakpus positions. The fourth section analyzes the nature of TNI reorganization. It is followed by a section that concentrates on the political engagements between President Jokowi and retired military officers that arguably facilitated Jokowi's political consolidation. This article concludes by explaining the implications of the TNI promotional patterns on Indonesia's military development and the prospects of military change during Jokowi's tenure.

General Trend of Recent Military Personnel Reshuffles

Between 2014 to 2021, there were a total of 101 reshuffle decisions (indicated by the total number of Surat Keputusan [SK] Panglima TNI or decision letters) with an average of fifty-five officers affected per reshuffle. The highest number of officers involved in the reshuffle occurred in 2020 with 1,104 officers repositioned during the year, and the lowest being 2017 with only 359 officers reshuffled.

A second finding indicates an upward trend in the number of officers affected for each reshuffle each year; starting from thirty-one officers per decision in 2014 to a striking number of 109 officers per decision in 2021.[6] There is a likelihood that these trends will continue given that more officers tend to be affected by SK issued from 2014 onward (fifty-nine officers in September 2014, eighty-four officers affected in a July 2015 decision letter, and then in June 2016, involving 116 officers).[7] During the leadership of Air Chief Marshal Hadi, this upward trend seemed to persist given that he had rotated 181 officers with the use of just a single SK in 2020.[8] Moreover, it is very likely that the ascendant trend will persist under the commandership of General Andika. Within a few days after General Andika's inauguration as Panglima TNI, he had reshuffled a total of 103 officers in November and December 2021.[9]

---

[5] See, The Editors, "Current Data on the Indonesian Military Elite," *Indonesia*, no. 98 (October 2014): 91–139.

[6] The number of officers reshuffled in 2021 seems to point to an anomaly. The average number of officers rotated per decision letters from 2014 to 2021 only amounts to fifty-five officers per decision letter.

[7] SKEP Panglima TNI No. Kep/643/IX/2014; SKEP Panglima TNI No. Kep/593/VII/2015; SKEP Panglima TNI No. Kep/463/VI/2016.

[8] SKEP Panglima TNI No. Kep/588/VII/2020.

[9] SKEP Panglima TNI No. Kep/1029/XI/2021 and SKEP Panglima TNI No. Kep/1028/XII/2021.

Table 1: Number of Officers Affected by Personnel Reshuffle

2014–21	Reshuffle by Year	Army	Navy	Air Force	Total Officers Affected
2014	19	287	195	107	589
2015	11	299	122	142	563
2016	7	184	129	84	397
2017	7	172	100	87	359
2018	16	387	194	185	766
2019	15	316	220	193	729
2020	16	617	254	233	1,104
2021	10	617	260	219	1,096
	101	2,879	1,474	1,250	5,603

For the years 2014–21, the majority of the officers reshuffled came from the army, impinging on an overall average of 45.9 percent of officers. It is also worth mentioning that, aside from an increase of 226 navy officers for 2014, the number of air force and navy personnel that were reshuffled remained relatively stable.

The third finding highlights that the number of reshuffled personnel varies with the size of the academy class (counted by the year of the graduation from the academy). As displayed by Table 2, each class size varies from year to year depending on the intake policy that was decided by the TNI (or ABRI, during the New Order Era) leadership. Based on our observations, an officer who graduated from the military academy has to serve for a period of twenty-five years in order to attain a high rank.

Regarding the effect on the academy class size on the personnel reshuffle, our observation from 2014 to 2021 (see Table 3) demonstrates that academy graduates of the 1988 cohort had the most officers reshuffled, followed by the classes of 1986 and 1987, respectively. One explanation regarding such a pattern is that the military, naval, and air force academies had presided over two batches of graduating classes in 1988, thus making the class size much larger than previous years.

Another explanation to this pattern is the TNI top leadership's preference to promote their fellow classmates to high-ranking appointments. For example, army officers that belonged to the class of 1981 were affected by reshuffle decisions more than other classes when General Moeldoko (class of 1981) had been in charge of the TNI from 2013 to 2015. Similarly, when Air Chief Marshal Hadi Tjahjanto (class of 1986) was commander (2018–21), there was a notable increase of air force officers graduating in 1986 who were beneficiaries of the reshuffles.

However, our hypothesis on how TNI top leadership had affected the officer promotion patterns was unproven in two instances. First, our data demonstrates that General Gatot Nurmantyo (class of 1982) did not promote a significant number of his classmates, as the size of the 1982 class was smaller compared to classes from 1983

Table 2: Number of Academy Graduates, 1977–96

	Military Academy	Navy Academy	Air Force Academy	Subtotal
1977	79	30	39	148
1978	99	28	23	150
1979	no intake	no intake	no intake	
1980	98	37	40	175
1981	153	38	48	239
1982	84	50	34	168
1983	184	87	63	334
1984	237	53	58	348
1985	254	63	67	384
1986	223	73	56	352
1987	277	92	69	438
1988	540	182	137	859
1989	261	86	71	418
1990	273	108	73	454
1991	290	106	60	456
1992	297	116	85	498
1993	275	137	93	505
1994	251	148	102	501
1995	296	140	109	545
1996	322	148	151	621

onward. Second, we do not account for the impact of General Andika Perkasa's (class of 1987) appointment because at the time of writing, he had only been TNI commander for two months.

We also observe that the leadership factor might be influential in affecting personnel reshuffles at the service headquarters level (Markas Besar Angkatan, Mabes Angkatan). As indicated by Table 4, several positions that fall into the categories of service leadership assistants, service main executive agencies, and commanders of main service commands belong to officers that graduated in the same year as their respective service leaders.

The President and the Dynamics of TNI Leadership

In this section, the Editors examine the appointment of TNI leadership positions and the civil-military relations dynamic surrounding these reshuffles. We specifically examine those positions that were directly chosen by the president, namely, appointments for TNI commander-in-chief and the chiefs of staffs from each military service. Apart from the appointments made by the president, the designation of high-level positions at TNI

Table 3: Number of Army, Navy, and Air Force Officers Reshuffled Based on Academy Graduation Year, 2014–21

Academy Graduation Year	Army								Navy								Air Force							
	2014	2015	2016	2017	2018	2019	2020	2021	2014	2015	2016	2017	2018	2019	2020	2021	2014	2015	2016	2017	2018	2019	2020	2021
1977	1	0	0	0	0	0	0	0	0	0	0	0	0	0	0	0	0	0	0	0	0	0	0	0
1978	12	0	0	0	0	0	0	0	0	0	0	0	0	0	0	0	4	0	0	0	0	0	0	0
1980	28	10	0	0	0	0	0	0	20	7	0	0	0	0	0	0	12	2	0	0	0	0	0	0
1981	53	55	7	0	0	0	0	0	28	13	3	0	0	0	0	0	18	18	3	0	0	0	0	0
1982	34	31	12	6	1	0	0	0	27	15	8	7	1	0	0	0	16	20	6	2	2	0	0	0
1983	52	49	35	22	21	3	0	0	40	41	29	7	11	1	0	0	15	28	16	9	11	1	0	0
1984	40	30	34	32	50	46	5	0	27	11	16	11	19	18	2	0	17	28	10	6	33	29	10	0
1985	33	47	24	17	57	60	58	9	17	11	13	15	26	26	16	4	12	9	9	23	28	32	14	5
1986	15	37	24	23	68	58	82	81	15	11	14	9	32	30	40	23	5	14	14	17	29	33	29	25
1987	10	13	19	22	56	43	99	111	14	4	13	15	19	31	27	37	4	5	10	7	22	18	40	27
1988	7	21	18	28	62	47	141	177	6	6	29	20	41	50	90	87	3	14	10	14	24	26	53	58
1989	2	3	6	9	32	24	64	70	1	3	3	7	12	22	24	22	1	2	4	3	17	20	25	30
1990	0	3	2	9	19	12	54	51	0	0	1	5	20	18	24	29	0	1	1	4	8	18	23	24
1991	0	0	3	3	11	10	53	54	0	0	0	3	10	12	11	17	0	1	1	1	3	10	11	10
1992	0	0	0	1	5	7	29	29	0	0	0	1	3	7	12	21	0	0	0	1	5	5	12	16
1993	0	0	0	0	5	6	28	21	0	0	0	0	0	4	5	9	0	0	0	0	3	1	6	9
1994	0	0	0	0	0	0	2	11	0	0	0	0	0	1	3	5	0	0	0	0	0	0	7	7
1995	0	0	0	0	0	0	2	2	0	0	0	0	0	0	0	4	0	0	0	0	0	0	3	5
1996	0	0	0	0	0	0	0	1	0	0	0	0	0	0	0	2	0	0	0	0	0	0	0	3

Table 4: TNI Leadership Structure Based on Service and Academy Graduation Year, as of December 31, 2021

TNI Headquarters

Academy Graduation Year	Leadership	Leadership Assistant	Central Executive Agency	Commander, TNI Main Command	Chief-of-Staff, TNI Main Command
1985	0	0	0	0	0
1986	0	1	1	1	0
1987	1	4	0	0	0
1988	0	2	2	1	0
1989	0	3	1	2	2
1990	0	0	2	0	1
1991	0	0	0	0	1
1992	0	0	0	0	1
1993	0	0	0	0	0
1994	0	0	1	0	0
1995	0	0	0	0	0
1996	0	0	0	0	0

Army Headquarters

Academy Graduation Year	Leadership	Leadership Assistant	Central Executive Agency	Commander, Main Command	Chief-of-Staff, Main Command
1985	0	0	0	0	0
1986	0	1	0	0	0
1987	1	4	4	4	1
1988	1	2	7	5	4
1989	0	2	1	3	3
1990	0	0	0	2	3
1991	0	1	0	2	4
1992	0	0	0	3	2
1993	0	0	1	1	2
1994	0	0	0	0	0
1995	0	0	0	0	0
1996	0	0	0	0	1

Navy Headquarters

Academy Graduation Year	Leadership	Leadership Assistant	Central Executive Agency	Commander, Main Command	Chief-of-Staff, Navy Main Command
1985	0	0	0	0	0
1986	0	0	0	0	0
1987	0	1	1	0	0
1988	2	7	2	3	1
1989	0	0	1	0	1
1990	0	0	0	2	1
1991	0	0	1	1	1
1992	0	0	1	0	1
1993	0	0	0	0	0
1994	0	0	0	0	0
1995	0	0	0	0	0
1996	0	0	0	0	0

Air Force Headquarters

Academy Graduation Year	Leadership	Leadership Assistant	Central Executive Agency	Commander, Main Command	Chief-of-Staff, Main Command
1985	0	1	0	0	0
1986	0	0	0	1	1
1987	2	3	1	2	0
1988	0	3	0	0	1
1989	0	1	1	1	0
1990	0	0	0	2	1
1991	0	1	1	0	2
1992	0	0	0	0	0
1993	0	0	0	0	0
1994	0	0	0	0	0
1995	0	0	0	0	0
1996	0	0	0	0	0

headquarters—including in each service headquarters—will be studied carefully in this section. The method of selection for these candidacies hint at the political dynamics unfolding at the national level where political negotiation and collusion between civilian and military leaders to reach a quid pro quo consensus became the focal point.

To give readers some context, governments in post-authoritarian Indonesia have been characterized by coalitional politics and party rivalries. Political candidates would have to secure the support of a political party or party coalition to be eligible to contest in the country's presidential election. Consequently, elected presidents since 1999 have had to form a party coalition, which in turn impacts policy decisions. Furthermore, ministerial portfolios are prized for their utility in political "horse-trading" (or to use the Indonesian term *dagang-sapi*) and to maintain a strong base of support in parliament.

Since taking office in October 2014, Jokowi, who was largely an outsider in the realm of national politics, had struggled to impose his authority on political party patrons and parties that supported him—particularly the PDIP and former President Megawati Sukarnoputri. For instance, in January 2015, pressure was brought to bear from Megawati, who was widely believed to have forced Jokowi to nominate her former aide, Police Commissioner-General Budi Gunawan, to be the next National Police (Polri) chief, despite the cloud of suspicion hanging over him due to an investigation by the Corruption Eradication Commission (KPK).[10]

Within this context, the changes of Indonesian key military leadership from November 2014 to August 2015 could be better understood in the context of President Jokowi's desire for political "autonomy" and the consolidation of his powerbase. During his first hundred days in office, the newly elected President Jokowi replaced the key leaders of the Indonesian navy and air force. After serving more than two years, the then-Navy Chief of Staff, Admiral Marsetio, was slated to retire in January 2015. Vice Admiral Ade Supandi (1983 class), Vice Admiral Didit Herdiawan (1984 class), and Vice Admiral Desi Albert Mamahit (1984 class) were among the strongest candidates for appointment as the next navy chief of staff. The three admirals held equally high-ranking positions within the military establishment. Didit and Mamahit were, respectively, navy deputy chief and rector of the Indonesian Defence University (Universitas Pertahanan, Unhan), while Ade had served as the TNI chief of general staff (Kepala Staf Umum, Kasum TNI).

On December 31, 2014, President Jokowi appointed Ade Supandi as Admiral Marsetio's successor. Apart from his seniority, several factors could have contributed to this decision. His competitors had shortcomings. First, Mamahit had never held a command position with any of the navy's strategic commands—including Eastern and Western Fleets. Second, Vice Admiral Didit Herdiawan who was an adjutant of former president Yudhoyono from 2004 to 2009 but to his disadvantage claimed to have supported Prabowo Subianto's candidacy during the 2014 presidential election. Third, Ade Supandi—among his younger colleagues—had maintained a relatively neutral relationship with all the major political groupings.

Under the leadership of Ade Supandi, the naval academy alumni class of 1983 had occupied the bulk of strategic posts at navy headquarters. These included Rear

[10] See, "Standoff over Budi Could Linger for Weeks," *The Jakarta Post*, February 14, 2015.

Admiral Arie Henrycus Sembiring (assistant for naval planning), Commodore Karma Suta (assistant for naval personnel), Rear Admiral Arie Soedewo (coordinator, expert staff to the navy chief, who later became assistant for naval operations), Commodore Harry Pratomo (assistant for naval logistics), Brigadier General (Marine) Tommy Basari Natanegara (newly created assistant for maritime potential), Brigadier General (Marine) Buyung Lalana (commander of marine corps), Rear Admiral Tri Prasodjo (the navy inspector general), and Rear Admiral Didik Wahyudi (expert staff coordinator to navy chief).

Just two months after his installation, to consolidate his position, Admiral Ade transferred Vice Admiral Didit Herdiawan just two months after his installation to the National Resilience Institute (Lemhannas) to serve as its vice governor. Admiral Ade then promoted his classmate Rear Admiral Widodo (former Western Fleet commander) to be his deputy at navy headquarters in 2015. A year later, Widodo was transferred to the Defense Ministry and handed over his post in the navy to Arie Henrycus Sembiring. Admiral Ade also promoted Rear Admiral Achmad Taufiqoerrachman (1985 class) to replace Vice Admiral Sembiring who passed away due to a sudden illness in late 2016.

A new air force chief of staff was also installed on January 2, 2015. Prior to that, the then-TNI Commander-in-Chief General Moeldoko submitted the names of four high-ranking officers for consideration—marshals Felicianus Henry Bambang Sulistyo (head of National Search and Rescue Agency or Basarnas, 1982 class), Ismono Wijayanto (Defense Ministry's Inspector General, 1983 class), Agus Supriatna (deputy to the TNI inspector general, 1983 class), and Bagus Puruhito (Air Force Deputy Chief, 1984 class). While Puruhito was the youngest officer and second-in-command of the air force, Agus's rank was still Air Vice-Marshal or one level below the other candidates. Despite this anomaly, President Jokowi selected the latter to succeed Air Chief Marshal Ida Bagus Putu Dunia, who was then due for retirement in February that year.

For administrative purposes, Agus Supriatna was promoted to briefly assume the vacant TNI chief of general staff portfolio before being sworn in as the air force chief of staff. Despite Jokowi's aspiration for political autonomy, this decision had PDIP Chairwoman Megawati Sukarnoputri's fingerprints all over it. Agus, while Defence Attache in Singapore, had maintained a close relationship with the former Indonesian president and her late husband Taufik Kiemas, who regularly visited the city-state for medical treatment.[11] This factor would have influenced his career trajectory. Having led the Air Force Operational Command-II (Koopsau-II) for nearly two years, he was later reassigned to a position at the office of the TNI inspector general rather than being promoted to other strategic positions—while a natural progression would have been to be appointed either assistant for air force operations or National Air Defense (Kohanudnas) commander.

From 2015 to 2016, Air Chief Marshal Agus Supriatna sought to fill air force headquarters with officers he felt were reliable and trustworthy. He handpicked his classmate Hadiyan Sumintaatmadja as the air force deputy chief, in the process replacing

---

[11] See, "Pilihan Presiden Penopang Program," *Gatra*, January 6, 2015.

Air Marshal Puruhito.[12] Other 1983 class officers include Air Vice-Marshal Mochamad Safi'i (Assistant for Air Force Planning), Air Vice-Marshal Mochamad Nurullah (Assistant for Air Force Logistics), Air Vice-Marshal Masmun Yan Manggesa (Assistant for Air Force Intelligence), and Air-Rear-Marshal Ras Rendro Bowo (Air Force Inspector General).

President Jokowi's quest for autonomy was evinced in the appointment of the new TNI Commander. Based on the Law No. 34/2004, any incumbent or former chiefs of army, navy, and air force would be legitimate candidates for the military's top leadership position. The existing regulation also implied a rotational practice among the chiefs of military services to preside over TNI headquarters. Between 2004 and 2014, air force, army, and navy chiefs had taken their turns to serve as the military's top leader (see Table 5). Given the post-authoritarian military tradition, and the fact that the incumbent Panglima TNI was an army officer, it was expected that Air Chief Marshal Agus Supriatna would be next in line to lead the TNI.

Instead, President Jokowi nominated the then-Army Chief of Staff General Gatot Nurmantyo (1982 class) to succeed General Moeldoko (1981 class) in July 2015. President Jokowi cited recent geopolitical changes, the need to consolidate military leadership, and even stressed that the nomination of a TNI commander-in-chief was his "prerogative right."[13] Yet, the decision was played out against the backdrop of political struggles between President Jokowi and the leaders of his principal political backers, the PDIP, over the appointment of a new national police chief.

Some observers speculated that the close ties between Air Chief Marshal Agus Supriatna and PDIP Chairwoman Megawati motivated Jokowi to opt for Gatot's nomination. Despite a brief public debate over the need to maintain a norm that required the rotation of the TNI commander-in-chief's position among the military service chiefs, the Indonesian parliament eventually approved the newly sworn president's decision.[14] The installation of General Gatot not only demonstrated Jokowi's political autonomy to the public at large, but also marked a sharp departure from the precedent established under the Yudhoyono administration.[15]

In an effort to avoid a situation where Gatot would hold a dual appointment within the military establishment, President Jokowi swiftly appointed the new military chief to take primary charge of army headquarters. At that juncture, the five eligible candidates included lieutenant generals Sonny Widjaja (commander of TNI Command and Staff College, Komandan Sesko TNI, 1982 class), Syafril Mahyudin (TNI inspector general, 1982 class), Muhammad Munir (army deputy chief, 1983 class), Mulyono (commander of Army Strategic Command, Panglima Kostrad, 1983 class) and Ediwan Prabowo (secretary general to the Ministry of Defense, 1984 class). While the first two senior officers would enter mandatory retirement age in less than ten months, a Munir or

---

[12] Interestingly, both Handiyan and Puruhito used to serve in the inner circle of former president Yudhoyono. While the latter was an adjutant in his first term, the former served as a presidential military secretary from 2011 to 2013.

[13] See "Alasan Jokowi Tunjuk Gatot sebagai Calon Panglima TNI," *Tempo*, June 10, 2015.

[14] See "House Endorse Gatot as New TNI Chief," *The Jakarta Post*, July 2, 2015.

[15] See "TNI Chief Nomination Seen as Reform Setback," *The Jakarta Post*, June 11, 2015).

Table 5: TNI Commanders after the 2004 TNI Law

Name	Class	Service Background	Duration
Djoko Suyanto	1973	Air Force	Feb. 16, 2006–Dec. 28, 2007
Djoko Santoso	1975	Army	Dec. 28, 2007–Sept. 28, 2010
Agus Suhartono	1978	Navy	Sept. 28, 2010–Aug. 30, 2013
Moeldoko	1980	Army	Aug. 30, 2013–July 8, 2015
Gatot Nurmantyo	1982	Army	July 8, 2015–Dec. 8, 2017
Hadi Tjahjanto	1986	Air Force	Dec. 8, 2017–Nov. 17, 2021
Andika Perkasa	1987	Army	Nov. 17, 2021–present

Ediwan appointment would come with its own unique complications as they served, respectively, as adjutant and private secretary of former president Yudhoyono.

Only a week after the new TNI commander-in-chief was sworn in on July 8, 2015, Jokowi promoted and installed Lieutenant General Mulyono as the new army chief of staff.[16] His tour of duty included a long career in the army's educational institutions before a short stint as assistant for army operations (2013) and then significantly later, the key strategic appointment as Jakarta commander (2014) a month before the then-Governor Jokowi began his run for the presidency. The four-star general was well-known for adopting a low profile and his particular aversion for commenting on non-military matters. Prior to his promotion as army chief of staff, Mulyono had also succeeded Gatot Nurmantyo as the commander of the Army Strategic Command in 2014.

Soon after assuming his new role, General Gatot Nurmantyo began to stamp his authority by reshuffling the commanding officers of strategic posts and positioning his aides within TNI headquarters. While we will discuss the rationale for reshuffling these commanders later in the section on executive commands and agencies, at this juncture it is important to highlight the objectives behind General Gatot's appointments relating to strategic positions within TNI Headquarters.

Graduating from the military academy in 1982, Gatot relied significantly on his classmates to assist him in his leadership role. They were Major General Setyo Sularso (TNI inspector general), Air Vice-Marshal Bambang Samoedro (assistant for military personnel), as well as Air Vice-Marshal Nugroho Prang Sumadi (assistant for military logistics).

The strategy of promoting and placing classmates in key positions was also utilized by General Mulyono at army headquarters. Early in his tenure as army chief, General Mulyono promoted Brigadier General Ibnu Darmawan as assistant for army intelligence and Brigadier General Musa Bangun as the coordinator of expert staff to army chief. Nonetheless, General Gatot Nurmantyo also exerted his authority to influence army headquarters in order to ensure they aligned closely with his interests. He replaced

---

[16] See "Letjen Mulyono Resmi Jabat KSAD," *Kompas*, July 15, 2015.

Lieutenant General Muhammad Munir, who was General Mulyono's academy classmate, with his own classmate Lieutenant General Erwin Syafitri as army deputy chief.

By the end of 2015, the installation of a new military leadership would be the first clear indication of President Jokowi's political consolidation and the stamping of his authority over the armed forces. Embroiled in a tussle with the ruling PDIP over the top leadership of national police, Jokowi adopted a typical Javanese leadership strategy of creating a counterbalance by using an influential army officer as a political balance or alternative powerbase. With General Gatot Nurmantyo presiding over TNI headquarters and all the service chiefs' graduates of the 1983 military academy class, the TNI maintained its practice of promotions based on patronage and seniority but also retained the alumni configuration of the military's high commands.

General Gatot Nurmantyo's tenure was marked with a number of contentious decisions and statements. There was the ambiguity surrounding General Gatot's "proxy war" narrative that would be characterized more for its abstruseness rather than providing coherent strategic policy guidance for the Indonesian public. Ratcheting up nationalistic impulses, he claimed that foreign powers were seeking to seize control over the country's natural resources—particularly energy, food, and water through the use of strategically placed domestic collaborators and subsidiaries.[17] His fiery hypothesis was frequently aired through his public speeches and social media messaging.[18] These comments became fuel for his detractors who would claim that General Gatot had a two-fold objective, which was to lay the groundwork for military role expansion while simultaneously promoting his political ambitions.[19]

The opportunity for political opportunism arrived during two mass protests in late 2016 where General Gatot gave the impression of standing in solidarity with street protesters who demanded the prosecution of then-Jakarta Governor *Basuki Tjahaja Purnama* for blasphemy. Gatot though rejected reports that he was linked to conservative Islamic groups and was planning a coup against the incumbent government.[20] Moreover, in a speech at the Golkar party's conference on May 22, 2017, Gatot recited a poem where he lamented the tremendous social injustice present in Indonesia. Not long after that, at a public lecture in Yogyakarta, he commented that the country's current practice of democracy was no longer in line with the principles of Pancasila and was the cause of social injustice for all Indonesian people.[21]

General Gatot's political maneuvers did not go unnoticed. Responding to his public comments, parliament members—including those from the ruling PDIP—noted that active service officers would be better off confining themselves to defense and military affairs rather than being involved in politics. Gatot also drew the ire of the TNI AU

---

[17] See, Keoni Marzuki, "Proxy Wars Narrative: TNI-AD's Quest for Relevance?" *RSIS Commentary*, no. 092, April 21, 2016; Muhamad Haripin, Adhi Priamarizki, and Keoni Indrabayu Marzuki, *The Army and Ideology in Indonesia: From Dwifungsi to Bela Negara* (London: Routledge, 2020).

[18] See "Pangkostrad Ingatkan Bahaya Proxy War," *SuaraMerderka.com*, April 30, 2014; "Indonesia Faces Proxy War: Army Chief," *The Jakarta Post*, March 10, 2015.

[19] See "President Reigning in 'Out of Control' Military Chief," *South China Morning Post*, January 9, 2017.

[20] See "TNI and Police Chiefs to Be Summoned over Treason Spat," *The Jakarta Post*, May 7, 2017.

[21] See "Saat Panglima TNI Membacakan Puisi di Rapimnas Golkar," *Kompas.com*, May 22, 2017; "Panglima TNI Sebut Demokrasi Indonesia Tak Sesuai Pancasila," *Kompas.com*, June 5, 2017.

leadership by promoting the screening of Pengkhianatan G30S/PKI, a 1984 Indonesian New Order era docudrama interpretation of the September 30, 1965 abortive coup, which discredited the air force, and there was also public dismay regarding whistleblowing actions related to his role in the AW-101 procurement corruption case.[22]

Beyond those actions, it was reported that President Jokowi had "reproached" the TNI commander during a close-door meeting for his unilateral suspension of defense cooperation with Australia.[23] Previously, in December 2016, the Indonesian military moved to suspend a language exchange program with its Australian counterparts following the discovery of "offensive" teaching material. However, the Presidential Palace later denied that the close-door meeting had taken place.[24]

While Gatot's politically motivated moves had made the incumbent president look ineffectual, any drastic measures employed would have had to be weighed carefully against the inevitable political fallout.[25] Short of dismissing the current TNI commander-in-chief, President Jokowi did the next best thing, which was to reassert his authority as the country's supreme commander-in-chief and behind the scenes groom a future leader of the armed forces. These moves on the part of Jokowi laid the platform for the swift rise of Air Marshal Hadi Tjahjanto (1986 class). In fact, Jokowi went back to his roots, and his cultivation of Hadi could be traced back to a relationship formed in Solo during his time as Mayor that coincided with Hadi's service as Adi Soemarmo Air Base commander (2010–11) and later as presidential military secretary (2015–16).

Hadi Tjahjanto's meteoric rise was further confirmed when Air Chief Marshal Agus Supriatna had almost concluded his active service on February 1, 2017. To replace him, General Gatot submitted the names of three high-ranking officers, specifically Air Marshal Hadiyan Sumintaatmadja (air force deputy chief), Air Marshal Bagus Puruhito (vice governor of Lemhannas), and Air Marshal Hadi Tjahjanto (Defence Ministry's inspector general).[26] Hadi's career path was quite different from the first two candidates. Hadi had never been in charge of air force strategic commands—either Koopsau-I or Koopsau-II—yet he still managed to attain a three-star promotion. Despite this shortcoming, on January 17 that year, President Jokowi handpicked his former military secretary as the new air force chief of staff, thereby paving the way for Hadi to become an eligible candidate for selection as the next Panglima TNI.[27]

Apart from his good "chemistry" with Jokowi, the promotion of Air Chief Marshal Hadi Tjahjanto broke the unspoken tradition that only an officer graduating in an odd-number year could serve as the air force chief. During his tenure, Hadi entrusted strategic positions at air force headquarters to his classmates Air Vice-Marshal Umar Sugeng Hariyono (air force inspector general), Air Vice-Marshal Fahru Zaini Isnanto

---

[22] See "Ditantang Gatot Nurmantyo Nobar Film G30SPKI, Ini Jawaban TNI AD," *Tempo.com*, September 21, 2018; and "Eks KSAU Tuding Gatot Nurmantyo Pembuat Masalah Korupsi Heli," *CNN Indonesia*, June 6, 2018.

[23] See "Indonesia's President Moves to Rein in 'Out of Control' Military Chief," *Reuters*, January 9, 2017.

[24] See "Palace Denied Jokowi-Gatot Spat over Australia," *The Jakarta Post*, January 11, 2017.

[25] Gatot also triggered displeasure among TNI AU leadership due to his idea of screening of the New Order's September 30, 1965 incident movie, which heavily discredits the air force.

[26] See "Jokowi to Announce New Air Force Chief," *The Jakarta Post*, January 17, 2017.

[27] See "New Air Force Chief to Succeed Gatot," *The Jakarta Post*, January 19, 2017).

(assistant for air force planning), and Air Commodore Kisenda Wiranatasumah (assistant for air force security). Moreover, the newly appointed air force chief in late 2015 led the investigation over an alleged corruption case relating to the purchase of AW-101 transport helicopters. Although the case would involve several air force personnel and lead to financial losses of around US$ 16.52 million incurred by the state, he stressed that the acquisition was made by his predecessor to meet the service's need for combat search and rescue capabilities.

Meanwhile, General Gatot proceeded to order major personnel turnovers from February to October 2017 involving 1985 class alumni to hold several leadership positions at TNI and service headquarters. These are Vice Admiral Achmad Taufiqoerachman (navy deputy chief), Air Vice-Marshal Dedy Permadi (assistant for military personnel), and major generals Lodewyk Pusung (assistant for military operations) and Wiyarto (assistant for territorial affairs). These positions were supposed to function as pathways to prepare the 1985 graduates for strategic appointments in the future.

In addition, the military's high command also embarked on some important restructuring in 2017 enabling other 1986 class alumni to rise within the ranks. These were Major General Tatang Sulaiman and Air Marshal Yuyu Sutisna, who, respectively, held the positions of deputy chiefs of army and air force. At the army headquarters, General Mulyono had also appointed new military aides, namely major generals Supartodi (assistant for territorial affairs, 1985 class), Sudirman (assistant for army operation, 1986 class), and Irwan Zaini (assistant for army logistics, 1987 class). He also appointed two 1988 graduates—namely Brigadier General Subiyanto and Major General Muhammad Nur Rahmad—as his respective assistants for army personnel and security affairs.

The Air Chief Marshal Hadi's nomination in December 2017 to take command of the military coincided with General Gatot's decision to overhaul the leadership of several key military units and commands. Gatot's last reshuffle decision that affected eighty-five officers and was characterized by a lack of coordination with the military headquarters, which led to some criticism and speculation that these personnel changes were part of Gatot's personal maneuvers.[28]

A day after receiving parliamentary approval on December 7, President Jokowi inaugurated Air Chief Marshal Hadi Tjahjanto to succeed General Gatot Nurmantyo. Serving for the first time at TNI headquarters, his first order of business came on December 19. The new commander-in-chief amended his predecessor's controversial personnel reshuffle decree.

Next, the newly designated TNI commander-in-chief issued an additional decree for personnel reshuffles particularly in military intelligence and the inspectorate to consolidate his power over matters relating to intelligence and internal affairs. This decision involved the promotion of army Major General Muhammad Herindra (1987 class) on March 2, 2018 to replace Lieutenant General Dodik Widjanarko as TNI's

---

[28] See "Gatot Bantah Mutasi 85 Perwira Sebagai Manuver Pribadi," *Media Indonesia*, December 6, 2017; "Putusan Mutasi Sebelum Perintah Jokowi," *Media Indonesia*, December 7, 2017); "Dikritik Elit PDIP, Gatot Jelaskan Alasan di Balik Mutasi 85 Pati TNI," *JawaPos.com*, December 8, 2017.

inspector general. The appointment was designed to oversee the handling of the corruption case pertaining to the AW-101 helicopter acquisition.

As President Jokowi entered the final year of his presidency in 2018, his preparations to revamp TNI began first with air force headquarters. Hadi Tjahjanto nominated three candidates as his successor, namely air marshals Muhammad Syaugi (head of National Search and Rescue Agency or Basarnas, 1984 class), Bagus Puruhito (deputy governor of Lemhannas), and his 1986 classmate, Yuyu Sutisna (air force deputy chief). While Bagus had served as a B-737 maritime patrol aircraft pilot and was nominated for the position back in 2015, Syaugi and Yuyu were both squadron leaders commanding the F-16 and F-5 jetfighters. However, Syaugi was scheduled to retire by the end of that year. On January 17, the incumbent president selected Yuyu Sutisna as the new air force chief of staff. Interestingly, the change of command coincided with a third reshuffle of Jokowi's cabinet members with more military men brought into his inner circle with retired generals Moeldoko to be the presidential chief of staff and Megawati confidant Agum Gumelar a member of the presidential advisory council.[29]

During his term, Air Chief Marshal Yuyu Sutisna entrusted key positions to the 1986 class to lead the air force. After promoting Wieko Syofyan as his deputy, he appointed marshals Johannes Berchman Widjayanto (former commander of Kodiklatau), Asep Dian Hermawan (then-assistant for military communication and electronics), and Abdul Wahab (former head of air force procurement) as his respective assistants for air force operations, planning, and logistics. In sum, during Air Chief Marshal Hadi's tenure as TNI chief and Air Chief Marshal Yuyu as air force chief, many officers of the 1986 cohort rose to prominence. These officers not only held various positions within TNI and air force headquarters but also held appointments within the air force executive agencies' main commands, as we will soon discuss in the next section.

At navy headquarters, Admiral Ade Supandi had approached his retirement age in May 2018. In a late January 2018 press conference, Admiral Ade presented five potential candidates to become the next navy chief—namely vice admirals Arie Soedewo (head of Maritime Security Agency or Bakamla, 1983 class), Didit Herdiawan (Kasum TNI, 1984 class), Achmad Taufiqoerrachman (navy deputy chief, 1985 class), Raden Mas Trusono (Sesko TNI commander), and Siwi Sukma Adji (TNI Academy commanding general, 1985 class). Arie's promotion was a nonstarter because his time of active duty ended on the same day as Admiral Ade. Second, Vice Admiral Didit had been nominated for the position back in 2014, and the outcome was unsuccessful. Both Vice Admiral Taufiqoerrachman and Marine Lieutenant General Trusono were scheduled to retire by the end of October 2019, allowing them little time to oversee naval development plans. Jokowi's options were thus limited, leading him to assign Vice Admiral Siwi Sukma Adji as the new navy chief of staff on May 23, 2018. Although Siwi had graduated a year earlier than Hadi Tjahjanto, he still had a further two years to serve, allowing him adequate time to manage infrastructure projects for the newly created third fleet and third marine force.

Unlike his air force counterpart, the newly sworn in navy chief of staff included his younger colleagues into the naval headquarters personnel structure. These included

---

[29] See "Tak Hanya KSAU, Presiden Jokowi Lantik Menteri Baru Pagi Ini," *Tempo.co*, January 17, 2018.

rear admirals I Nyoman Mandra (assistant for naval personnel, 1986 class), Moelyanto (assistant for naval logistics, 1986 class), Didik Setiyono (assistant for naval operation, 1987 Class), Djoko Erwan Prihatmoko (navy inspector general, 1987 class), and Supriatno Irawan (assistant for navy security, 1988 class). Admiral Siwi also made Rear Admiral Wuspo Lukito (former governor of the Naval Academy, 1986 class) his deputy chief. He also retained his classmate Rear Admiral Arusukmono Indra Sucahyo as his assistant for naval planning.

On September 23, 2018, the campaign period for the 2019 Presidential and Legislative Elections began and lasted until April 13, 2019. A day after the official opening of the campaign period, Air Chief Marshal Hadi began the process of reshaping the higher command, starting with his military aides. These included Major General George Elnadus Supit (assistant for territorial affairs), Major General Ganip Warsito (assistant for military operation), and Major General Andjar Wiratma (assistant for military intelligence). In early 2019, Hadi introduced more 1986 graduates into TNI headquarters. After opting to retain Vice Admiral Didit Herdiawan for another year (note that Didit was then the longest-serving TNI chief of general staff, having served for more than three years), Air Chief Marshal Hadi promoted Major General Joni Supriyanto as the military's chief of general staff. This way, he maintained the *reformasi* norm of rotation within the Indonesian armed forces that when either an air force or navy officer becomes Panglima TNI (TNI Commander), an army officer would be appointed as the military's chief of general staff and vice versa (see Table 6 below). Additionally, Air Chief Marshal Hadi appointed Rear Admiral Kukuh Sudibyanto and Air Vice-Marshal Lutfi Syaefullah as his respective assistants for military logistics and electronic communication.

The most significant event took place in late November 2018 at army headquarters. With General Mulyono soon to reach his mandatory retirement age, there were six eligible candidates for the next army chief—namely, lieutenant generals Agus Surya Bakti (1984 class), Doni Monardo (1985 class), Tatang Sulaiman (1986 class), Muhammad Herindra (1987 class), Andika Perkasa (1987 class), and Anto Mukti Putranto (1987 class). The appointment would not be without controversy. On November 16, a coalition of civil society organizations demanded the National Commission on Human Rights (Komnas HAM) review the military careers of the ten senior army officers, who might become Mulyono's successor. A week later, President Jokowi decided to install his former commander of Paspampres Andika Perkasa as the new army chief of staff. This move preempted further public uproar over the army leadership change, while avoiding any risk to political stability during an election year.

A month after the transfer of the ceremonial baton, General Andika sought to consolidate his position with the appointment of his classmates to army headquarters. He withdrew Brigadier General Dominicus Agus Riyanto's previous assignment to army inspector general and retained him as his assistant for army planning; instead, the new army chief appointed his classmate Major General Suko Pranoto to take up Riyanto's position as the army inspector general. Later, in early 2019, he promoted his classmate Major General Bakti Agus Fadjari (1987 class), who previously held no significant appointment, as his assistant for territorial affairs.

During the 2019 election year, there were few military leadership changes involving the air force and air force deputy chiefs, where Air Marshal Wieko Syofyan and Vice

Table 6: TNI Commanders and Chiefs of General Staff, 2006–19

TNI Commander	Service Background	TNI Chief of General Staff	Service Background
Endriartono Sutarto (June 7, 2002–Feb. 16, 2006)	Army	Wartoyo (Mar. 16, 2004–Dec. 29, 2005)	Air Force
Djoko Suyanto (Feb. 16, 2006–Dec. 28, 2007)	Air Force	Endang Suwarya (Dec. 29, 2005–Sept. 4, 2007)	Army
		Erwin Sudjono (Sept. 4, 2007–Dec. 27, 2007)	Army
Djoko Susanto (Dec. 28, 2007–Sept. 28, 2010)	Army	Tedjo Edhy Purdijatno (Dec. 27, 2007–July 1, 2008)	Navy
		Y. Didik Heru Purnomo (July 1, 2008–Oct. 23, 2008)	Navy
		Edy Harjoko (Oct. 23, 2008–Mar. 1, 2011)	Air Force
Agus Suhartono (Sept. 28, 2010–Aug. 30, 2013)	Navy	Yohannes Suryo Prabowo (Mar. 1, 2011–Aug. 1, 2012)	Army
		Daryatmo (Aug. 1, 2012–Apr. 18, 2013)	Air Force
		Boy Syahri Qamar (Apr. 18, 2013–May 12, 2014)	Air Force
Moeldoko (Aug. 30, 2013–July 8, 2015)	Army	Ade Supandi (May 12, 2014–Dec. 30, 2014)	Navy
		Agus Supriatna (Dec. 30, 2014–Feb. 6, 2015)	Air Force
Gatot Nurmantyo (July 8, 2015–Dec. 4, 2017)	Army	Dede Rusamsi Feb. 6, 2015–Oct. 22, 2015)	Air Force
		Didit Herdiawan (Oct. 22, 2015–Jan. 25, 2019)	Navy
		Joni Supriyanto (Jan. 25, 2019–today)	Army
Hadi Tjahjanto (Dec. 4, 2017–Nov. 17, 2021)	Air Force	Muhamad Herindra (Oct. 27, 2020–Dec. 23, 2020)	Army
		Ganip Warsito (Feb. 1, 2021–June 9, 2021)	Army
Andika Perkasa (Nov. 17, 2021–present)	Army	Eko Margiyono (June 9, 2021–present)	Army

Admiral Wuspo Lukito were replaced by Air Marshal Fahru Zaini Isnanto and Vice Admiral Mintoro Yulianto. However, it is safe to say that the Indonesian military had been consolidated under the leadership of Air-Chief Marshal Hadi Tjahjanto by the end of January 2019. Leaving nothing to chance, Air Chief Marshal Hadi filled TNI headquarters with his academy classmates and supplemented them with their younger colleagues, thereby ensuring that his loyalists were entrenched within the HQ establishment.

Moreover, this TNI establishment was relatively insulated from political intervention during 2019 legislative and presidential elections. At an annual leadership meeting held on January 29 that year, President Jokowi felt confident to assert that active military and police officers would be required to remain politically neutral in the upcoming elections. Back in November 2018, the TNI's high command also reiterated their commitment to maintain its political neutrality at a troop readiness ceremonial event. These calls were echoed throughout the chain of command during the campaign period. This way, Prabowo loyalists were held in check, enabling the incumbent President Jokowi to maintain effective control over the armed forces.

By the start of his second presidential term, Jokowi had sidelined all top brass officers who held high-ranking positions under the previous administration and those who had blatantly shown political ambition to challenge the president (see Table 7). By the end of 2019 and early 2020, the competition for the position of air force and navy chiefs began in earnest as air chief marshals Yuyu and Admiral Siwi were approaching their end of tenure.

As the race for these positions began, the severe acute respiratory syndrome coronavirus 2 (SARS-CoV-2, or simply COVID-19) pandemic began to infect the Indonesian population in late February 2020. President Jokowi then formed a national COVID-19 task force just two weeks after he announced Indonesia's first COVID-19 case. To lead the task force, he appointed Lieutenant General Doni Monardo, who had replaced Rear Admiral Willem Rampangilei (1980 class) as the head of the Indonesian National Disaster Relief Agency in 2019.[30] We will further discuss the involvement of the TNI in COVID-19 management in the later part of this paper.

As the COVID-19 began to wreak havoc on Indonesia's failing health sector, the race for the newer generations of TNI leadership had become centralized around officers who made substantial contributions toward the national pandemic response. The first to come to prominence was Vice Admiral Yudo Margono, whose dual role commanding Kogabwilhan I and Kogasgabpad TNI placed him in a useful position to play a coordinating role in national pandemic management. Next was Major General Eko Margiyono, the commanding officer of Kodam Jaya and Kogasgabpad Jakarta, who contributed substantially to managing the national field hospital for COVID-19 patients at Kemayoran Athletes Village. Third to come to prominence was Air Marshal Fadjar Prasetyo—commander of Kogabwilhan II—who assisted with East Java pandemic management efforts supervised by the provincial government.

---

[30] Back in 2019, President Jokowi had issued a new regulation on the organization of National Disaster Relief Agency (BNPB) on January 8, 2019. See, "Perpres Baru Atur Keterlibatan TNI di BNPB," *Media Indonesia*, January 9, 2019. It was argued that Lieutenant General Monardo's appointment as head of BNPB was meant to sideline him from the race for TNI leadership due to his prior appointment as one of the heads of Yudhoyono's presidential security details.

Table 7: TNI Commanders and Service Chief, 2014–21

TNI Commander	Class	Service	Army Chief	Class	Air Force Chief	Class	Navy Chief	Class
Moeldoko Aug. 30, 2013–July 8, 2015	1981	Army	Gatot Nurmantyo July 8, 2015–Dec. 4, 2017	1982	Ida Bagus Putu Dunia Dec. 17, 2012 –Jan. 2, 2015	1981	Marsetio Dec. 17, 2012–Dec. 31, 2014	1981
Gatot Nurmantyo July 8, 2015–Dec. 4, 2017	1982	Army	Mulyono July 15, 2015–Nov. 22, 2018	1983	Agus Supriatna Jan. 2, 2015–Jan. 18, 2017	1983	Ade Supandi Dec. 31, 2014–May 23, 2018	1983
Hadi Tjahjanto Dec. 4, 2017–Nov. 17, 2021	1986	Air Force			Hadi Tjahjanto Jan. 18, 2017–Jan. 17, 2018	1986		
			Andika Perkasa Nov. 22, 2018–Nov. 17, 2021	1987	Yuyu Sutisna Jan. 17, 2018–May 20, 2020	1986	Siwi Sukma Adji May 23, 2018–May 20, 2020	1985
Andika Perkasa Nov. 17, 2021–present	1987	Army	Dudung Abdurachman Nov. 17, 2021–present	1988	Fadjar Prasetyo May 20, 2020–present	1988	Yudo Margono May 20, 2020–present	1988

In May 2020, President Joko Widodo appointed both Vice Admiral Yudo Margono and Air Marshal Fadjar Prasetyo as chiefs of navy and air force, replacing Admiral Siwi and Air Chief Marshal Yuyu who were retiring within the same month. As explained, both Admiral Yudo and Air Marshal Fadjar were both the inaugural commanders of the newly commissioned Joint-Defense Regional Command (Komando Gabungan Wilayah Pertahanan, Kogabwilhan) I and II. Such experience is considered valuable as both air force and navy chief past nominees usually do not have three-star operational command positions, unlike the army, which has Kostrad. Apart from the newly appointed navy and air chiefs, Major General Eko Margiyono also received a three-star promotion as Kostrad commander in late July 2020.

The newly appointed air force and navy chief also followed the example of General Andika in seeking to consolidate their leaderships within their respective service headquarters. From his appointment up to December 2020, the army chief selected nine of his classmates to hold the majority of all high-ranking positions—apart from his deputy chief and the assistant for army operations position—within the army headquarters. Lieutenant General Tatang Sulaiman—who had been serving under General Mulyono— was replaced by Major General Mochammad Fachrudin (class of 1985) in April 2020 and served until the end of his tenure in November 2020. However, the candidate for deputy army chief, Lieutenant General Herman Asaribab, passed away before the transfer could be affected.[31] As a result, the then-Lieutenant General Fachrudin's tenure as deputy army chief was lengthened until January 2021.

Back at navy and air force headquarters, both Air Chief Marshal Fadjar and Admiral Yudo—like the army chief—sought to consolidate their leadership by installing their classmates into the key positions within their respective service headquarters. Throughout 2020 alone, Admiral Yudo had introduced Major General (Marine) Widodo Dwi Purwanto, Rear Admirals Puguh Santoso, Irwan Achmadi, and Sunaryo to be his assistants for maritime potential, logistics, personnel, and navy deputy inspector general, respectively. In addition, Admiral Yudo also appointed his Vice Admiral Ahmadi Heri Purwono as the navy deputy chief. The air force chief had also introduced air vice-marshals Henri Alfiandi, Agustinus Gustaf Brugman, Fadjar Sumarijadji, Djamaluddin, and Kusworo to be the assistants for air force personnel, intelligence, logistics, and air-space potentials, respectively. All in all, the appointment of both Air Chief Marshal Fadjar and Admiral Yudo brought a substantial boost to the presence of military academy graduates of 1988 within air force and navy headquarters.

At the TNI main headquarters, the TNI chief of general staff position was handed over from Lieutenant General Joni Supriyanto to Lieutenant General Muhammad Herindra (class of 1987) in October 2021. With this reshuffle, Lieutenant General Herindra handed the TNI inspector general position to Lieutenant General (Marine) Bambang Suswantono. However, when Lieutenant General Herindra was appointed as deputy minister for defense, the position of TNI chief of general staff would remain vacant until 2021.

Entering the year 2021, the race for the TNI commander position had intensified as Air Chief Marshal Hadi Tjahjanto would retire in November 2021. Out of the three

---

[31] See "Lt. Gen. Herman Asaribab, Papua-Born Army Deputy Chief-of-Staff, Dies in Jakarta," *The Jakarta Post*, December 15, 2020.

service chiefs, only two names emerged as strong contenders: General Andika (the army chief) and Admiral Yudo Margono (the navy chief of staff). Based on the balance of service time before retirement, Admiral Yudo was in the most advantageous position due to his relatively younger age. In addition, the previous pattern of TNI commander reshuffles during the Reformasi era—that followed a rotation between the three services—would tip the balance in favor Admiral Yudo. However, being the son-in-law of A. M. Hendropriyono meant that General Andika would have the stronger political backing compared to Admiral Yudo.

Regardless, throughout 2021, the race for TNI commander came with its fair share of mixed signals. For instance, analysts speculated that A. M. Hendropriyono's meeting with President Jokowi at the presidential palace on May 7, 2021 was an attempt to lobby on behalf of Andika.[32] To balance the ledger and support Admiral Yudo's candidacy, Vice-President Ma'aruf Amin was allegedly overheard to address Admiral Yudo as "Panglima," indirectly signaling his preferences.[33] Yet, the clearest signal that President Jokowi was going to appoint General Andika came when General Andika stood in for Air Chief Marshal Hadi to escort the president as he embarked on his flight to the G20 meeting in Rome.

Apart from the appointment of TNI commander, there were also several notable sideshows in the lead-up to the race for the TNI leadership in 2021. First, lobbying for next new army chief began soon after the Presidential Letter concerning General Andika's appointment as the new TNI Commander was delivered to the Indonesian Parliament. Second, there would be two rounds of changes to the TNI chief of general staff. Third, the deputy service chiefs within the army and air force headquarters would also be replaced.

Out of several three-star army generals, three strong candidates appeared as possibilities to lead the Indonesian army.[34] The first was Lieutenant General Dudung Abdurachman (class of 1988), a former Kodam Jaya commander who in mid-2021 had been promoted as Kostrad commander, replacing Lieutenant General Eko Margiyono. The second was Eko Margiyono, the previous Kostrad commander who was then appointed as TNI chief of general staff. And finally was Lieutenant General Bakti Agus Fadjari, who was the army deputy chief and was installed in 2021, replacing Lieutenant General Mochammad Fachrudin. Eventually, the president selected Lieutenant General Dudung as General Andika's replacement in 2021. Dudung caught the attention of Jokowi following the former Kodam Jaya Commander's action of dismantling hundreds of banners welcoming hardline cleric Habib Rizieq who had returned to Indonesia following a period of self-imposed exile in Saudi Arabia and urged the disbanding of the Islamic Defenders Front (FPI) in November 2020.[35] Those actions made a positive

---

[32] See "Jalan Jenderal Andika Jadi Calon Panglima TNI, dari Hendropriyono ke Istana hingga Antar Jokowi," *Kompas*, November 3, 2021.

[33] See "Cerita Ma'ruf Amin Panggil KSAL Yudo Margono Sebagai Panglima TNI," *Tempo*, September 19, 2021.

[34] See "Ini Dia Tiga Nama Calon Kuat KASAD Pengganti Jenderal TNI Andika Perkasa," *KompasTV*, November 3, 2021.

[35] See "Sepak Terjang Mayjen Dudung Melawan FPI hingga Promosi Jadi Pangkostrad," *Kompas.com*, May 26, 2021.

impression on Jokowi, giving him the inkling that he had found a reliable partner to combat the conservative camp—many of whom are part of Jokowi's opposition.

At TNI headquarters, there were two rounds of changes affecting the TNI chief of general staff appointment that occurred throughout 2021. From December 2020, Air Chief Marshal Hadi took over the position in the absence of a suitable candidate and was able to resolve the situation in February 2021 when he appointed Lieutenant General Ganip Warsito (class of 1986). Lieutenant General Ganip was previously appointed as commander of Kogabwilhan III and served as the TNI chief of general staff up to June 2021 when he was appointed as head of BNPB. The position was then passed on to Kostrad Commander Lieutenant General Eko Margiyono. Having appointed lieutenant generals Ganip and Eko Margiyono, Air Chief Marshal Hadi was able to stay true to the reformasi service rotation norm.

On top of these two developments, two service headquarters had also appointed new deputy chiefs. With Lieutenant General Fachrudin's retirement, army headquarters promoted Major General Bakti Agus Fadjari in March 2021. Next, air force headquarters appointed Air Marshal Agustinus Gustaf Brugman as the new deputy chief in September 2021, whose previous appointment was assistant for TNI personnel affairs. Both Major General Fadjari and Air Marshal Brugman were the classmates of General Andika and Air Chief Marshal Fadjar, respectively.

The dynamics of TNI leadership under President Jokowi hint at the continuing relevance of political factors in the appointment of officers for TNI leadership positions. In trying to understand these political factors it is also important to know why and how certain officers can be promoted up the TNI leadership ladder. In the next section, we will discuss how and why officers are being promoted as leaders of TNI strategic executive agencies and main commands.

TNI Executive Agencies and Main Commands

In this section, the Editors highlight several key rotation patterns pertaining to strategic positions related to Kotama TNI and Balakpus TNI. Officers appointed to these positions are significant because they oversee TNI force deployment and its day-to-day activities. Relating to the previous section on TNI leadership changes and rotational patterns, we can infer those promotions related to Kotama and Balakpus TNI follow a consistent pattern where they are still influenced by close relationships to political leaders or their TNI seniors.

Close relationship to political leaders—whether it involves the president or his political allies—is a major determining factor due to the president's constitutional prerogative to appoint high-ranking officers. At the same time, collegial relationships with TNI leaders also matter for promotions due to their role on the promotions board (Dewan Kepangkatan dan Jabatan Tinggi, Wanjakti). Throughout the years, promotion criteria that revolves around collegial preferences—to include colleagues, classmates, and former subordinates—persists as a norm. Yet not all officers are promoted based on these criteria; TNI leaders also use these command positions as a "reward" for high-achieving officers.

This section briefly discusses the tenure of General Moeldoko and then turns its focus on the leadership period of General Gatot and Air Chief Marshal Hadi Tjahjanto premised on two reasons. First, General Moeldoko was appointed as TNI commander by the former President Yudhoyono and thus seen as a legacy appointment of the previous regime. Second, the appointment for strategic offices between 2014 and 2015 were more likely driven by President Jokowi's desire to consolidate his grip on the TNI rather than General Moeldoko's personal ambitions.

Nevertheless, there were several notable changes to the leadership of Kotama and Balakpus TNI during Moeldoko's leadership in 2014. First, Moeldoko promoted Major General Mulyono to serve as Kostrad commander to replace General Gatot Nurmantyo in September 2014. Moeldoko had also promoted his classmate Major General Harry Purdianto as the TNI academy commanding general (Komandan Jenderal Akademi TNI) in late October 2014. Just before the 2014 presidential inauguration on October 20, 2014, Moeldoko promoted Brigadier General Andika Perkasa (1987 class) as the commander of Presidential Guards (Paspampres).[36]

At the end of his tenure as TNI Commander in mid-2015, General Moeldoko issued several decrees on promotion affecting several strategic posts within the Balakpus and Kotama ranks. Apart from positions related to Kodam commanders, none of Moeldoko's decrees on promotion that came later affected leaders serving in TNI's executive agencies and the higher command. The majority of the Balakpus and Kotama leadership were in place by late 2014. Arguably, these patterns indicated Moeldoko's confidence with personnel holding these strategic positions.

General Gatot Nurmantyo's Leadership

General Nurmantyo's first priority was to overturn the appointments within the ranks of Balakpus and Kotama that were made during the by then-retired Moeldoko. While doing this, Gatot demonstrated a preference for his military academy classmates of 1982. He appointed Major General Yayat Sudrajat (Class 1982) as the new Armed Forces Strategic Intelligence Agency head (KABAIS) replacing Major General Erwin Syafitri.[37] At the same time another classmate, Major General Bayu Purwiyono was promoted as TNI Academy commanding general replacing General Moeldoko's classmate Major General Harry Purdianto. Later, a 2016 organizational change made the TNI Academy commander a three-star ranked position.[38] Interestingly some of Gatot's classmates such as Lieutenant General Sony Widjaja (Sesko TNI commander) would hold on to their positions for quite some time.

---

[36] This promotion was likely also motivated by the incoming President Jokowi's preferences. Jokowi also appointed Colonel Maruli Simanjuntak (1992 class) to take charge of Group-A Paspamres, which is responsible for safeguarding the president and his family. Interestingly, both Andika Perkasa and Maruli Simanjuntak are, respectively, the sons-in-law of Abdullah Mahmud Hendropriyono and Luhut Binsar Panjaitan—retired four-star army generals and senior advisors of Jokowi. See "Hendropriyono's Son-in-Law Named Top Presidential Guard, *The Jakarta Post*, October 16, 2014); "Kolonel Inf Maruli Simanjuntak Jabat Komandan Grup A Paspampres," *Detik.com*, October 21, 2014.

[37] See SKEP Panglima TNI No. 593/VII/2015.

[38] See Presidential Regulation (Perpres) No. 62/2016 on changes on TNI's organizational structure.

Gatot also rewarded his classmates with promotions to strategic positions within the ranks of the army's upper echelons. These included Major General Erwin Syafitri as the deputy army chief and Brigadier General Pratimun to lead the Army Command and Staff College (Sesko TNI AD). For the time being, the new army chief of staff General Mulyono (class of 1983) had to be content with Gatot's appointments for the army leadership structure. Later, General Mulyono would assert his own authority to shape and restructure the leadership within the army's strategic commands and units according to his preferences. This involved appointing Major General Meris Wiryadi as Kostrad chief of staff.

Aside from General Gatot and General Mulyono's classmates, the new TNI leadership also propelled juniors with ties to them to attain prominent strategic positions within the army. One of General Gatot's earliest rotation initiatives involved Major General Edy Rahmayadi (1985 class), who was promoted as Kostrad Commander replacing General Mulyono and Brigadier General Muhammad Herindra (1987 class) who in turn replaced Major General Doni Monardo (1985 class) as Kopassus commanding general.[39] Before his promotion, in 2014 Edy Rahmayadi held the appointment as Kostrad 1st Infantry Division commander and then immediately was given the North Sumatera Command.[40]

In addition, Edy oversaw the organization of TNI's anniversary ceremonies in 2015 and 2017, both which were held during the Gatot era.[41] Traditionally, such positions are usually only designated for a highly decorated officer. This act also underlined General Gatot's confidence in Edy. Apart from Edy, another within this generation who was also promoted was Major General Agus Sutomo (1984 class), replacing the retiring Lieutenant General Lodewijk Freidrich Paulus (1981 class) as the new commander of Army Doctrine, Education and Training Leadership Command (Kodiklatad).

The following month, in mid-August 2015, General Gatot initiated another round of reshuffles affecting several officers holding key appointments within strategic military institutions.[42] These were promotions creating a pathway for certain army officers to attain key appointments. It involved Major General Dedi Kusnadi Thamim (1983 class), who replaced Marine Major General Sturman Panjaitan as commander of TNI's Doctrine, Education, and Training Leadership Command (Kodiklat TNI). Major General Dedi, though, only held this position for three months. In the same promotion exercise, Gatot also appointed his classmate Brigadier General Edy Sudarmanto as commander of TNI's Communication and Electronic Unit.

---

[39] Presidential Regulation (Perpres) No. 62/2016 on changes on TNI's organizational structure.

[40] Such a promotion made Edy Rahmayadi's two-star tenure (as major general) unique by having the shortest command tenure for a Major general—just one year. Interestingly, in November 2016, Edy, with strong support from the newly designated TNI commander-in-chief, was able to thwart the then-retired General Moeldoko's desire to gain control of the Football Association of Indonesia (Persatuan Sepak Bola Seluruh Indonesia, PSSI). See "Jadi Calon Ketua PSSI, Pangkostrad Dapat Restu Panglima TNI," *Tempo.co*, August 30, 2016; "Kalahkan Moeldoko, Edy Rahmayadi Jadi Ketua Umum PSSI," *Tempo.co*, November 10, 2016). As argued elsewhere, the Chairmanship of the PSSI is a prized possession for TNI generals. See James M. Dorsey and Leonard C. Sebastian, "The Politics of Indonesian and Turkish Soccer: A Comparative Analysis," *Soccer and Society* 14, no. 5, (September 2013): 615–34.

[41] See "Mengenal Pangkostrad Edy Rahmayadi, Komandan Upacara HUT ke-72 TNI," *Detik*, October 5, 2017.

[42] See SKEP Panglima TNI No. 662/VIII/2015.

Apart from these early developments, the army's executive agencies and commands also saw considerable regeneration patterns. Among the younger officers promoted to hold strategic positions in the army were Brigadier General Sudirman and Brigadier General Ganip Warsito, both from the 1986 class, who were appointed to command Kostrad's 1st and 2nd infantry divisions, respectively. Interestingly, both had served under General Gatot on different occasions. Brigadier General Sudirman had served as Kostrad's inspector under Gatot when he was Kostrad commander while Brigadier General Ganip was commander of the Army Combat Training Office (Pusat Latihan Tempur, Puslatpur) at Kodiklatad when Gatot held an appointment as Kodiklatad commander from 2011 to 2013. General Gatot also promoted Brigadier General Hartomo as the governor of the Military Academy. He was Army Intelligence Centre (Pusat Intelijen Angkatan Darat, Pusintelad) chief during Gatot's tenure as army chief of staff. These appointments were further evidence that Gatot tended to reward his previous subordinates with strategic appointments, and this was the pattern of decision-making Gatot consistently demonstrated throughout his tenure as TNI commander-in-chief.

None of General Gatot's air force and navy classmates received promotions to three-star rank or high-profile positions within the central military command early in his tenure as Panglima TNI. Within the air force ranks, there had been some regular personnel rotation for both upper and lower high-ranked officer positions.[43] The designated positions for more senior officers included the Air Force Operational Commands (Komando Operasi TNI AU, Koopsau), National Air Defense Command (Kohanudnas), Air Force Education Command (Kodikau), Air Force Maintenance Command (Koharmatau), Air Force Special Force (Korpaskhas), Air Force Command and Staff College (Sesko TNI AU), and the Air Force Academy (Akademi Angkatan Udara). The intermediate positions between upper and lower high-ranked positions included service chief or deputy assistant under the air force headquarters. Meanwhile the younger generation officers usually commanded various units below the abovementioned commands and agencies, positions like air base and air defense sectoral commanders.

During Air Chief Marshal Agus Supriatna's leadership, he promoted his classmates to these strategic commands: air vice-marshals Adrian Wattimena (Paskhas commander), Ras Rendro Bowo (Kodikau commander, then air force inspector general), Anang Murdianto (Sesko TNI AU commander), and Agus Dwi Putranto who later took Anang Murdianto's post (Sesko TNI AU commander). Similar to the situation with Air Vice-Marshal Ras Rendro Bowo, Agus Supriatna also promoted Air Vice-Marshal Abdul Muis (1985 class) twice in 2015: first as governor of the Air Force Academy replacing Air Vice-Marshal Sugihardjo (1982 class), then as Kohanudnas commander replacing Air Vice-Marshal Hadiyan Sumintaatmadja.

When it came to appointments for strategic positions, Air Chief Marshal Agus Supriatna promoted people he was familiar with to replace his classmates. These included Air Vice-Marshal Yuyu Sutisna's appointment as commander of Air Force Operational Command I to replace the air force chief of staff's classmate Air Vice-Marshal Agus Dwi

---

[43] High-ranked positions here refer to one-star general and above. Lower high-ranked officers indicate those who just got their one-star promotion. Meanwhile, upper high-ranked officers are those who have been serving within the star ranks for more than a year.

Putranto; and Air-Commander Barhim (1984 class) to assume Air Vice-Marshal Abdul Muis's position as Koopsau-II commander before the latter went on to command the Air Force Academy. In the same year, Air Vice-Marshal Barhim passed the baton to Air Commodore Dody Trisunu (1986 class). In mid-2015, Supriatna opted to promote Air Commodore Eko Supriyanto to fill the post left vacant by Air Vice-Marshal Ras Rendro Bowo's move to the Air Force Education Command (Kodikau).

Familiarity was the operative word when it came to Air Chief Marshal Supriatna's decisions regarding appointments. Both Agus Dwi Putranto and Barhim had consecutively served as Supriatna's chief of staff when he was commander of Koopsau II Jakarta. Supriatna was well known to Air Commodore Abdul Muis, as they both had served in Makassar. During that time, Agus Supriatna commanded Hasanuddin Air Base while Abdul Muis commanded the Air Defence Sectoral Command II (Kosekhanudnas-II), both located in Makassar. This tour of duty involved them in an operation to force down a trespassing Pakistani plane.[44] Beside these three appointments, Supriatna also used less-strategic appointments to promote his classmates who were stuck at the colonel rank and promising younger generation officers to hold high-ranked positions.

Meanwhile, Admiral Ade Supandi made some appointments within the navy strategic commands. At that time, the designated strategic positions for senior officers included commands of the Navy Western Fleet, Eastern Fleet, Transport Command (Komando Lintas Laut Militer, Kolinlamil), the Naval Academy, Marine Corps, and Navy Command and Staff College. Early in his tenure, Admiral Ade appointed Rear Admiral Achmad Taufiqoerochman (1985 class) and Rear Admiral Darwanto (1984 class) to fill the vacant Navy Western Fleet and Eastern Fleet commander positions, respectively. These posts were occupied by Admiral Ade's classmates who he had appointed to hold strategic positions, as previously highlighted. Before assuming his new position, Rear Admiral Taufiqoerrochman assumed the position as expert staff coordinator for two navy chiefs: the retiring Admiral Marsetio and Admiral Ade. Replacing Rear Admiral Darwanto as Navy Transport commander, Admiral Ade appointed Commodore Aan Kurnia. Admiral Ade also promoted Marine Brigadier General Buyung Lalana to replace Marine Major General Achmad Faridz Washington as commander of the Marine Corps. Both marine generals are Admiral Ade's 1983 Naval Academy classmates.

Apart from these appointments, Admiral Ade also promoted several academy classmates and promising juniors to hold various posts under the navy operational and educational commands. In 2015 alone, he rotated twelve out of fourteen naval base (Pangkalan Utama TNI AL, Lantamal) commanders, nine of which involved promoting colonel-ranked officers to hold their first flag-rank appointments. Within these nine promotions, Ade slipped in three classmates who were still at the colonel rank: Marine Colonel Leonard W. Supit and navy colonels Heru Santoso and Dindin Kurnadi. Apart from naval base commander appointments, Ade also promoted three of his classmates to lead naval service agencies and the Surabaya garrison chief of staff, which was traditionally designated to be filled by naval officers. In sum, Ade had been quite successful in balancing between his personal interests in consolidating the navy leadership and the need to continuously regenerate his pool of high-ranking naval officers.

---

[44] See "Pakistani Plane Forced to Land in Indonesia," *The Jakarta Post*, March 8, 2011.

Entering the year 2016, General Gatot had been successful in advocating, at that time, the most recent organizational changes when President Jokowi issued Presidential Decree 62 Year 2016 (Perpres No. 62 Tahun 2016).[45] The Presidential Decree also marked President Jokowi's attempts at reorganizing the TNI, moving on from the earlier regulations formulated during President Yudhoyono's administration. The reorganization, arguably, was supposed to increase effectiveness and efficiency within the TNI organization. However, in reality, the real importance of the initiative was to make new posts available for high-ranking officers across the three services, alleviating promotional bottlenecks.[46]

As the previous section had suggested, General Gatot made some controversial decisions regarding the appointments of some army officers. He appointed Major General Hartomo (former governor of the Military Academy, 1986 class) as the head of the military's strategic intelligence body (BAIS), replacing Major General Yayat Sudrajat. Meanwhile, Major General Yayat was also promoted to become the secretary of the Coordinating Ministry of Political, Legal and Security Affairs (Menko Polhukam). These decisions had prompted criticism from civil society groups due to the human rights record of these two army officers.[47] While Hartomo was indicted for the assassination of Theys Hiyo Eluay, a community leader in West Papua and the chairperson of Papuan Council Presidium, Yayat had been accused of crimes against humanity in East Timor.[48]

Nevertheless, the new presidential decree regarding the composition of TNI was not without its advantages to Major General Bayu Purwiyono, who happened to command the TNI Academy at the time. Among General Gatot's military academy classmates, Major General Yayat and Major General Bayu Purwiyono were the last to be appointed to three-star positions. At the same time, it is also interesting to see whether there were some continuities and progression for 1983 class officers' careers during General Mulyono's tenure as army chief of staff. Among his classmates, Major General Nugroho Widyotomo managed to gain promotion as the secretary general for the National Resilience Council (Sesjen Wantannas). More importantly, from 2016 to the end of 2017, none of the aging 1982 and 1983 class got promoted to significantly important commands or agencies.

General Gatot's tenure marked a shift of generation from the classes 1982 and 1983 to the younger generations. Positions such as the leadership of Kodiklatad and Kopassus shifted from Lieutenant General Agus Sutomo and Major General Herindra to Major General Agus Kriswanto (1984 class) and Brigadier General Madsuni (class 1988), respectively. Lieutenant General Agus Sutomo was designated to replace the retiring Sesko TNI commander Lieutenant General Sonny Widjaja in his second three-star assignment. Apart from these high-ranking promotions, organizational changes that had occurred within TNI also benefitted some of the army's executive agencies. Among the

[45] See Peraturan Presiden (Perpres) Republik Indonesia No. 62 Tahun 2016 tentang Susunan Organisasi Tentara Nasional Indonesia.

[46] See Evan Laksmana, "Reshuffling the Deck? Military Corporatism, Promotional Logjams, and Post-Authoritarian Civil-Military Relations in Indonesia," *Journal of Contemporary Asia* 49, no. 5 (2019), 806–36.

[47] See "Activists Question Hartomo's Promotion," *The Jakarta Post*, September 24, 2016.

[48] See "Terlibat Bunuh Theys dan Dipecat, Hartomo Kini Jadi Kabais," *Tempo.co*, September 21, 2016; "Indonesia Court Acquits Military Officer," Associated Press, December 30, 2002.

units that benefitted, for example, the commander of army aviation became a two-star appointment from 2016 onward.

These situations were replicated at the navy headquarters. Within the navy ranks, the positions earmarked for promotion included the newly installed assistant for maritime potentials to the navy chief, chief of the Navy Hydro-Oceanographic Centre (Ka Pushidrosal) and commander of the Naval Doctrine, Education and Training Leadership Command (Dan Kodiklatal). In 2016, the navy headquarters rotated four key strategic positions, namely the commanders of Navy Western Fleet, Navy Transport Commands, Naval Aviation Center, and chief of the Navy Hydro-Oceanographic Centre. Throughout the year, navy chief of staff Admiral Ade rotated the commander of the Navy Western Fleet two times: Rear Admiral Achmad Taufiqqoerochman was replaced by Rear Admiral Siwi Sukma Adji (1985 class), who in turn was replaced by Rear Admiral Aan Kurnia (1987 class). Both rear admirals Achmad Taufiqqoerochman and Siwi Sukma Adji were appointed as assistant for planning to the navy chief and the commander general of the Armed Forces Academy, respectively. Meanwhile, Admiral Ade replaced Rear Admiral Aan Kurnia at the Navy Transport Command with Commodore I. G. Putu Wijamahadi (1984 class), who previously held the position of deputy assistant for operations to the navy chief. The retiring chief of the Navy Hydro-Oceanographic Centre, Rear Admiral Daryanto (1982 class) was replaced by Commodore Harjo Susmoro (1987 class best graduate) just two months after the former got promoted as a two-star officer. Lastly, the command of the Naval Aviation Center was passed from Commodore Sigit Setiyanta (1987 class) to Commodore Manahan Simorangkir (1986 class). At this point, the fast-moving rotational patterns affirmed Admiral Ade's efforts, which no longer focused on promoting his classmates to strategic positions, but to further enlarging the pool of high-ranking naval officers.

The promotion pattern within the air force ranks was diametrically opposite to the army and navy services. Apart from the overall 2016 organizational changes that also affected some air force high-ranking positions, for example the newly installed assistant for airspace potentials to the air force chief (asisten potensi kedirgantaraan, aspotdirga) and commander of Air Force Doctrine, Education and Training Leadership Command (Komando Pembinaan Doktrin, Pendidikan dan Latihan, Kodiklatau), there had been several intragenerational appointments among the air force strategic commands. For promotions to air force strategic positions, Air Chief Marshal Agus Supriatna appointed Air Vice-Marshal Haryoko (1982 class) to lead the Air Force Maintenance Command (Koharmatau), replacing the latter's classmate, Air Vice-Marshal Robert Soter Marut. Supriatna also utilized a strategy of replacing a batch of classmates simultaneously. Air Vice-Marshal Dody Trisunu (1986 class), who had been appointed to lead Air Force Operational Command II the previous year, was replaced together with his classmate Air Vice-Marshal Umar Sugeng Hariyono in late 2016. This strategy had the effect of constraining the air force high-ranking officer's corps from enlarging their talent pool. To some extent, these decisions paved the way to ensure upward mobility for Air Marshal Hadi, who was then appointed as the Ministry of Defense inspector general that year and subsequently succeeded Air Chief Marshal Agus Supriatna as air force chief of staff later in January 2017.

Compared to 2016, many significant appointments occurred during the last years of General Gatot's TNI leadership in 2017. Apart from a few controversial decisions on promotion that he made late in December 2017, General Gatot promoted two navy officers, Marine Major General Raden Mas Trusono and Vice Admiral Siwi Sukma Adji, to become commander of Sesko TNI and the TNI academy, respectively. Those two positions were generally dominated by army officers. Arguably, these positions were also targeted to lay the platform for the appointment of the in-coming navy chief by ensuring the presence of more three-star navy officers to be considered when Admiral Ade stepped down in 2018. Beyond that, some of the important decisions within the three services need to be further elaborated.

First, within the top army establishment, there were two promotion appointments for the positions of deputy army chief: first, Major General Hinsa Siburian (1986 class) was promoted in April 2017, before he was then retired and replaced by his classmate Major General Tatang Sulaiman. Next, General Gatot also promoted and rotated some of the key positions within Kostrad. These involved Major General Benny Susianto (1987 class) replacing Major General Cucu Somantri (1984 class) as Kostrad chief of staff in April 2017. Major General Benny was then replaced by Major General Imam Edy Mulyono (1984 class) in October 2017, who in turn was replaced by Major General Bambang Taufik (1984 class) in December 2017. Tellingly, before Major General Benny was appointed as Kostrad chief of staff, he commanded Kostrad's 1st Infantry Division at the same time his classmate Major General A. M. Putranto commanded Kostrad's 2nd Infantry Division. These two were then replaced by officers of the 1988 class, brigadier generals Ainurrahman and Agus Suhardi, respectively.

Additionally, within the army leadership, General Mulyono handed over the Army Territorial Centre (Pusterad) from his classmate Hadi Prasodjo to Hartomo on October 27, 2017. Major General Hartomo's previous position as head of BAIS was to have been filled by General Mulyono's intelligence aide, Major General Ilyas Alamsyah (1988 class), before the new TNI Commander-in-Chief Air Chief Marshal Hadi cancelled the promotion orders issued by Gatot. Instead, Air Vice-Marshal Kisenda Wiranatakusumah became the new head of BAIS and a senior officer without a major portfolio, Major General Joni Supriyanto (1986 class), then became Air Vice-Marshal Kisenda's deputy. The decision was a source of consternation for the former TNI Commander-in-Chief General Gatot, who would later argue that he had selected the best men to fill these appointments.[49]

Before Air Chief Marshal Hadi was installed as TNI commander-in-chief, he had promoted several high-ranking officers to air force strategic commands. These included his classmate Air Vice-Marshal Yuyu Sutisna as Kohanudnas commander in February 2017, who he later promoted to become his deputy in October 2017. Apart from Air Marshal Yuyu Sutisna, Air Chief Marshal Hadi also appointed his classmate Air Vice-Marshal Yadi Indrayadi to command Koopsau-II, replacing another 1986 class graduate, Air Vice-Marshal Umar Sugeng Hariyono. Beyond selecting his classmates, Hadi also chose promising younger officers like Air Vice-Marshal Imran Baidirus (1988 class) who took over Air Vice-Marshal Yuyu's former post at Koopsau-I. Later in 2017, Hadi also promoted Marshal Imran Baidirus for a second time again to follow in Air Vice-Marshal Yuyu's wake as Kohanudnas commander. Air Chief Marshal Hadi trusted Imran

[49] See "Manuver Hadi 'buang' Pengaruh Gatot," *Pinter Politik*, January 2, 2018; "Di Acara Prabowo, Gatot Nurmantyo Keluhkan Kondisi TNI Saat Ini," *Tempo*, April 12, 2019.

Baidirus; their relationship was forged during the time the latter served as his deputy assistant for operations. The beneficiaries of Air Chief Marshal Hadi's favorable attitude toward Air Vice-Marshal Imran Baidirus were some of the officers from the 1988 class. Those who benefited from a career boost were Air Commodore Nanang Santoso, who replaced Air Vice-Marshal Imran Baidirus at Koopsau-I, and Air Commodore Heraldy Dumex Dharma, who became Kohanudnas chief of staff.

The situation was quite different within the navy ranks. First, the major appointments had only involved the replacement of Marine Major General R. M. Trusono as the commander of the Marine Corps (Kormar) with Marine Major General Bambang Suswantono (1987 class). Previously, Major General Bambang Suswantono was the commander of Presidential Guards (Dan Paspampres). The position was then passed on to promote another Marine Brigade-General Suhartono (1988 class). In the later part of 2017, Admiral Ade also began to appoint several officers to strategic positions within the navy: Rear Admiral Darwanto would replace his retiring classmate Rear Marshal I. G. Putu Wijamahadi as Kodiklatal commander, Commodore Didik Setiyono (1987 class) replaced Admiral Darwanto as Eastern Fleet commander, and Commodore Yudo Margono (1988 class) became the Naval Transport commander. The former Naval Transport commander Rear Admiral Agung Prasetyawan (1987 class) was lined up to replace Rear Admiral Siwi Sukma Adji as the assistant for general military planning.

To summarize his time in office, General Gatot Nurmantyo had maintained a balance between each service allowing the service chiefs' autonomy to appoint the officers qualified for strategic posts while exerting his prerogative when it came to specific appointments. However, toward the end of his tenure, apart from the amended TNI Commander's decree (SKEP Panglima TNI), General Gatot had valid reasons for his decision-making for service appointments, which were motivated by a combination of professional and personal merit.

Hadi Tjahjanto's Leadership

Being an air force officer, Air Chief Marshal Hadi Tjahjanto had to start his appointment by doing something out of the ordinary in order to consolidate his leadership over the TNI. First on his agenda was the amendment of General Gatot's last promotion orders, cancelling sixteen high-ranking officer appointments.[50] Nevertheless Hadi gave his assurance that the amendment was not based on personal preferences and citing that the respective units still needed such appointments to cover officers either redeployed or retiring from their positions. Next, the newly designated TNI commander-in-chief issued an additional decree for personnel reshuffles, particularly in military intelligence and the inspectorate, to consolidate his power over the intelligence and internal affairs sectors. This involved appointing his trusted classmate from the 1986

---

[50] The annulled decision involved the appointments of generals Sudirman (assistant for army operations) and Hasanudin (Marine Corps chief of staff, 1989 class). Initially, they would replace, respectively, Lieutenant General Edy Rahmayadi (Kostrad commander) and Major General Bambang Suswantono (Marine Corps commander, 1987 class). Edi Rahmayadi had tendered his resignation from active service in a bid for the upcoming North Sumatera gubernatorial election. See "New Military Chief Partially Cancels Gatot's Major Reshuffles," *The Jakarta Post*, December 20, 2017; "Mengapa Panglima TNI Membatalkan Mutasi 16 Perwira Tinggi," *Beritagar.id*, December 20, 2017.

class, Air Vice-Marshal Kisenda Wiranatakusumah, to helm BAIS, who had previously served as his security aide during his time as air force chief.[51]

As the TNI commander, Air Chief Marshal Hadi Tjahjanto had a dominant role in continuing TNI reorganizational efforts. In early 2018, he inaugurated eleven development programs for TNI.[52] It should be noted, however, that Air Chief Marshal Hadi enjoyed President Jokowi's political backing and was seen as his instrument to shape and make changes within the TNI organization from the very outset.

Compared to General Gatot's achievements in pursuing TNI reorganizational efforts, Air Chief Marshal Hadi's efforts would be viewed as more successful. During his tenure, he advocated the implementation of two major regulations pertaining to TNI organization in 2019, marked by Presidential Decree No. 42 Year 2019 and Presidential Decree No. 66 Year 2019. According to the latest regulations on TNI's organizational structure—Peraturan Presiden No. 66/2019—Balakpus consists of twenty-three agencies from TNI Staff and Command College (Sesko TNI) to the latest TNI Special Operations Command (Komando Operasi Khusus, Koopsus).[53]

The latest regulation also gave TNI a roadmap in developing an organizational structure. Before the new regulation came into force, TNI often engaged itself in what could be dubbed as organizational tinkering through a process of validation that simply raised a designated office holder's rank by moving them one rank upward. While this process had been fruitful, enabling the high-ranking officers to occupy more positions, it was not a healthy development for the overall benefit of TNI in the long run.

The latest regulation also marked the enactment of new Kotama units placed directly under the TNI headquarters, namely the three Joint-Defense Regional Commands (Kogabwilhan) located in Riau Islands, East Kalimantan, and Papua.[54] Aside from the three Kogabwilhan, the new regulations also raised the status of the navy's Marine Corps (Komando Marinir, Kormar) to become one of TNI's Kotama. Previously, Kormar was always considered a second-tiered force within navy service subordinated to each naval fleet command. The accession of the Marine Corps as a new major operational command would mean that the TNI commander-in-chief could now directly mobilize the Marine Corps to handle security contingencies.

Nevertheless, these regulations provide a framework and allow us a reference point to study which command structures and agencies will grow in importance. Apart from the existing operational commands and executive agencies prominent during General

---

[51] This leadership change is noteworthy considering the poor coordination between BAIS and security-related institutions during General Gatot Nurmantyo's tenure. In June 2016, for instance, senior defense officials mulled over a plan to form a new defense intelligence body, suggesting a lack of information exchanges with their military counterparts. See "Intelijen Pertahanan Usulan Komandan," *Majalah Tempo*, July 4–9, 2016. Even worse, a year later, miscommunication between the military intelligence and national police led to public uproar over the alleged import of thousands of illegal firearms. See "Jokowi and Gatot Discuss Controversial Remarks," *The Jakarta Post*, September 27, 2017.

[52] See "Panglima Hadi Tjahjanto Tetapkan 11 Program Prioritas Pembangunan TNI," *Kompas*, January 25, 2018.

[53] See Peraturan Presiden (Perpres) Republik Indonesia No. 66 Tahun 2019 tentang Susunan Organisasi Tentara Nasional Indonesia.

[54] See Iis Gindarsah, "Joint Defense Regional Commands, a Maritime Focus," *The Jakarta Post*, October 5, 2019.

Gatot's leadership, observers will now also need to look at the four new commands that we have previously mentioned and became operational in 2019. One of the more interesting operational commands to begin our analysis is the army's Kostrad. In 2018 alone, the position of Kostrad commander was held by three different officers: Lieutenant General Agus Kriswanto (1984 class), Lieutenant General Andika Perkasa (1987 class), and Major General Besar Harto Karyawan (1986 class). Previously General Andika's appointment to this position was controversial, as it was viewed more as a political appointment enabling him to gain the credentials to succeed General Mulyono as the army chief.

Apart from Kostrad's top leadership, the army headquarters also passed on its prestigious infantry division commanderships to younger army officers. At this time, TNI Commander-in-Chief Marshal Hadi inaugurated a new Kostrad 3rd Infantry Division in Makassar.[55] Command of Kostrad's 1st, 2nd, and 3rd Infantry Divisions were handed to Brigadier General Agus Rohman (1988 class), Brigadier General Marga Taufiq (1987 class), and Major General Achmad Marzuki (1989 class), respectively. Before General Mulyono's retirement in November 2018, to lay the platform for the in-coming army chief, Major General Marga Taufiq, who happened to be Lieutenant General Andika Perkasa's classmate, was promoted in December 2018 to take charge of the significantly resourced Pattimura Territorial Command in the Moluccas. Replacing Major General Marga Taufiq, the new army chief, Lieutenant General Andika Perkasa, installed Brigadier General Tri Yuniarto (1989 class best graduate) to command Kostrad's 2nd Infantry Division.

A similar situation also occurred within the Kopassus leadership. Major General Madsuni, who had assumed this position since 2016, had passed the baton of command to his junior Major General Eko Margiyono (1989 class). In early 2018, a retiring General Mulyono also rotated the deputy commander position, which was viewed as one of the most prestigious appointments for a new one-star officer. Brigadier General Richard Tampubolon (1992 graduate) handed over his position as Kopassus deputy commander to 1993 graduate, Colonel Mohamad Hasan.

The situation within the navy was quite different. In 2018, Admiral Ade passed on the navy leadership to Vice Admiral Siwi Sukma Aji (1985 class). To fill Admiral Siwi's previous role in the TNI Academy, Air Chief Marshal Hadi promoted Rear Admiral Aan Kurnia (1987 class), who then relinquished his position as assistant for naval operations. Among the naval operational commands, Air Chief Marshal Hadi also oversaw some organizational changes. In addition to the western and eastern fleets, he inaugurated an additional third naval fleet in Sorong, West Papua. Located within the third fleet was a new Marine Corps Division (Pasukan Marinir, Pasmar). The naval fleet configuration was then re-designated as 1st Fleet (Jakarta), 2nd Fleet (Surabaya), and 3rd Fleet (Sorong).

At the same time, these organizational changes enabled a regeneration process within the navy's officer corps. The Naval Transport Commander Rear Admiral Yudo Margono assumed a new position as the 1st Fleet commander in May 2018, replacing Rear Admiral Aan Kurnia who took up a new posting as the navy chief's assistant for operations. At the same time, the navy chief promoted Rear Admiral Yudo's

[55] See "Hadi Kukuhkan Tiga Panglima dan Satu Komandan Satuan Baru di Wilayah Timur," *Kompas*, May 11, 2018.

classmate, Commodore R. Achmad Rivai, to become the Naval Transport commander. Rear Admiral Rivai then passed this post to another 1988 graduate, Commodore Heru Kusmanto. The new navy chief of staff also handed over 2nd fleet commandership from Rear Admiral Didik Setiyono to Rear Admiral Mintoro Yulianto (1986 class) in September 2018. The navy chief of staff also later promoted another 1986 graduate, Rear Admiral Mintoro Yulianto, as his new deputy. The previous deputy, Vice Admiral Achmad Taufiqoerrochman, who previously was viewed as a strong contender for the position of navy chief of staff, was instead deployed to lead the maritime security agency (Bakamla).

Within the air force ranks, Air Chief Marshal Hadi and Air Chief Marshal Yuyu's classmates took charge of the key air force strategic appointments. For instance, the air force academy class of 1986 took charge of nine of the twenty-one air force central executive bodies: Aeronautics (Wisnu Dewantoko), Aerospace Potential (Hari Budianto), Communication and Electronic (Bambang Hengki), Education (Andjar Sungkowo and later Umar Rudianto), Flight and Operational Safety (Agung Heru Santoso), Operation Development (Irawan Nurhadi), Personnel Wellbeing (Trusta Yuniarta), Procurement (Hento Budi Sarjono), and Research and Development (Rochmadi Saputro). However, regarding the air force operational commands, early in 2018, air force chief of staff Air Chief Marshal Yuyu Sutisna mostly favored the 1988 graduates. In February 2018, the air force chief of staff promoted Air Commodore Fadjar Prasetyo to replace Air Vice-Marshal Yadi Indrayadi to take charge of Koopsau II. Marshal Fadjar Prasetyo was to be later appointed to lead the prestigious Koopsau-I in Jakarta, replacing his classmate Air Vice-Marshal Nanang Santoso. Another 1988 graduate, Commodore Henri Alfiandi, was promoted to fill the former's previous position at Koopsau II. The consolidation of the air force high command was completed in May 2018, when Air Chief Marshal Hadi promoted 1989 graduate Air Commodore Tamsil Gustari Malik as the newly inaugurated Koopsau III commander. These patterns infer that Air Chief Marshal Hadi and Air Chief Marshal Yuyu had managed to augment their classmates' careers into the air force high-ranking officer's corps while at the same time managing a regeneration process within the various air force commands.

As Indonesia approached the 2019 general election, TNI headquarters announced a major personnel reshuffle in January 2019. On January 25, 2019, Air Chief Marshal Hadi promoted then-Kodam Jakarta commander, Major General Joni Supriyanto, as TNI chief of general staff, replacing Vice Admiral Didit Herdiawan who became Defense Ministry inspector general. Within the army ranks, Hadi also replaced Major General Hartomo's position as army territorial center commander with Major General Arif Rahman. Hadi filled Arif Rahman's previous post—Kodam V/Brawijaya commander—with Major General R. Wisnoe Prasetja Boedi, handed Kodam Jakarta commander to Major General Eko Margiyono, and appointed Major General I Nyoman Cantiasa as Kopassus commandant general. At the navy executive agency, Hadi replaced both Naval Academy governor and vice governor Rear Admiral Muhammad Ali and Brigadier General (Marine) Nuri Andrianis Djatmika with Vice Admiral Edi Sucipto and Brigadier General (Marine) Endi Supardi.

Air Chief Marshal Hadi had only begun to reshuffle officers that led the air force commands in March 2019. He replaced Koopsau III commander Air Vice-Marshal Tamsil Gustari Malik with the younger Air Commodore Andyawan Martono Putra. It was also observed that Air Chief Marshal Hadi did not make any important reshuffles during the election month in April 2019.

In May 2019, Hadi reshuffled the presidential military secretary, Air Vice-Marshal Trisno Hendradi, and rewarded him with a three-star position as Sesko TNI commander, as the previous holder, Vice Admiral Deddy Muhibah Pribadi, was retiring.[56] Throughout June and July 2019, Hadi had also reshuffled Kodiklatau commander Air Vice-Marshal Andjar Sungkowo with Air Commodore Diyah Yudanardi (class 1988) and appointed Brigadier General Rochadi to be the first commander for the newly inaugurated TNI special operations command (Komando Operasi Khusus TNI, Koopsus TNI).[57] By the end of August 2019, Hadi had also swapped Air Vice-Marshal Donny Ermawan's position as Seskoau commander with Air Vice-Marshal Henri Alfiandi's position as Koopsau II commander. In the same month, he also transferred the position of Kodam XVII/Cenderawasih commander to Major General Herman Asaribab after waves of riots in Papua.[58]

In September 2019, Hadi announced a major reshuffle that involved the three newly inaugurated Kogabwilhan. He promoted Rear Admiral Yudo Margono, Air Vice-Marshal Fadjar Prasetyo, and Major General Ganip Warsito to hold three-star appointments as commanders of Kogabwilhan I, II, and III, respectively. Such a promotion initiative laid the groundwork for another round of reshuffles within the TNI executive agencies and main commands: Yudo's previous post as Koarmada I commander was handed over to Rear Admiral Muhammad Ali and the Koopsau I leadership was handed from Fadjar to Air Commodore Khairil Lubis (class of 1990). Hadi also appointed Rear Admiral Heru Kusmanto to replace Mintoro Yulianto—who became navy deputy chief—as Koarmada II commander. Heru Kusmanto's previous post as Kolinlamil commander was handed over to Commodore Ahmadi Heri Purwono. On top of those reshuffles, Hadi had also promoted Air Vice-Marshal Dedy Permadi as Sesko TNI commander while retiring the now three-star officer Trisno Hendradi.

The TNI did not make major reshuffles nearing the day of the presidential inauguration on October 20, 2019. However, the position of Kodam III/Siliwangi was handed over to Major General Nugroho Budi Wiryanto (class of 1987) just a few days after the inauguration. At the end of the year, Hadi also promoted Brigadier General Kasim Genawi as the last Kodiklat TNI commander, who held a two-star rank before it was validated as a three-star position in 2020.

In early January 2020, the army headquarters had reshuffled two Kodam commanders posted in the island of Sulawesi. The commando-experienced Major General Santos Gunawan Matondang replaced Major General Tiopan Aritonang as Kodam XIII/Merdeka commander, who would be responsible for supervising territorial defense covering Central to North Sulawesi.[59] Meanwhile, Major General Andi Sumangerukka substituted

---

[56] Air Vice-Marshal Trisno had acted as the presidential military secretary since 2016 and his three-star promotion was considered a reward for his service with the president.

[57] The Editors discuss Koopsus further in the next section.

[58] By August 2019, both Kodam commanders in Papua (Kodam XVII/Cenderawasih and Kodam XVIII/Kasuari) were held by "Papua natives."

[59] Major General Matondang was commander of the renowned Kopassus anti-terror unit, Detachment-81, and tasked to quell the remaining Mujahidin Indonesia Timur (MIT) terrorism threat in Poso.

Major General Surawahadi as Kodam XIV/Hasanudin Commander, who would cover South and Southeast Sulawesi. At the end of January 2020, TNI headquarters had to pick a replacement for TNI academy commander, as Vice Admiral Aan Kurnia was appointed to take charge of Bakamla. To fill this position, TNI headquarters then promoted Major General (Marine) Bambang Suswantono, who had command experience with both Paspampres and the Marine Corps.

From February to mid-March, the positions that involved TNI main commands and executive agencies were not reshuffled. The reshuffle only began on March 31, 2020, when command of Kodam Iskandar Muda was handed from Major General Teguh Arief Indratmoko to Major General Hassanudin. In April, TNI headquarters announced some important changes to the holders of key commands and agencies: the Army Territorial Center (Pusterad), the Naval Command and Staff College, Kostrad's 3rd Infantry Division, and few territorial commands. Command of Pusterad went from Major General Arif Rahman to Major General Joppye Onesimus Wayangkau.[60] Seskoal's new commander was Commodore Iwan Isnurwanto, who took over command from Rear Admiral Amarulla Octavian. Kostrad's Infantry Division-3 commander was changed with Major General Achmad Marzuki, handing over command to Brigadier General Wanti Waranei Franky Mamahit. Kodam V/Brawijaya and Kodam XVIII/Kasuari commanders were, respectively, handed from Major General R. Wisnoe Prasetija Boedi to Major General Widodo Iryanyah and from Major General Joppye Wayangkau to Major General Ali Hamdan Bogra.

The reshuffles in May 2020 were particularly significant compared to the May reshuffles in the previous year due to the creation of potentially prestigious new commands. First, the leadership of both Kogabwilhan I and II were accessible, as Yudo Margono and Fadjar Prasetyo were appointed as chiefs of the navy and air force, respectively. Their replacements were Rear Admiral I Nyoman Gede Ariawan and Air Vice-Marshal Imran Baidirus. Then, several key positions within the navy ranks were also reshuffled due to the changes in TNI upper ranks. Muhammad Ali's position as Koarmada I commander was passed on to Commodore Ahmadi Heri Purwono, while I Nyoman Gede Ariawan's Koarmada III commandership was given over to Rear Admiral Dadi Hartanto. At the same time, the position of Kolinlamil commander was made available by Ahmadi Heri Purwono handing over command to accommodate the newly promoted Commodore Abdul Rasyid Kacong. The rotation also affected the key command positions within the air force, namely Seskoau; Koopsau I, II, and III; as well as Kohanudnas. Air Vice-Marshal Henri Alfiandi, the Seskoau commander, was replaced by Air Vice-Marshal Samsu Rizal. The commanders of Koopsau I, II, and III were passed from Air Commodore Khairil Lubis to Air Commodore Tri Bowo Budi Santoso, Air Commodore Donny Ermawan to Air Commodore Minggit Tribowo, and Air Vice-Marshal Andyawan Martono Putra to Air Vice-Marshal Novyan Samyoga. Lastly, Kohanudnas commander was handed from Air Vice-Marshal Imran Baidirus to Air Vice-Marshal Khairil Lubis.

The reshuffles from June to July 2020 were as important as May 2020. Within the TNI headquarters, BAIS deputy head and Koopsus TNI commander were handed from Major

---

[60] By 2020, Pusterad commander became a three-star position due to Perpres 66/2019. This reshuffle made Major General Wayangkau the first Papuan native to hold a three-star appointment.

General Handy Geniardi to Brigadier General Gina Yoginda and Major General Rochadi to Major General Richard H. T. Tampubolon, respectively. The reshuffles within the army ranks had received greater attention, where Kostrad, the military academy, Seskoad, the army infantry center, as well as several key Kodam leaderships were also reshuffled. The Kostrad commandership was passed from Lieutenant General Besar Harto Karyawan to Major General Eko Margiyono, while its Infantry Division-1 was handed over from Major General Agus Rohman to Brigadier General Dedy Kusmayadi. Within the education agencies, the military academy governor was given from Major General Dudung Abdurachman to Brigadier General Totok Imam Santoso, the Seskoad commander was passed from Major General Kurnia Dewantara to Major General Anton Nugroho, while the commander of the army infantry center was handed over from Major General Teguh Pudjo Rumekso to Lieutenant General Besar Harto Karyawan.[61] In addition, the seven Kodam leaderships that saw new appointments included Kodam Jaya, I/Bukit Barisan, II/Sriwijaya, IV/Diponegoro, VI/Mulawarman, IX/Udayana, and XVI/Patimura. The new commanders were respectively generals Dudung Abdurachman, Irwansyah, Agus Suhardi, Bakti Agus Fadjari, Heri Wiranto, Kurnia Dewantara, and Agus Rohman.

During the June–July period, navy headquarters also amended some of the previous appointments regarding its main command. Rear Admiral Ahmadi Heri Purwono—who commanded Koarmada I—was promoted as navy deputy chief. In turn, Koarmada I leadership then passed on to Rear Admiral Abdul Rasyid Kacong. To fill Abdul Rasyid Kacong's position at Kolinlamil, the navy headquarters then appointed Commodore Irwan Achmadi.

Fewer positions were reshuffled during the August–September 2020 period. First, Major General Sudirman was appointed as Kodiklat TNI commander, replacing Major General Kasim Genawi.[62] Next, Lieutenant General R. Wisnoe Prasetija Boedi replaced the retiring Major General Joppye Wayangkau as Pusterad commander. The most prestigious reshuffle within this time frame was Major General Mohamad Hasan's promotion as Kopassus commander, replacing I Nyoman Cantiasa. Major General Cantiasa was then appointed as Kodam XVIII/Kasuari commander, as his experience in special operations was considered highly valuable in conflict regions like West Papua.

From October to December 2020, there were several important reshuffles due to the changes in the TNI leadership explained in the previous section.[63] First, Air Chief Marshal Hadi appointed Lieutenant General Joni Supriyanto (formerly TNI Chief of General Staff, 1986 class) as head of BAIS, replacing the retiring Air Marshal Kisenda Wiranatakusumah. In addition, Hadi also appointed Air Vice-Marshal Tamsil Gustari Malik to replace Bambang Suswantono as TNI academy commanding general in October 2020. Next, Hadi promoted Brigadier General Agus Subiyanto as Paspampres commander in November 2020.

---

[61] Lieutenant General Besar Harto was the first three-star army infantry center commander since Perpres 62/2019 took effect. The army infantry center commander was previously held by a two-star general.

[62] Major General Sudirman was General Gatot's choice back in 2017 to replace Edy Rahmayadi as Kostrad commander. He was eventually promoted to a three-star general after the Kodiklat TNI commander was validated into a three-star position.

[63] See the previous section on the promotion of Lieutenant-Generals Herindra and Suswantono as TNI chief of general staff and inspector general, respectively.

Within the navy, Commodore Tunggul Suropati and Rear Admiral Nyoman Gede Sudihartawan were promoted as Naval Academy governor and Koarmada II commander, respectively, in October 2020.[64] In addition, the navy headquarters also promoted Commodore Irvansyah as Kolinlamil commander, replacing Rear Admiral Irwan Achmadi, who became assistant for navy personnel affairs in November 2020.

Army headquarters installed a new Kodam V/Brawijaya commander, Major General Suhariyanto, in place of the retiring Major General Widodo Iryansyah in October 2020. Next, army headquarters appointed army generals Hassanudin, Ignatius Yogo Triyono, and Achmad Marzuki as, respectively, Kodam I/Bukit Barisan, Kodam XVII/ Cenderawasih, and Kodam Iskandar Muda commanders in November 2020. In addition, the former Paspamres commander, Maruli Simanjuntak, was also appointed as Kodam IX/Udayana commander in the same month.As previously explained, Air Chief Marshal Hadi's successor as the TNI commander was decided when the Indonesian Parliament received the presidential recommendation letter on November 3, 2021. However, the race to select new service chiefs—regardless of which of the three services leaders got appointed as the new TNI commander—began as early as January 2021. Thus, several strategic main command positions would be reshuffled to ensure an adequate pool of capable service chiefs to expand the range of candidates who could qualify for consideration as service chiefs.

In the first quarter of 2021, TNI headquarters promoted two high-ranking officers at the two-star level to three-star positions within the TNI main commands and executive agencies: Major General Arif Rahman (class 1988) would be appointed to command the army infantry center while Major General Agus Rohman (class 1988) would become Kogabwilhan III commander. The second quarter of 2021 saw further reshuffles, with five officers appointed to three-star positions within the TNI main commands and executive agencies. These were Air Vice-Marshal Diyah Yudanardi (Sesko TNI commander) and Major General Tiopan Aritonang (Kodiklat TNI commander), who both began their new appointments in April 2021. In addition, Major General Dudung Abdurachman and Major General Teguh Arief Indratmoko were promoted as Kostrad commander and Pusterad commander in May 2021.[65] Finally, in the last four months before Hadi's retirement—between July and October 2021—only three more appointments were made for newly created three-star positions. These were Rear Admiral Muhammad Ali (Kogabwilhan I commander), Major General Jeffry Apoly Rahawarin (Kogabwilhan III commander), and Major General Madsuni (Kodiklat TNI commander).

Unsurprisingly, these ten names were among the candidates in line to become service chiefs. The possibility that Fadjar Prasetyo might replace Hadi was set aside when Parliament announced that the next TNI commander candidates would be narrowed down to Andika Perkasa and Yudo Margono.[66] Therefore, the remaining eligible

---

[64] Commodore Suropati replaced Edi Sucipto who was transferred to Lemhannas. Meanwhile, Rear Admiral Sudihartawan replaced Rear Admiral Heru Kusmanto who in turn was appointed as Assistant for Military Planning by TNI Commander Hadi.

[65] Major General Dudung's tenure as Kodam Jaya commander was relatively short (approximately ten months). In addition, for some observers, Major General Dudung's appointment was also unexpected. See "Mengulik Jabatan Pangkostrad yang Kini Diduduki Dudung Abdurachman," *Tirto*, June 9, 2021.

[66] See "Calon Kuat Panglima TNI di DPR: Masih KSAD Andika Perkasa dan KSAL Yudo Margono," *Kumparan*, September 12, 2021).

candidates to replace the army and navy chiefs were nine navy and seventeen army officers holding three-star positions.[67] Of these officers, three navy officers and eight army officers belonged to either TNI or service main commands and executive agencies. A key takeaway from the above is that being reshuffled into these strategic positions is an important stepping stone for a TNI officer's late-career progression.

Personnel Reshuffle and TNI Major Reorganization

During Jokowi's first-term administration, the Indonesian government had issued two amendments to the existing Presidential Regulation (Perpres) No. 10/2010 on TNI's organizational structure. There were four strategic factors that made it necessary for the introduction of these organizational amendments. *First*, the proliferation of cyber capabilities as a "cost-effective" asymmetric weapon. A 2011 study by Washington-based Center for Strategic and International Studies identified thirty-three countries that had incorporated cyberwarfare into their military planning and organization.[68] Common elements in the military doctrines include the use of cyber capabilities for reconnaissance, information operations, critical network and service disruptions, as well as a complement to electronic warfare. Given the importance of "power balance" in cyberspace, the TNI leadership formed a cyberwarfare unit (Satuan Siber, Satsiber TNI) to develop relevant capabilities and doctrine in 2017.

Second, the adoption of new arms and military technologies. Over the past decade, the Indonesian military had acquired sophisticated weapons such as attack helicopters, main battle tanks, vertical launch system-capable frigates, and beyond visual range anti-air missile systems. In theory, these enable the TNI to modify its existing field manuals and develop new war-fighting doctrines and capabilities, including tank warfare, close combat air support, ship-borne air defense, and long-range air combat maneuvers. For that purpose, the military's high command had recently reorganized its existing institutions for doctrinal development, education, and training (Kodiklat) at armed forces headquarters. Moreover, the navy and air force established a new department to oversee their respective operational exercises (Dinas Operasi dan Latihan TNI AL, Disopslatal and Dinas Operasi dan Latihan TNI AU, Disopslatau).

Third, increased military cooperative engagements. For Indonesia, diplomacy is the first line of defense. A recent study noted that between 2009 and 2015, the country's defense and military officials have participated in 447 multilateral events; 37 percent of which are intra-Southeast Asian defense and security dialogues. Bilaterally, it also conducted 385 defense interactions or military-to-military exchanges with a total of thirty-six regional and extra-regional countries.[69] The idea was to build amicable relationships among military establishments, while promoting national defense interests. Hence, back in 2013, TNI headquarters created an International Cooperation Center (Pusat Kerjasama Internasional, Puskersin) to consolidate all military international cooperation initiatives. Moreover, due

[67] See "Jajaran Jenderal TNI AL Calon Suksesor KSAL Yudo Margono," *Kumparan*, September 12, 2021; "Sederet Jenderal Calon KSAD Penerus Jenderal Andika Perkasa," *Kumparan*, September 12, 2021.

[68] See James A. Lewis and Katrina Timlin, "Cybersecurity and Cyberwarfare: Preliminary Assessment of National Doctrine and Organization," *UNIDIR Resources* (2011).

[69] See Iis Gindarsah, "Strategic Hedging in Indonesia's Defense Diplomacy," *Defense and Security Analysis* 32, no. 4 (2016): 342–43.

to its strategic role in maritime diplomacy and coupled with the intensification of border talks, the navy elevated the status of its Hydrographic and Oceanographic Department (Dinas Hidro Oseanografi TNI Angkatan Laut, Dishidrosal) in 2016.

Fourth, the legislation of new laws on military and security affairs. In addition to the existing military penal codes, the Indonesian government had approved the Law No. 25/2014 on military discipline. The Supreme Court's data showed that from 2004 to 2017, the military courts—who are in charge of adjudicating in lawsuits involving TNI personnel—issued a total of 16,842 decisions or an average of 1,295 decisions per year. While the majority of these cases (45 percent) were military criminal law violations, 33 percent of them were cases involving violations of general penal codes.[70] In an effort to further strengthen law enforcement within the defense establishment, the Indonesian government had recently revitalized the role of military police corps through the establishment of a Military Police Center (Puspom TNI) at TNI headquarters. That being said, contrary to the views of some critics, TNI leadership remains consistent and strongly committed to eliminate the culture of impunity from the military.

Likewise, the latest amendment of Law No. 15/2003 included a provision on the military's counterterrorism role. Between 2007 and 2018, TNI headquarters had regularly held a combined military drill involving the air force, army, and navy's counterterrorism units. The latest exercise took place prior to the International Monetary Fund-World Bank annual meeting in Bali in October 2018. During the legislative deliberations on a new counterterrorism law, the TNI's high-command revived a plan to create a "joint special operation command." It came into being as part of Perpres No. 42/2019, which related to the second amendment of the military's organizational structure. It stipulates that Koopsus TNI can "conduct and engage in support operations that require rapid and precise use of force to safeguard national interests both at home and abroad." Similar to its equivalent counterparts in foreign militaries, the spectrum of missions of the new military command may include more than one core activity, such as direct action, special reconnaissance, counterterrorism, counterinsurgency, unconventional warfare, security force assistance, hostage rescue and recovery, as well as military information support.[71]

Besides the four strategic factors, TNI also faced an internal challenge in the form of a plethora of non-job officers, creating promotional logjams. Political interference in senior officer appointments and the constant tinkering of its organizational structure were allegedly behind the career bottleneck issue within the Indonesian military.[72] The formation of new structures like Kogabwilhan and Koopsus TNI offered solutions for these problems. However, it should be noted that the establishment of Kogabwilhan and Koopssus was not designed solely to absorb excess manpower, but also to address strategic concerns and development issues.

TNI wants to utilize Kogabwilhan as a "first responder" in the event of regional conflict and to function as a "strike force" to deny foreign intrusion. Such important

---

[70] See Iis Gindarsah, "Strategic Drivers of TNI Reorganization," *The Jakarta Post*, July 31, 2019.

[71] Jokowi's administration, however, has not yet finalized the specific rules of engagement for Koopsus's involvement in countering terrorists, which consequently created a legal loophole. See Chaula R. Anindya, "Indonesia's Counterterrorism Policy: An Appraisal," *RSIS Commentary*, no. 188, September 26, 2019.

[72] See Evan Laksmana, "Reshuffling the Deck? Military Corporatism, Promotional Logjams, and Post-Authoritarian Civil-Military Relations in Indonesia," *Journal of Contemporary Asia* 49, no. 5 (2019): 806–36.

functions now make commanders of Kogabwilhan significant actors working directly under the command of Panglima TNI. In addition, to solve promotional logjam issues, the formation of Kogabwilhan can be attributed to major military developments in the region. The first is the increasing centrality of the maritime domain in Indonesia's defense strategy as the location of Kogabwilhan headquarters takes into account the country's Archipelagic Sea-Lanes (ALKI) and the disposition of existing military units, including the newly established army's Kostrad infantry division, the navy's third fleet and marine force, and the air force's new operational command overseeing the eastern part of Indonesia. Next, the Kogabwilhan is the operational structure that accommodates and operationalizes the TNI's emerging combined armed warfare doctrine. The new command employs relevant functions for command and control of future joint military operations involving different branches and capabilities of TNI. Third, Kogabwilhan's leadership appointment is a step in the right direction toward TNI's continued professionalization with the predominance of a merit-based system shaping military personnel policy where career history, military skill, and tactical acumen become preeminent when it comes to determining the selection criteria for promotion.[73]

In the past, notably in the 1950s, the Indonesian armed forces had the Regional Defence Command (Komando Wilayah Pertahanan, Kowilhan), a structure almost similar to the Kogabwilhan. Unlike the current version of Kogabwilhan, the 1950–58 Kowilhan was divided into seven operational areas (two in Sumatera, West Java, Central Java, East Java and Bali, Kalimantan, and the eastern part of Indonesia, except West Papua). After the 1969–70 reorganization, the Kowilhan in reality entrenched army domination as leaders of key territories, such as Sumatera, Java, and Sulawesi, were nominated by the service. Furthermore, Kowilhan commanders had significant authority as they practically owned their own troops, as each command owned a chief of staff from the different services.[74] The absence of meritocracy in determining Kowilhan leaders had exacerbated the situation, as many of them were appointed due to their roots in the region or personalistic ties with some Jakarta elites. Back in 1970, the late Benedict Anderson coined the term "regional warlordism" to describe a chaotic chain of command due to the extensive power held by these Kowilhan commanders.[75]

The Indonesian authorities have learned the lessons of history and taken note of the messy situation created by the Kowilhan structure in the past. To avoid repeating past mistakes, new norms would be adopted. First, merit-based appointments will become the norm for selecting commanders for the existing Kogabwilhan. Career backgrounds will serve as the most compelling element in determining leaders of a Kogabwilhan. The first three Kogabwilhan commanders appointed, namely Vice Admiral Yudo Margono, Air Marshal Fadjar Prasetyo, and Lieutenant General Ganip Warsito, have demonstrated a similar tour of duty pattern, particularly serving as naval fleet commander, air force operational commander, and army territorial commander,

---

[73] See Iis Gindarsah, "Joint Defense Regional Commands, a Maritime Focus," *The Jakarta Post*, October 5, 2019.

[74] See Ben Anderson, "Current Data on the Indonesian Military Elite after the Reorganization 1969–1970," *Indonesia*, no. 10 (October 1970): 199.

[75] See Ben Anderson, "Current Data on the Indonesian Military Elite," *Indonesia*, no. 40 (October 1985): 131.

respectively.[76] Next, Kogabwilhan commanders have less power compared to Kowilhan commanders. Kogabwilhan structures do not possess any designated troops on their own and need to request permission from TNI headquarters to utilize any unit within their operational jurisdictions. Furthermore, the formation of Koopsus, which aims to assist the National Police in countering terrorism, which remains its primary duty, can in reality also absorb a number of top brass military officers.[77] For example, the commander and vice commander of Koopssus will be two-star general and one-star general, respectively.

TNI and the National War against the COVID-19 Pandemic[78]

In July 2021, former TNI Commander ACM Hadi Tjahjanto labeled the current COVID-19 pandemic as a war in which cooperation from all segments of society would be required to attain victory.[79] Now we turn our attention to the implications of military role expansion in the context of the Indonesian military's significant involvement in efforts to mitigate the COVID-19 outbreak. The Indonesian government's decision to utilize the TNI to support the nationwide efforts in mitigating the epidemic was both odd and problematic. First, the military is not designed to have strong expertise on medical and public health affairs, as its major function deals with defense affairs. Secondly, the existing regulatory frameworks—Defense Law (Law 3/2002) and the TNI Law (Law 34/2004)—do not permit the military to operate in non-natural disaster management. However, leaving these considerations aside, the TNI has in its possession a vast array of military installations and assets across the archipelago that might be proven to be useful in helping the government at times of emergency. In addition, some of these military installations are embedded in territorial commands that are currently and operationally reporting to the larger Kogabwilhan.[80] This consideration led the government to produce an "emergency" ordinance that allows military utilization in mitigating the pandemic.

As stipulated in the existing regulation, the government of Indonesia may employ the TNI under the framework of military operations other than war (MOOTW) for disaster management purposes. Yet, the pandemic situation opened a possible scenario whereby GOI would require the TNI to conduct missions contributing to the support of overall civilian governance. Such a scenario might require the TNI to perform civic missions and to deliver humanitarian aid. Considering the regulatory gap, President Joko Widodo enacted Presidential Decree (Keppres) 12/2020 that declared the COVID-19 pandemic as a national disaster. By enacting the presidential decree, there was no longer any regulatory gap preventing the government from utilizing the TNI to engage in non-defense missions within the pandemic context.

---

[76] See Iis Gindarsah, "Joint Defense Regional Commands, A Maritime Focus."

[77] However, the assistance will only be extended when the police are deemed inadequate to respond to an emergency. See "Jokowi Revives Special Military Force to Help Police Combat Terrorism," *The Jakarta Post*, July 25, 2019.

[78] The analysis in this part of the paper covers the beginning of the COVID-19 outbreak in Indonesia until the end of Hadi Tjahjanto's tenure as Panglima, in line with the article's timeline coverage.

[79] See "Panglima TNI Nyatakan Saat ini Peperangan, Musuhnya Tak Terlihat [TNI Commander Labelled the Current Situation as War, against an Invincible Enemy]," *DetikNews*, July 16, 2021.

[80] See Tiola, "New Joint-Command Faces First Test under COVID-19," *The Jakarta Post*, May 20, 2020.

As argued by Iis Gindarsah, the TNI can be deployed in three scenarios of operation during the pandemic.[81] First, the government might involve the TNI in civic actions (*operasi bakti*) under a relatively stable scenario where the government has ensured political stability, maintained social cohesion, and controlled the spread of the epidemic. The second scenario comes into play if epidemic cases spike leading to an increase in the probability of a social crisis. In this second scenario, the TNI operates under the umbrella of an assistance operation (*tugas perbantuan*) supporting the civilian authority—particularly in medical, transportation, custom and immigration affairs, as well as police functions in enforcing the established health protocols. The third and final scenario requires the conduct of an internal security operation (*operasi keamanan dalam negeri*), which only applied if the pandemic caused unstable domestic security.

President Jokowi mandated the Chief of Operational Staff to TNI Commander-in-Chief (Asisten Operasi, Asops Panglima TNI) to be deputized alongside the Chief of Operational Staff to Chief of POLRI (Asops Kapolri) within the COVID-19 Task Force. In addition, the president instructed KSAD General Andika Perkasa to become a deputy head within the COVID-19 Management Committee. In addition, Commander of Joint Defense Area Command I (Panglima Komando Gabungan Wilayah Pertahanan, Pangkogabwilhan), Vice Admiral Yudo Margono also formed four Integrated Joint Task Commands (Komando Tugas Gabungan Terpadu, Kogasgabpad) in March 2020, which worked under the coordination of COVID-19 Task Force.[82]

Each Kogasgabpad functions under different TNI main operational commands (Komando Utama Operasional, Kotama Ops TNI) and plays a unique role in supporting the central government's COVID-19 mitigation plans. The Kogasgabpad I works under the auspices of the Greater Jakarta Regional Military Command (Komando Daerah Militer Jayakarta, Kodam Jaya), which was commanded by Major General Eko Margiono and then passed on to Major General Dudung Abdurachman. Based in Jakarta, Kogasgabpad I has the responsibility to work hand-in-hand with various civilian agencies in Wisma Atlet, an athlete accommodation center modified as an emergency hospital. Kogasgabpad II would work under the 1st Air Force Operations Command (Komando Operasi TNI Angkatan Udara, Koopsau I), which was under the command of Air Vice-Marshal M. Khairil Lubis who then passed on his command to Air Vice-Marshal Tri Bowo Budi S. Kogasgabpad II, who would be responsible for the preparing and running of daily activities for the newly built quarantine facility in Natuna Air Base, Riau Islands Province. Kogasgabpad III was based in Sebaru Island, Jakarta, and under the management of the Navy First Fleet (Komando Armada, Koarmada I). Koarmada I was commanded by Rear Admiral Muhammad Ali, who was later replaced by Rear Admiral Ahmadi Heri Purwono. Providing health care and managing isolation and quarantine facilities in Sebaru Island became the duties of Kogasgabpad III. Lastly, Kogasgabpad IV, which operates under the aegis of Kodam I/Bukit Barisan, would run emergency hospitals on Galang Island, Riau Islands. Kogasgabpad IV was led by Major

[81] See, Iis Gindarsah, "Operasi Militer Selain Perang (OMSP) di Masa Pandemi COVID-19 [Military Operations Other than War (MOOTW) in Times of COVID-19 Pandemic]," in *Indonesia dan COVID-19: Pandangan Multi Aspek dan Sektoral* [Indonesia and COVID-19: Perspectives on multiple aspects and sectorals], ed. Fajar B. Hirawan (Jakarta: CSIS, 2020).

[82] See "Pangkogabwilhan I: Empat Kogasgabpad Dibentuk untuk Tangani COVID-19 [Commander of TNI's Joint-Defence Area Command I: Four Integrated Joint-Task Force Command are Formed to Handle COVID-19]," *Antara News*, March 23, 2020.

General Mohamad Sabrar Fadhilah before he passed on his command to Major General Irwansyah.

Apart from establishing four Kogasgabpad, the military was also involved in missions that evolved out from several government initiatives, like providing military facilities, equipment, manpower, and even expertise. For instance, TNI became involved in the distribution of medical equipment—including vaccine distribution—across the archipelago. In the early phase, the air force flew its C-130 plane to Shanghai, China, to collect medical equipment that was purchased by the Ministry of Defense in March 2020.[83] Apart from logistical support, TNI was deployed as auxiliary enforcers to implement the government's large-scale social restriction (PSBB) policy. Together with POLRI, President Jokowi ordered TNI to enforce the implementation of health protocols in a variety of locations. In June 2020, TNI Commander Marshal Hadi Tjahjanto stated that TNI–POLRI personnel would be deployed in about 1,800 spots (150,000 TNI officers and 190,000 POLRI officers) around the archipelago, including commercial centers, traditional markets, and tourist sites.[84]

In August 2020, the central government formed the National Economic and COVID-19 Recovery Committee (KPCPEN) and appointed General Andika Perkasa as deputy head of the committee. President Jokowi hoped the inclusion of the military would aid KPCPEN in enforcing strict health protocols for the benefit of the public.[85] Former Minister of Health Lt. Gen. Terawan Agus Putranto in early 2021 attempted to promote his *Vaksin Nusantara*, where research for the project was conducted at the Army Hospital Gatot Soebroto. Nonetheless, the National Agency of Drug and Food Control (BPOM) did not permit the circulation of *Vaksin Nusantara* due to the lack of clinical proof.[86] After, TNI headquarters denied any involvement in the project, though the research was done at one of its facilities.[87] Later, the military was involved in the national vaccination plan through conducting vaccinations in its 803 hospitals and other facilities across the nation, including mobilizing 10,867 vaccinators.[88]

At the provincial level, the TNI coordinated with regional leaders through the so-called Forkopimda (Regional Leaders Coordination Forum). This would serve as a crucial channel of coordination between civilian leaders and military as well as police officers at the regional level. For an example, Kodam Jayakarta in Jakarta often conducted health protocol socialization events together with the Jakarta regional police (Polda Metro Jaya).[89] In West Java, Kodam Siliwangi with Governor Ridwan Kamil and Forkopimda

---

[83] See "TNI Berangkatkan Hercules Jemput Alat Kesehatan Covid-19 di Shanghai [TNI deploys Hercules Transport Aircraft to pick-up COVID-19 medical equipments in Shanghai]," *Merdeka News*, March 21, 2020.

[84] See "Troop Deployment Plan Stokes Fear of Return to Hard Tactics, Dwifungsi," *The Jakarta Post*, June 4, 2020.

[85] See "Jokowi Picks Army Chief as National COVID-19 Committee's Vice Chairman," *The Jakarta Post*, August 11, 2020.

[86] See "4 Alasan Mengapa Vaksin Nusantara Tidak Lulus Uji Klinik Fase 1 [4 Reasons of the 1st Clinical Test Failure of *Vaksin Nusantara*]," *Kompas*, April 28, 2021.

[87] See "Tegas! Vaksin Nusantara Terawan Bukan Program TNI [Terawan's *Vaksin Nusantara* is not TNI's Program]," *CNBC Indonesia*, April 19, 2021.

[88] See "TNI-POLRI Bantu Percepatan Vaksinasi COVID-19 [TNI-POLRI Helps Acceleration of COVID-19 Vaccination]," *Satgas COVID-19*, August 18, 2021.

[89] See "Forkopimda DKI Jakarta Launching Penerapan Pendisiplinan Prokes COVID-19 Berbasis Komunitas," *Kodam Jaya*, September 11, 2020.

regularly toured several cities and regencies in West Java—such as Bandung regency, Banjar city, Cirebon city, and Karawang regency—raising the population's awareness and distributing logistical support during the pandemic. In general, the military's participation in COVID-19 management at the regional level revolved around the building of emergency medical infrastructure, campaigning to raise public awareness, and enforcing health protocols. The TNI also could act independently to mitigate the pandemic from spreading within its ranks or embark on conducting civic actions such as hosting charity and blood donation events and even enacting public kitchens (*dapur umum*) with POLRI in various regional cities and regencies.

Changes and Continuities in Jokowi Era

The 2014 election had brought with it a significant change in Indonesia's political landscape. Sworn and ensconced in the state palace garbed in populist paraphernalia, Jokowi began his administration promising a fresh and clean start for Indonesia. However, as he sought to pursue political autonomy, Jokowi found himself needing to balance the competing interests of political and business oligarchs who supported him during the election period.[90] This balancing act was quite evident in the first two cabinet reshuffles, which in turn resulted in a peculiar constellation of Indonesian elite interests best represented by 2014–19 Working Cabinet (Kabinet Kerja).[91] The same process was also at work during Jokowi's quest to strengthen his grip over TNI. At first, Jokowi maintained an orthodox strategy primarily aimed at removing his predecessor's appointees—a process dubbed *de-Yudhoyono-isasi*—which aimed to galvanize Jokowi's influence within the TNI. Unlike Yudhoyono, who often engaged in micromanaging the TNI's high-ranking officers' career development, Jokowi preferred to retain TNI's autonomy, allowing them to pick their own "Big Man."[92] This preference was clearly seen in the nomination of Gatot Nurmantyo as Panglima TNI, who had strong support from within the military's ranks. Instead of nominating the PDIP-backed candidate Air Chief Marshal Agus Supriatna, Jokowi opted for Gatot to lead TNI. However, Gatot's political maneuvers sounded the alarm bell for the state palace that, if left alone to his own devices, a "Big Man" could easily undermine political stability. With these concerns to consider, Jokowi then opted to groom his own loyal supporter, making him the military "Big Man" and thereby consolidating his influence over TNI.

As a continuation of a strategy that sought to emphasize his quest for political autonomy and power base consolidation, Jokowi made several maneuvers that impacted the TNI. First, like his predecessors, Jokowi used his prerogative to appoint the new military top brass to consolidate his hold on the TNI. Interestingly, the consolidation of the TNI elite took place during Hadi's tenure as Panglima TNI. On the one hand, Jokowi wanted to establish firm influence over the military. On the other hand, the

---

[90] See Leonard C. Sebastian, Emirza Adi Syailendra, and Keoni Indrabayu Marzuki, "Civil-Military Relations in Indonesia after the Reform Period," *Asia Policy* 13, no. 3 (July 2018): 49–78.

[91] See "Melihat 4 'Reshuffle' Kabinet Pemerintahan Jokowi–JK," *Kompas.com*, August 15, 2018.

[92] In the cases of Melanesian and Polynesian political community, Big Man refers to the leadership systems opposed to legitimate chieftainship. These cases highlight that leader might not attain his legitimacy to lead a community from a passed down lineage but the ability to provide welfare and popularity within his community. See Marshall D. Sahlins, "Poor Man, Rich Man, Big-Man, Chief: Political Types in Melanesia and Polynesia," *Comparative Studies in Society and History* 5, no. 3 (1963): 283–303.

president seemed reluctant to push for abrupt change among TNI leadership, most certainly to avoid any unnecessary political turmoil and resistance from the armed forces, while Gatot Nurmantyo was still Panglima TNI. Jokowi did sign Perpres 62/2016 on TNI Structural Change. However, the presidential regulation did not radically alter TNI structure and was merely focused on meeting each service's long-time aspirations: establishing an Army Preparedness Department (Dislaikad) for TNI AD, establishing maritime potential staff at navy headquarters and a Hydro-Oceanographic Center (Pushidros TNI AL) for TNI AL, and establishing air space potential staff at air force headquarters and Operational and Training Department (Disoplatau) for TNI AU.[93] Nonetheless, Presidential Regulations 42/2019 and 66/2019 significantly expanded TNI organizational structure. The two presidential regulations, respectively, mandated the establishment of Koopsus TNI and the new appointment of a deputy TNI commander position.[94] Furthermore, the placement of officers following the appointment of Air Chief Marshal Hadi strengthened the general belief that the president's choice predominated over those promoted by *geng Solo* (Solo gang referring to Jokowi's inner circle comprising confidants originating from Solo) and political cliques surrounding Jokowi, notably Luhut Pandjaitan and A. M. Hendropriyono. Retired military officers, like Luhut and Hendropriyono have managed to preserve their considerable political influence, maintaining their connections and networks to local politicians and working their own levers of power, which have played a critical role in sustaining the president's political position.[95]

We have also witnessed a rapid structural expansion of the Indonesian armed forces after Hadi's appointment at TNI headquarters. The establishment of the Kogabwilhan structure vividly reflected the development. However, it should be noted that the augmentation of TNI was mandated by the Minimum Essential Force (MEF) doctrine. The initiative not only recommended the formation of regional joint-command structures, but also the introduction of new divisions, such as a third air force command plus additional Kostrad and Marine Corps divisions and units in each TNI service.[96] This certainly indicated that Jokowi's TNI development policy was also a continuation from a policy that had its origins in the previous administration and raised further questions over the president's commitment toward an already withering Global Maritime Fulcrum (GMF) concept.[97] Therefore, there is no solid basis to support any argument suggesting that the current TNI structural developments were a consequence of the need to fulfill GMF aspirations.

---

[93] See "Susunan Baru Organisasi TNI AD Setelah Perpres 62/2016 Diteken Jokowi," *Tribunnews*, January 20, 2017; "Perpres 62/2016 Diteken, Berikut Susunan Baru Organisasi TNI Angkatan Laut," *Tribunnews*, January 20, 2017; "Susunan Terbaru Organisasi TNI Angkatan Udara Berdasarkan Perpres 62/2016," *Tribunnews*, January 20, 2017.

[94] The current Minister for Religious Affairs Fachrul Razi, a founder of the Hanura Party, was the last Deputy Commander of the TNI serving from 1999 to 2000.

[95] See Keoni Marzuki, "Old Soldiers Never Die: Retired Officers Behind Jokowi, Prabowo," *RSIS Commentary*, no. 17, January 30, 2019.

[96] See *Postur Pertahanan Negara 2009–2029*.

[97] Jokowi offered GMF as his vision to build Indonesia's maritime sector. See Iis Gindarsah and Adhi Priamarizki, *Indonesia's Maritime Doctrine and Security Concerns* (Singapore: S. Rajaratnam School of International Studies, 2015). See also relevant articles on maritime security in Leonard C. Sebastian and Jonathan Chen, eds., "Indonesia's Foreign and Maritime Policies under Joko Widodo," special issue of *Journal of Asian Security and International Affairs*, 8, no. 3 (December 2021).

Second, elite appeasement has turned out to be Jokowi's primary strategy in securing support from TNI. The president has been known for his lack of a power base, which compelled him to forge an alliance with the military in exchange for political support. Jokowi permitted various interest groups with linkages to active duty TNI officers to fill strategic positions, grooming these personnel as "Big Men" within the military structure. These officers included the current TNI commander General Andika Perkasa and the current General Maruli Simadjuntak, who are, respectively, sons-in-law of A. M. Hendropriyono and Luhut Pandjaitan.

Third, several attempts at organizational tinkering that occurred during the first year of Jokowi's presidency provided little evidence of that, the former Jakarta Governor was taking seriously a shift toward a maritime-focus defense planning stance. We see that the TNI's new top brass are mostly dominated by high-ranking army officers rather than members of the other two services, particularly the navy. Combining this observation with the abovementioned fact that maritime defense infrastructure was mandated by MEF rather than Jokowi, we can argue that Indonesian civilian authorities seemed to lack a commitment to build a maritime-oriented defense posture or, at least for the moment, place a low priority in realizing the idea.

Concluding Remarks

Despite notable institutional progress, some observers are still concerned over setbacks to military reform in Indonesia over the past decade. Central to these concerns are issues relating to the military's political neutrality, the place of operations other than war in an environment where military reforms have stalled, and active officer appointments to positions beyond defense and military sector. Our findings indicated the continued trend of the TNI military's commitment to professionalism, which were highlighted by the Editors in the 2014 edition of the "Current Data on the Indonesian Military Elite." Such circumstances consequently minimize any potential military intervention into civilian affairs. Moreover, a close observation of the recent strategic landscape shows that the threats to national defense are increasingly dynamic, multidimensional, and technologically sophisticated. The outbreak of the COVID-19 pandemic in early 2020 has also galvanized the central role of TNI in handling nontraditional security issues.[98]

Hence, upgrading combat capability and modernizing the armaments of TNI is likely to become the leading objective for future organizational changes within the defense establishment. On another note, appointments within TNI do indicate growing promotional trends based on meritocracy, particularly for Balakpus and Kotama appointments. Besides merit and skills gained from past tours of duty, reward and appeasement are also considerations for the promotion. Some officers who are considered as *putra daerah* or sons of the soil also have been rewarded territorial positions in their respective regions.

In addition to the abovementioned issues, the reelected President Jokowi has to address outstanding issues in the military realm. The memorandum of understanding between the TNI and national police chiefs on handling social unrest, for instance,

---

[98] Chaula R. Anindya and Sigit S. Nugroho, "Jokowi's War on Pandemic: Growing Dependence on TNI?" *RSIS Commentary*, no. 088, May 11, 2020.

serves as an ad-hoc mechanism because the law or government regulation on military secondments has still not been formalized since 2004. Hence, the Indonesian government needs to complete the implementing regulations of Law No. 3/2002 and Law No. 34/2004 on defense and military affairs, particularly in relation to operations other than war. Moreover, with an average of 5 percent economic growth, the Indonesian government could only afford 0.82 percent of gross domestic product (GDP) or 5.09 percent of the annual budget to cover defense spending over the past five years. Another notable challenge is the relatively slow process of arms procurement. Aside from meeting a target of 1.5 percent of GDP, Jokowi's second-term administration has to fast-track the country's military modernization, including the acquisition of 4.5 generation of jetfighters to replace the outdated F-5 combat squadron.

The discussion in the previous sections also indicate that Jokowi and his inner circle have managed to consolidate their influence at the TNI leadership level. During the early days of his first presidential term, Jokowi opted for caution by not significantly shaping the elite composition within the Indonesian military. The departure of Gatot Nurmantyo and the ascendancy of Hadi Tjahjanto, and in due course Andika Perkasa, provides the president and the consolidated political cliques surrounding him the confidence to revise TNI's structure as well as pursue other agenda, including the abovementioned modernization program.

A no less important issue is the revitalization of Indonesia's indigenous defense industry. At a presidential debate in late March 2019, Jokowi interpreted the military's arms modernization strategy as an "investment" to build capacity for research, production, and maintenance of military equipment at home. In addition to state funding to encourage defense research and development and imposing offset requirements on the country's major arms importers, the Indonesian government has to find ways to make domestic defense firms become more capable and competitive in the global arms market. Taken as a whole, the completion of these issues will not only reinforce a professional identity within the TNI and bolster its capabilities as an integrated armed force, but also constitute the "legacy" of the Jokowi administration to the Indonesian people.

Appendix

Position	Commanding Officer (*succession*)
Commander in Chief (*General, Admiral, Air Chief Marshal*)	General Gatot Nurmantyo * March 13, 1960 *Akmil 1982 *Infantry *July 8, 2015 *Army Chief of Staff
	Air Chief Marshal Hadi Tjahjanto *8 November 1963 *AAU 1986 *Aviators d *Air Force Chief of Staff
	General Andika Perkasa *December 21, 1964 *Akmil 1987 *Infantry *November 17, 2021 *Army Chief of Staff
Chief of the General Staff (*Lieutenant General, Vice Admiral, Air Marshal*)	Vice Admiral Ade Supandi (*promotion*) *May 26, 1960 *AAL 1983 *Seaman *May 12, 2014 *Assistant for Navy Planning
	Air Vice-Marshal Agus Supriatna (*promotion*) *January 28, 1959 *AAU 1983 *Aviators *December 30, 2014 *Deputy of TNI Inspector General
	Air Vice-Marshal Dede Rusamsi (*promotion*) *December 19, 1957 *AAU 1981 *Aviators *February 6, 2015 *Deputy Governor of Lemhannas
	Vice Admiral Didit Herdiawan *September 13, 1961 *AAL 1984 *Seaman *October 22, 2015 * Deputy Governor of Lemhannas

Position	Commanding Officer (*succession*)
	Major General Joni Supriyanto (*promotion*) *June 6, 1964 *Akmil 1986 *Infantry *January 25, 2019 *Commander, Kodam Jaya
	Lieutenant General Muhammad Herindra *November 30, 1964 *Akmil 1987 *Infantry *October 27, 2020 *Armed Force Inspector General
	Lieutenant General Ganip Warsito *November 23, 1963 *Akmil 1986 *Infantry *February 1, 2021 *Commander, Joint-Defence Regional Commands III
	Lieutenant General Eko Margiyono *May 12, 1967 *Akmil 1989 *Infantry *May 25, 2021 *Commander, Kostrad
Inspector General (*Lieutenant General, Vice Admiral, Air Marshal*)	Major General Syafril Mahyudin (*promotion*) *Akmil 1982 *Infantry *May 19, 2014 *Special Staff to TNI Commander
	Major General Setyo Sularso (*promotion*) *May 27, 1959 *Akmil 1982 *Infantry *April 25, 2016 *Commander, Kodam IX/Udayana
	Major General Dodik Widjanarko (*promotion*) *July 1, 1963 *Akmil 1985 *Military Police *July 28, 2017 *Commander, Military Police
	Major General Muhammad Herindra (*promotion*) *October 28, 1964 *Akmil 1987 *Infantry *March 2, 2018 *Special Staff to TNI Commander

continued

Position	Commanding Officer (*succession*)
	Lieutenant General (Marine) Bambang Suswantono *July 25, 1965 *AAL 1987 *Marines *October 21, 2020 *Commander, Sesko TNI
Commander, Military Joint-Defence Area Command (Komando Gabungan Wilayah Pertahanan, Kogabwilhan) I (*Lieutenant General, Vice Admiral, Air Marshal*)	Rear Admiral Yudo Margono (*promotion*) *November 26, 1965 *AAL 1988 *Seaman *September24, 2019 *Commander, Koarmada I
	Rear Admiral I Nyoman Gede Ariawan (*promotion*) *March 8, 1963 *AAL 1986 *Seaman *May 26, 2020 *Commander, Koarmada III
	Rear Admiral Muhammad Ali (*promotion*) *April 9, 1967 *AAL 1989 *Seaman *August 2, 2021 *Assistant for Navy Planning
Commander, Military Joint-Defence Area Command II	Air Vice-Marshal Fadjar Prasetyo (*promotion*) *April 9, 1966 *AAU 1988 *Aviators *September24, 2019 *Commander, Koopsau I
	Air Vice-Marshal Imran Baidirus (*promotion*) *September 3, 1964 *AAU 1988 *Aviators *May 26, 2020 *Commander, Kohanudnas
Commander, Military Joint-Defence Area Command III	Major General Ganip Warsito (*promotion*) *November 23, 1963 *Akmil 1986 *Infantry *September24, 2019 *Assistant for TNI Operations

Position	Commanding Officer (*succession*)
	Major General Agus Rohman (*promotion*) *August 15, 1953 *Akmil 1988 *Infantry *February 21, 2021 *Commander, Kodam XVI/Pattimura
	Major General Jeffry Apoly Rahawarin (*promotion*) *January 21, 1964 *Akmil 1988 *Infantry *August 2, 2021 *Commander, Kodam XVI/Pattimura
Commanding General, Military Academy (*Akademi TNI*) (*Major General, Rear Admiral, Air Vice-Marshal*)	Major General Harry Purdianto *May 10, 1957 *Akmil 1981 *Infantry *October 31, 2014 *Chief of Staff, Kostrad
	Major General Bayu Purwiyono (*promotion*) *September 16, 1959 *Akmil 1982 *Infantry *July 25, 2015 *Commander, Kodam IV/Diponegoro
	Rear Admiral Siwi Sukma Adji (*promotion*) *May 14, 1962 *AAL 1985 *Seaman *September 28, 2017 *Assistant for General Planning
	Rear Admiral Aan Kurnia (*promotion*) *July 22, 1965 *AAL 1987 *Seaman *May 23, 2018 *Assistant for Navy Operation
	Major General (Marine) Bambang Suswantono (*promotion*) *July 25, 1965 *AAL 1987 *Marines *January 31, 2020 *Assistant for Maritime Potentials to Navy Chief of Staff

continued

Position	Commanding Officer (*succession*)
	Air Vice-Marshal Tamsil Gustari Malik (*promotion*) *May 31, 1963 *AAU 1987 *Aviators *October 21, 2020 *Assistant for Intelligence to Air Force Chief of Staff
	Air Vice-Marshal Andyawan Martono Putra (*promotion*) *April 30, 1967 *AAU 1989 *Aviators *May 25, 2021 *Assistant for Planning to Air Force Chief of Staff
Commander, Military Command and Staff College (Sesko TNI) (*Lieutenant General, Vice Admiral, Air Marshal*)	Major General Sonny Widjaja (promotion) *January 1, 1958 *Akmil 1982 *Infantry *August 15, 2014 *Assistant for Army Operation
	Major General Agus Sutomo (promotion) *August 14, 1960 *Akmil 1984 *Infantry *February 1, 2016 *Commander, Kodiklatad
	Major General Raden Mas Trusono (promotion) *October 29, 1960 *AAL 1985 *Marines *February 23, 2017 *Commander, Marine Corps
	Rear Admiral Deddy Muhibah Pribadi (promotion) *May 16, 1961 *AAL 1985 *Seaman *October15, 2018 *Coordinator of Expert Staffs to Navy Chief of Staff
	Air Vice-Marshal Trisno Hendradi (promotion) *October 14, 1961 *AAU 1986 *Aviators *May 27, 2019 *Presidential Military Secretary

Position	Commanding Officer (*succession*)
	Air Vice-Marshal Dedy Permadi (promotion) *April 3, 1963 *AAU 1985 *Aviators *September 24, 2019 *Assistant for Personnel to TNI Commander
	Air Vice-Marshal Diyah Yudanardi (promotion) *December 13, 1964 *AAU 1988 *Aviators *April 26, 2021 *Assistant for Personnel to TNI Commander
Assistant for Military Personnel (*Major General, Rear Admiral, Air Vice-Marshal*)	Rear Admiral Sugeng Darmawan *October 1, 1957 *AAL 1981 *Seaman *February 28, 2018 *Expert Staff, Lemhannas
	Air Vice-Marshal Bambang Samoedro *May19, 1959 *AAU 1982 *Aviators *October 22, 2015 *Expert Staff, Lemhannas
	Air Vice-Marshal Dedy Permadi *April 3, 1963 *AAU 1985 *Aviators *May 31, 2017 *Assistant for Air Force Personnel
	Air Vice-Marshal Diyah Yudanardi *December 13, 1964 *AAU 1988 *Aviators *September 24, 2019 *Commander, Air Force Education and Training Command
	Air Vice-Marshal Agustinus Gustaf Brugman *December 15, 1965 *AAU 1988 *Aviators *April 26, 2021 *Assistant for Air Force Personnel to Air Force Chief of Staff

continued

Position	Commanding Officer (*succession*)
	Air Vice-Marshal Kusworo *February 12, 1967 *AAU 1988 *Aviators *September 13, 2021 *Assistant for Aerospace Potential to Air Force Chief of Staff
Assistant for General Planning (*Major General, Rear Admiral, Air Vice-Marshal*)	Major General Sumedy *October 15, 1960 *Akmil 1983 *Cavalry *October 10, 2014 *Special Staff to TNI Commander
	Rear Admiral Agung Pramono *September 6, 1960 *AAL 1984 *Seaman *August 18, 2015 *Assistant for Navy Planning
	Rear Admiral Siwi Sukma Adji *May 14, 1962 *AAL 1985 *Seaman *August 1, 2016 *Commander, Koarmada II
	Rear Admiral Agung Prasetiawan *June 6, 1964 *AAL 1987 *Seaman *September 28, 2017 *Commander, Kolinlamil
	Rear Admiral Heru Kusmanto *March 31, 1966 *AAL 1988 *Seaman *October 1, 2020 *Commander, Koarmada II
Assistant for Military Operations (*Major General, Rear Admiral, Air Vice-Marshal*)	Major General Indra Hidayat R. *August 6, 1957 *Akmil 1981 *Infantry *August 4, 2014 *Chief of Staff, Kostrad
	Major General Fransen G. Siahaan *May 27, 1958 *Akmil 1983 *Infantry *August 18, 2015 *Commander, Kodam XVII/Cendrawasih

Position	Commanding Officer (*succession*)
	Major General Agung Risdhianto *April 22, 1961 *Akmil 1985 *Infantry *May 20, 2016 *Commander, Kodam XII/Tanjungpura
	Major General Lodewyk Pusung *September 27, 1960 *Akmil 1985 *Infantry *February 22, 2017 *Commander, Kodam I/Bukit Barisan
	Major General Ganip Warsito *November 23, 1963 *Akmil 1986 *Infantry *September 24, 2018 *Special Staff to TNI Commander
	Major General Tiopan Aritonang *November 16, 1963 *Akmil 1986 *Infantry *January 9, 2020 *Commander, Kodam XIII/Merdeka
	Major General Syafruddin *August 3, 1964 *Akmil 1989 *Infantry *April 26, 2021 *Chief of Staff, Kogabwilhan I
Assistant for Military Logistics (*Major General, Rear Admiral, Air Vice-Marshal*)	Air Vice-Marshal Karibiyama *March 16, 1957 *AAU 1981 *Air Force Engineer *October 31, 2013 *Expert Staff to TNI Commander
	Air Vice-Marshal Nugroho Prang Sumadi *February 5, 1959 *AAU 1982 *Air Force Engineer *March 30, 2015 *Commander, Koharmatau
	Major General Gadang Pambudi *September 4, 1959 *Akmil 1984 *Infantry *February 20, 2017 *Assistant for Army Logistics

continued

Position	Commanding Officer (*succession*)
	Rear Admiral Bambang Nariyono *January 17, 1961 *AAL 1984 *Naval Engineer *September 28, 2017 *Special Staff to Navy Chief of Staff
	Air Vice-Marshal Kukuh Sudibyanto *December19, 1962 *AAU 1986 *Air Force Engineer *February 27, 2019 *Expert Staff to TNI Commander
	Air Vice-Marshal Dento Priyono *March 28, 1963 *AAU 1986 *Air Force Engineer *December 28, 2020 *Expert Staff to TNI Commander
	Air Vice-Marshal Sujatmiko Gatot Sriyatno *August 20, 1964 *AAU 1987 *Air Force Engineer *24 March 2021 *Expert Staff to TNI Commander
Assistant for Military Intelligence (*Major General, Rear Admiral, Air Vice-Marshal*)	Major General Amri Husaini *April 7, 1957 *AAL 1981* *Marines *March 21, 2014 *Deputy Coordinator for State Defence, Security Affairs
	Coordinating Ministry for Politics, Law and Major General A. Faridz Washington *December 27, 1959 *AAL 1983 *Marines *March 30, 2015 *Commander, Marine Corps
	Major General Benny Indra Pujihastono *December 2, 1961 *Akmil 1984 *Field Artillery *June 9, 2016 *Commander, Kodam VI/Mulawarman

Position	Commanding Officer (*succession*)
	Major General Agus Surya Bakti *August 17, 1961 *Akmil 1984 *Infantry *July 13, 2018 *Commander, Kodam XIV/Hasanuddin
	Major General Andjar Wiratma *February 21, 1965 *Akmil 1987 *Infantry *September 24, 2018 *Vice Head of BAIS TNI
Assistant for Military Territorial Affairs (*Major General*)	Major General Ngakan Gede Sugiartha Garjitha *July 14, 1957 *Akmil 1981 *Infantry *January 30, 2014 *Expert Staff to Head of BIN
	Major General Wiyarto *October 3, 1959 *Akmil 1985 *Infantry *August 3, 2015 *Commander, Kodam XVI/Pattimura
	Major General Kustanto Widiatmoko *March 16, 1957 *Akmil 1987 *Cavalry *October 27, 2017 *Commander, Kodam V/Brawijaya
	Major General George Elnadus Supit *July 22, 1962 *Akmil 1985 *Infantry *September 24, 2018 *Commander, Kodam XVII/Cendrawasih
	Major General Madsuni *February 14, 1964 *Akmil 1988 *Infantry *July 27, 2020 *Expert Staff to TNI Commander
	Major General Sapriadi *March 1, 1965 *Akmil 1989 *Infantry *September 13, 2021 *Deputy Commander, TNI Academy

continued

Position	Commanding Officer (*succession*)
Assistant for Military Electronic Communications (*Major General, Rear Admiral, Air Vice-Marshal*)	Air Vice-Marshal Bambang Agus Margono *March 27, 1957 *AAU 1981 *Aviators *February 28, 2014 *Deputy of TNI Inspector General
	Air Vice-Marshal Muhammad Yunus *June 19, 1958 *AAL 1981 *Administration *March 30, 2015 *Expert Staff, Lemhannas
	Air Vice-Marshal Bonar H. Hutagaol *May 28, 1961 *AAU 1984 *Aviators *October 22, 2015 *Expert Staff, Lemhannas
	Air Vice-Marshal Asep Dian Hermawan *November 15, 1962 *AAU 1986 *Air Force Electronics *July 2, 2018 *Expert Staff to TNI Commander
	Rear Admiral Lutfi Syaefullah *April 11, 1963 *AAL 1986 *Seaman *January 25, 2019 *Expert Staff to TNI Commander
	Rear Admiral Atok Dushanto *August 6, 1964 *AAL 1987 *Seaman *April 28, 2021 *Assistant for Electronic Communication to Navy Chief of Staff
Head of Strategic Intelligence Body (BAIS) (Before 2020: *Major General, Rear Admiral, Air Vice-Marshal*; 2020–onward: *Lieutenant General, Vice Admiral, Air Marshal*)	Major General Yayat Sudrajat *June 15, 1959 *Akmil 1982 *Infantry *July 25, 2015 *Assistant for Army Security
	Major General Hartomo *March 1, 1963 *Akmil 1986 *Infantry *September 16, 2016 *Governor, Military Academy

Position	Commanding Officer (*succession*)
	Major General Ilyas Alamsyah *April 11, 1966 *Akmil 1988 *Infantry *October 27, 2017 *Assistant for Army Security
	Air Vice-Marshal Kisenda Wiranatakusumah (*promotion*) *August 1, 1962 *AAU 1986 *Special (Intelligence) *December 19, 2017 *Assistant for Air Force Security
	Lieutenant General Joni Supriyanto *June 6, 1964 *Akmil 1986 *October 21, 2020 *Chief of General Staff
Deputy Head of BAIS (*Major General, Rear Admiral, Air Vice-Marshal*)	Air Vice-Marshal Amarullah *May18, 1957 *AAU 1981 *November 18, 2013 *Commander, Korpaskhas
	Air Commodore Supomo (*promotion*) *February 7, 1959 *AAU 1983 *April 24, 2015 *Deputy Assistant for Air Force Security
	Air Commodore Benedictus Widjanarko (*promotion*) *March 27, 1959 *AAU 1983 *August 18, 2015 *Expert Staff to TNI Commander
	Air Commodore Wieko Syofyan (*promotion*) *April 4, 1964 *AAU 1986 *August 1, 2016 *Head of Air Force Public and Media Relations Department
	Air Commodore Donny Ermawan Taufanto (*promotion*) *December12, 1965 *AAU 1988 *June 9, 2017 *Chief of Staff, Koopsau I

continued

Position	Commanding Officer (*succession*)
	Major General Joni Supriyanto (*promotion*) *June 6, 1964 *Akmil 1986 *Infantry *December 19, 2017 *Special Staff to Army Chief of Staff
	Brigadier General Andjar Wiratma (*promotion*) *February 21, 1965 *Akmil 1987 *Infantry *March 2, 2018 *Deputy Assistant for Military Intelligence
	Brigadier General Handy Geniardi (*promotion*) *December 6, 1964 *Akmil 1987 *Infantry *September 24, 2018 *Director A BAIS TNI
	Brigadier General Gina Yoginda (promotion) *May 2, 1963 *Akmil 1986 *Cavalry *July 27, 2020 *Commander, Satinduk BAIS TNI
	Major General Achmad Riad *August 9, 1965 *Akmil 1988 *Cavalry *April 26, 2021 *Head, TNI Public and Media Relations Centre
Commander, Military Education and Training Command (Kodiklat TNI) (2010–20: *Major General, Rear Admiral, Air Vice-Marshal; 2020–onward: Lieutenant General, Vice Admiral, Air Marshal*)	Major General I Wayan Mendra *August 12, 1957 *AAL 1981 *Marines *January 30, 2014 *Expert Staff to TNI Commander
	Brigadier General Sturman Panjaitan (*promotion*) *October 17, 1959 *AAL 1983 *Marines *May 15, 2015 *Deputy Assistant for TNI Territorial Affairs
	Major General Dedi Kusnadi Thamim *August 31, 1958 *Akmil 1983 *Infantry *August 18, 2015 *Commander, Kodam III/Siliwangi

Position	Commanding Officer (*succession*)
	Major General Sumardi *February 20, 1959 *Akmil 1984 *Infantry *June 9, 2016 *Commander, Kodam V/Brawijaya
	Major General Agung Risdhianto *April 22, 1961 *Akmil 1985 *Infantry *February 22, 2017 *Assistant for Military Operation
	Major General Benny Indra Pujihastono *December 2, 1961 *Akmil 1984 *Field Artillery *July 13, 2018 *Assistant for Military Intelligence
	Brigadier General Kasim Genawi *December 28, 1962 *Akmil 1986 *Infantry *December 27, 2019 *Deputy Assistant for Military Logistics
	Major General Sudirman (*promotion*) *March 5, 1963 *Akmil 1986 *Infantry *September 26, 2020 *Coordinator of Expert Staffs to TNI Commander
	Major General Tiopan Aritonang (promotion) *November 16, 1963 *Akmil 1986 *Infantry *April 26, 2021 *Assistant for Military Operation
	Major General Madsuni (*promotion*) *February 14, 1964 *Akmil 1988 *Infantry *September 13, 2021 *Assistant for TNI Territorial Affairs
	Major General Bambang Isnawan (*promotion*) *July 31, 1966 *Akmil 1988 *Infantry *December 6 2021 *Commander, Kodam XVI/Pattimura

continued

Position	Commanding Officer (*succession*)
Commander, Presidential Guards (Paspampres) (*Major General*)	Brigadier General Andika Perkasa (*promotion*) *December 21, 1964 *Akmil 1987 *Infantry *October 14, 2014 *Head of Army Public and Media Relations Department
	Brigadier General Bambang Suswantono (*promotion*) *July 25, 1965 *AAL 1987 *Marines *May 20, 2016 *Deputy Commander, Paspampres
	Brigadier General Suhartono (*promotion*) *April 15, 1966 *AAL 1988 *Marines *February 23, 2017 *Commander, Lantamal XI
	Brigadier General Maruli Simanjuntak (*promotion*) *February 27, 1970 *Akmil 1992 *Infantry *November 29, 2018 *Chief of Staff, Kodam IV/Diponegoro
	Brigadier General Agus Subiyanto (*promotion*) *August 5, 1967 *Akmil 1991 *Infantry *November18, 2020 *Commander, Korem 061/Suryakancana Kodam III/Siliwangi
	Brigadier General Tri Budi Utomo (*promotion*) *February 6, 1971 *Akmil 1994 *Infantry *August 2, 2021 *Deputy Commander, Kopassus
Commander, TNI Special Operations Command (Koopsus TNI) (*Major General, Rear Admiral, Air Vice-Marshal*)	Brigadier General Rochadi (*promotion*) *July 1, 1962 *Akmil 1986 *Infantry *July 24, 2019 *Director A BAIS TNI

Position	Commanding Officer (*succession*)

	Major General Richard Horja Taruli Tampubolon
	  *May 24, 1969
	  *Akmil 1992
	  *Infantry
	  *July 27, 2020
	  *Chief of Staff, Kogabwilhan I

	Brigadier General Joko Purwo Putranto (*promotion*)
	  *October 2, 1966
	  *Akmil 1990
	  *Infantry
	  *December 6 2021
	  *Chief of Staff, Kodam Iskandar Muda

Head, Military Logistics Body (Babek) (*Brigadier General, Commodore, Air Commodore*)	Col. Sudarto (*promotion*)
	  *April 18, 1962
	  *Akmil 1985
	  *Field Artillery
	  *June 26, 2015
	  *Control Officer, Babek TNI

	Col. Fabian Albert Embran (*promotion*)
	  *July 24, 1961
	  *Akmil 1985
	  *Logistics
	  *August 18, 2015
	  *Control Officer, Babek TNI

	Commodore Sapto Adi
	  *October 22, 1961
	  *AAL 1986
	  *Naval Supply
	  *October 15, 2018
	  *Director for General Affairs, TNI Academy

	Brigadier General Gunawan Pakki
	  *May 4, 1963
	  *Akmil 1986
	  *Army Engineer
	  *July 1, 2019
	  *Commander, TNI Headquarters Detachment

	Air Commodore Sugeng Wiwoho
	  *November 6, 1965
	  *AAU 1988
	  *Air Force Engineer
	  *January 26, 2021
	  *Administration Officer, Directorate for Education, TNI Academy

continued

Position	Commanding Officer (*succession*)
Commander, Military Electronic Communication Unit (Satkomlek) (*Brigadier General, Commodore, Air Commodore*)	Brigadier General Edy Sudarmanto *October 2, 1959 *Akmil 1982 *Electronic communication *August 18, 2015 *Head of Army Information and Data Analysis
	Col. Umaryana Kasma (*promotion*) *August 30, 1959 *Akmil 1986 *Electronic communication *January 15, 2016
	Brigadier General Jumadi *October 10, 1960 *Akmil 1985 *Electronic communication *July 28, 2017 *Head of Security Maintenance Centre, Ministry of Defence
	Brigadier General Budi Prijono *June 16, 1966 *Akmil 1988 *Electronic communication *December 4, 2017 *Head of Army Communication Department
	Air Commodore Judy Sudrajat *November 23, 1965 *AAU 1988 *Electronic communication *June 12, 2019 *Deputy Commander, Satkomlek TNI
Commander, Peace Keeping Center (2007–20: *Brigadier General, Commodore and Air Commodore, 2020–onward: Major General, Rear Admiral and Air Vice-Marshal*)	Brigadier General Achmad Marzuki *February 24, 1967 *Akmil 1989 *Infantry *June 9, 2016 *Commander, Korem 174/ATW Kodam XVII/ Cendrawasih
	Brigadier General Victor Hasudungan Simatupang (*promotion*) *September 7, 1963 *Akmil 1987 *Military Police *March 9, 2018 *Officer, BIN
	Brigadier General Benedictus Benny K *November 29, 1968 *AAU 1990 *Aviators *July 19, 2021 *Deputy Commander, Peace Keeping Center

Position	Commanding Officer (*succession*)
Navy Chief of Staff (*Admiral*)	Vice Admiral Ade Supandi (*promotion*) *May 26, 1960 *AAL 1983 *Seaman *December 30, 2014 *Chief of General Staff
	Vice Admiral Siwi Sukma Adji (promotion) *May 14, 1962 *AAL 1985 *Seaman *May 23, 2018 *TNI Inspector General
	Vice Admiral Yudo Margono (*promotion*) *November 26, 1965 *AAL 1988 *Seaman *May 20, 2020 *Commander, Kogabwilhan I
Deputy Chief of Staff (*Vice Admiral*)	Rear Admiral Didit Herdiawan (*promotion*) *September 13, 1961 *AAL 1984 *Seaman *May 12, 2014 *Assistant for Navy Operation
	Rear Admiral Widodo (*promotion*) *June 30, 1959 *AAL 1983 *Seaman *February 6, 2015 *Commander, Koarmada I
	Rear Admiral Arie Henrycus Sembiring M. (*promotion*) *January 10, 1960 *AAL 1983 *Seaman *February 12, 2016 *Assistant for Navy Planning
	Rear Admiral Achmad Taufiqoerahman (*promotion*) *October 18, 1961 *AAL 1985 *Seaman *January 18, 2017 *Assistant for Navy Planning

continued

Position	Commanding Officer (*succession*)
	Rear Admiral Wuspo Lukito (*promotion*) *October 29, 1961 *AAL 1986 *Seaman *September 24, 2018 *Governor, Naval Academy
	Rear Admiral Mintoro Yulianto (*promotion*) *July 21, 1962 *AAL 1986 *Seaman *September 24,2019 *Commander, Koarmada II
	Rear Admiral Ahmadi Heri Purwono (*promotion*) *October 28, 1965 *AAL 1988 *Seaman *July 27, 2020 *Commander, Koarmada I
Assistant for Navy Personnel (*Rear Admiral, Major General*)	Commodore Djoko Teguh Wahojo (*promotion*) *June 4, 1958 *AAL 1983 *Seaman *February 28, 2014 *Expert Staff, Lemhannas
	Commodore Karma Suta (*promotion*) *August 28, 1960 *AAL 1983 *Seaman *June 9, 2016 *Expert Staff to Navy Chief of Staff
	Commodore I Nyoman Mandra (*promotion*) *November 20, 1962 *AAL 1986 *Seaman *July 31, 2018 *Expert Staff to Navy Chief of Staff
	Rear Admiral Irwan Achmadi *March 13, 1965 *AAL 1988 *Seaman *November 18, 2020 *Commander, Kolinlamil
Assistant for Navy Planning (*Rear Admiral, Major General*)	Rear Admiral Agung Pramono *September 6, 1960 *AAL 1984 *Seaman *May 12, 2014 *Commander, Koarmada II

Position	Commanding Officer (*succession*)
	Rear Admiral Arie Henrycus Sembiring M. *January 10, 1960 *AAL 1983 *Seaman *August 18, 2015 *Assistant for Navy Operation
	Rear Admiral Achmad Taufiqoerahman *October 18, 1961 *AAL 1985 *Seaman *June 9, 2016 *Commander, Koarmada I
	Rear Admiral Tri Wahyudi Sukarno *January 19, 1963 *AAL 1986 *Seaman *February 3, 2017 *Commander, Kodiklatal
	Rear Admiral Arusukmono Indra Sucahyo *November 10, 1962 *AAL 1985 *Seaman *October 27, 2017 *Commander, Seskoal
	Rear Admiral Muhammad Ali *April 9, 1967 *AAL 1989 *Seaman *May 27, 2020 *Commander, Koarmada I
	Rear Admiral Abdul Rasyid Kacong *September 28, 1964 *AAL 1988 *Seaman *August 3, 2021 *Commander, Koarmada I
Assistant for Navy Operation (*Rear Admiral, Major General*)	Rear Admiral Arief Rudianto *January 6, 1957 *AAL 1981 *Seaman *May 12, 2014 *Commander, Koarmada I
	Rear Admiral Arie Henrycus Sembiring M. *January 10, 1960 *AAL 1983 *Seaman *December 30, 2014 *Commander, Koarmada II

continued

Position	Commanding Officer (*succession*)
	Rear Admiral Ari Soedewo *May 1, 1960 *AAL 1983 *Seaman *August 18, 2015 *Coordinator of Expert Staffs to Navy Chief of Staff
	Rear Admiral I. N. G. N. Ary Atmaja *March 22, 1960 *AAL 1984 *Seaman *April 4, 2016 *Commander, Naval Doctrinal Development, Education and Training
	Rear Admiral Aan Kurnia *August 1, 2016 *AAL 1987 *Seaman *April 4, 2016 *Commander, Koarmada I
	Rear Admiral Didik Setiyono *May 2, 1964 *AAL 1987 *Seaman *September 24, 2018 *Commander, Koarmada II
	Rear Admiral Dadi Hartanto *August 30, 1966 *AAL 1988 *Seaman *June 23, 2021 *Commander, Koarmada III
Assistant for Navy Logistics (*Rear Admiral, Major General*)	Commodore Harry Pratomo (*promotion*) *April 17, 1958 *AAL 1983 *Naval Engineer *August 4, 2014 *Deputy Assistant for Navy Logistics
	Commodore Mulyadi (*promotion*) *March 25, 1961 *AAL 1985 *Naval Engineer *February 24, 2016 *Head, Navy Material Aptitude Department

Position	Commanding Officer (*succession*)
	Commodore Moelyanto (*promotion*) *May 12, 1963 *AAL 1986 *Naval Engineer *January 25, 2019 *Head, Naval Research and Development Department
	Commodore Puguh Santoso (*promotion*) *August 11, 1964 *AAL 1988 *Naval Engineer *October 21, 2020 *Deputy Assistant for Navy Logistics
Assistant for Navy Security (*Rear Admiral, Major General*)	Rear Admiral Agus Heryana *October 3, 1959 *AAL 1983 *Seaman *December 30, 2014 *Expert Staff to Navy Chief of Staff
	Commodore Supriatno Irawan (*promotion*) *March 19, 1965 *AAL 1988 *Seaman *October 27, 2017 *Head of Naval Security Department
	Commodore Angkasa Dipua (*promotion*) *March 19, 1965 *AAL 1988 *Naval Electronics *July 6, 2019 *Head of Naval Security Department
Assistant for Maritime Potential (*Rear Admiral, Major General*)	Brigadier General Tommy Basari Natanegara (*promotion*) *July 14, 1959 *AAL 1983 *Marines *August 3, 2016 *Head of Maritime Potential Department
	Brigadier General Gatot Triswanto (*promotion*) *March 3, 1960 *AAL 1985 *Marines *April 25, 2017 *Deputy Assistant for TNI Territorial Affairs

continued

Position	Commanding Officer (*succession*)
	Commodore Edi Sucipto (*promotion*) *August 11, 1965 *AAL 1988 *Seaman *March 2, 2018 *Commander, Lantamal V
	Maj. Gen. Bambang Suswantono *July 25, 1965 *AAL 1987 *Marines *November 29, 2018 *Commander, Marine Corps
	Brigadier General Yuniar Ludfi (*promotion*) *November 9, 1962 *AAL 1986 *Marines *February 2, 2020 *Director, National Counter-Terrorism Agency (BNPT)
	Brigadier General Widodo Dwi Purwanto (*promotion*) *June 26, 1965 *AAL 1987 *Marines *July 27, 2020 *Head, Naval Maritime Potentials Department
Assistant for Naval Electronic Communications (*Rear Admiral, Major General*)	Commodore Atok Dushanto (*promotion*) *August 6, 1964 *AAL 1987 *Seaman *July 31, 2020 *Head, Naval Electronic Communication Department
	Commodore I. N. G. Sudihartawan (*promotion*) *January 19, 1965 *AAL 1987 *Seaman *April 26, 2021 *Commander, Koarmada II
Commander, Naval Doctrinal Development, Education and Training Command (Kodiklatal) (2014–20: *Rear Admiral, Major General; 2020– onward: Vice Admiral, Lieutenant General*)	Rear Admiral I. N. G. N. Arie Atmaja *March 12, 1960 *AAL 1984 *Seaman *September 5, 2014 *Commander, Koarmada I

Position	Commanding Officer (*succession*)
	Rear Admiral Tri Wahyudi Sukarno *January 19, 1963 *AAL 1986 *Seaman *July 25, 2015 *Presidential Military Secretary
	Rear Admiral I. G. Putu Wijamahadi *November 8, 1959 *AAL 1984 *Seaman *February 3, 2017 *Commander, Kolinlamil
	Rear Admiral Dedy Yulianto *December 10, 1961 *AAL 1985 *Seaman *September 24, 2018 *Deputy, Lemhannas
	Rear Admiral Nurhidayat (*promotion*) *December 7, 1965 *AAL 1988 *Seaman *December 27, 2019 *Secretary General, Wantannas
Commander, Naval Command and Staff College (Seskoal) (*Rear Admiral*)	Commodore Herry Setianegara (*promotion*) *July 17, 1958 *AAL 1983 *Seaman *May 19, 2014 *Expert Staff, Lemhannas
	Commodore Arusukmono Indra Sucahyo (*promotion*) *November 10, 1962 *AAL 1985 *Seaman *July 29, 2016 *Inspector for Operation and Training, Kodiklatal
	Commodore Sulistyanto (*promotion*) *October 2, 1961 *AAL 1984 *Seaman *October 27, 2017 *Head of Naval Education Department
	Commodore Amarulla Octavian (*promotion*) *October 24, 1965 *AAL 1988 *Seaman *July 31, 2018 *Dean, Faculty of Defence Management, Defence University

continued

Position	Commanding Officer (*succession*)
	Commodore Iwan Isnurwanto (*promotion*) *November 9, 1965 *AAL 1988 *Seaman *April 9, 2020 *Chief of Staff, Koarmada II
	Rear Admiral Tunggul Suropati *May 21, 1965 *AAL 1988 *Seaman *April 26, 2021 *Governor, Naval Academy
Governor, Naval Academy (AAL) (*Rear Admiral*)	Commodore Achmad Taufiqoerahman (*promotion*) *October 18, 1961 *AAL 1985 *Seaman *April 9, 2014 *Chief of Staff, Koarmada I
	Brigadier General Guntur Irianto Ciptolelono (*promotion*) *December 30, 1961 *AAL 1985 *Marines *October 14, 2014 *Deputy Commander, Paspampres
	Commodore Wuspo Lukito (*promotion*) *September 24, 2018 *AAL 1986 *Seaman *December 22, 2016 *Special Staff to Navy Chief of Staff
	Commodore Muhammad Ali (*promotion*) *April 9, 1967 *AAL 1989 *Seaman *September 24, 2018 *Deputy Assistant for Navy Planning
	Commodore Edi Sucipto (*promotion*) *August 11, 1965 *AAL 1988 *Seaman *January 25, 2019 *Coordinator of Expert Staffs to Navy Chief of Staff

Position	Commanding Officer (*succession*)
	Commodore Tunggul Suropati (*promotion*) *May 21, 1965 *AAL 1988 *Seaman *October 1, 2020 *Deputy Head, TNI Public and Media Relations Centre
	Brigadier General Nur Alamsyah (*promotion*) *October 23, 1967 *AAL 1989 *Marines *April 26, 2021 *Deputy Commander, Marine Corps
Commander, Fleet Command (Koarmada) I or previously known as Western Fleet (*Rear Admiral*)	Rear Admiral I. N. G. N. Arie Atmaja *March 12, 1960 *AAL 1984 *Seaman *May 12, 2014 *Special Staff to Navy Chief of Staff
	Rear Admiral Widodo *June 30, 1959 *AAL 1983 *Seaman *September 5, 2014 *Commander, Kodiklatal
	Rear Admiral Achmad Taufiqoerahman *October 18, 1961 *AAL 1985 *Seaman *February 6, 2015 *Coordinator of Expert Staffs to Navy Chief of Staff
	Rear Admiral Siwi Sukma Adji *May 14, 1962 *AAL 1985 *Seaman *June 9, 2016 *Expert Staff, Lemhannas
	Rear Admiral Aan Kurnia *August 1, 2016 *AAL 1987 *Seaman *August 1, 2016 *Commander, Kolinlamil

continued

Position	Commanding Officer (*succession*)
	Rear Admiral Yudo Margono *November 26, 1965 *AAL 1988 *Seaman *March 2, 2018 *Commander, Kolinlamil
	Rear Admiral Muhammad Ali *April 9, 1967 *AAL 1989 *Seaman *September 24, 2019 *Coordinator of Expert Staffs to Navy Chief of Staff
	Rear Admiral Ahmadi Heri Purwono *October 28, 1965 *AAL 1988 *Seaman *May 26, 2020 *Commander, Kolinlamil
	Rear Admiral Abdul Rasyid Kacong *September 28, 1964 *AAL 1988 *Seaman *July 27, 2020 *Commander, Kolinlamil
	Rear Admiral Arsyad Abdullah *September 14, 1967 *AAL 1990 *Seaman *August 2, 2021 *Commander, Kolinlamil
Commander, Fleet Command II or previously known as Eastern Fleet (*Rear Admiral*)	Rear Admiral Sri Mohamad Darojatim *July 6, 1957 *AAL 1982 *Seaman *May 12, 2014 *Commander, Kolinlamil
	Rear Admiral Arie Henrycus Sembiring M. *January 10, 1960 *AAL 1983 *Seaman *October 31, 2014 *Commander, Kolinlamil
	Rear Admiral Darwanto *September 13, 1961 *AAL 1984 *Seaman *December 30, 2014 *Head of Naval Operation Department

Position	Commanding Officer (*succession*)
	Rear Admiral Didik Setiyono *May 2, 1964 *AAL 1987 *Seaman *October 27, 2017 *Head of Naval Operation Department
	Rear Admiral Mintoro Yulianto *July 21, 1962 *AAL 1986 *Seaman *September 24, 2018 *Expert Staff, Lemhannas
	Rear Admiral Heru Kusmanto *March 31, 1966 *AAL 1988 *Seaman *September 24, 2019 *Commander, Kolinlamil
	Rear Admiral I Nyoman Gede Sudihartawan *January 19, 1965 *AAL 1987 *Seaman *October 1, 2020 *Expert Staff, Lemhannas
	Rear Admiral Iwan Isnurwanto (*promotion*) *November 9, 1965 *AAL 1988 *Seaman *April 26, 2021 *Commander, Seskoal
Commander, Fleet Command III (*Rear Admiral*)	Rear Admiral I Nyoman Gede Ariawan *March 8, 1963 *AAL 1986 *Seaman *May 8, 2018 *Special Staff to Navy Chief of Staff
	Rear Admiral Dadi Hartanto *August 30, 1966 *AAL 1988 *Seaman *May 26, 2020 *Chief of Staff, Kogabwilhan III
	Rear Admiral Irvansyah *May 10, 1968 *AAL 1990 *Seaman *June 23, 2021 *Commander, Kolinlamil

continued

Position	Commanding Officer (*succession*)
Commander, Military Sea Transport Command (Kolinlamil) (*Rear Admiral*)	Commodore Arie Henrycus Sembiring M. (*promotion*) *January 10, 1960 *AAL 1983 *Seaman *May 12, 2014 *Deputy Assistant for Navy Operation
	Commodore Darwanto (*promotion*) *September 13, 1961 *AAL 1984 *Seaman *October 31, 2014 *Deputy Assistant for Navy Operation
	Commodore Aan Kurnia (*promotion*) *July 22, 1965 *AAL 1987 *Seaman *August 1, 2016 *Chief of Staff, Koarmada II
	Commodore I. G. Putu Wijamahadi (*promotion*) *November 8, 1959 *AAL 1984 *Seaman *August 1, 2016 *Deputy Assistant for Navy Operation
	Commodore Agung Prasetiawan (*promotion*) *June 6, 1964 *AAL 1987 *Seaman *February 3, 2017 *Deputy Assistant for Navy Planning
	Commodore Yudo Margono (*promotion*) *November 26, 1965 *AAL 1988 *Seaman *September 28, 2017 *Chief of Staff, Koarmada I
	Commodore R. Achmad Rivai (*promotion*) *October 26, 1965 *AAL 1988 *Seaman *March 2, 2018 *Special Staff to Navy Chief of Staff
	Commodore Heru Kusmanto (*promotion*) *March 31, 1966 *AAL 1988 *Seaman *December 20, 2018 *Chief of Staff, Koarmada I

Position	Commanding Officer (*succession*)
	Commodore Ahmadi Heri Purwono (*promotion*) *October 28, 1965 *AAL 1988 *Seaman *September 24,2019 *Chief of Staff, Koarmada II
	Commodore Abdul Rasyid Kacong (*promotion*) *September 28, 1964 *AAL 1988 *Seaman *May 26, 2020 *Commander, Lantamal I/Medan
	Commodore Irwan Achmadi (*promotion*) *March 13, 1965 *AAL 1988 *Seaman *July 27, 2020 *Commander, Kodikopsla
	Commodore Irvansyah *May 10, 1968 *AAL 1990 *Seaman *November 18, 2020 *Deputy Assistant for Naval Operations to Navy Chief of Staff
	Rear Admiral Arsyad Abdullah *September 14, 1967 *AAL 1990 *Seaman *June 23, 2021 *Chief of Staff, Kogabwilhan III
	Commodore Erwin S. Aldedharma (*promotion*) *May 5, 1970 *AAL 1991 *Seaman *August 2, 2021 *Chief of Staff, Koarmada I
Commander, Marine Corps (*Major General*)	Brigadier General Buyung Lalana (*promotion*) *July 8, 1958 * AAL 1983 *Marines *March 30, 2015 *Commander, Lantamal XI
	Brigadier General Raden Mas Trusono (*promotion*) *October 29, 1960 *Marines *AAL 1985 *June 15, 2016 *Commander, Lantamal III

continued

Position	Commanding Officer (*succession*)
	Maj. Gen. Bambang Suswantono *July 25, 1965 *AAL 1987 *Marines *February 23, 2017 *Commander, Paspampres
	Major General Suhartono *April 15, 1966 *AAL 1988 *Marines *November 29, 2018 *Commander, Paspampres
Air Force Chief of Staff (*Air Chief Marshal*)	Air Marshal Agus Supriatna (*promotion*) *January 28, 1959 *AAU 1983 *Aviators *January 2, 2015 *Chief of General Staff
	Air Marshal Hadi Tjahjanto (*promotion*) *November 8, 1963 *AAU 1986 *Aviators *January 16, 2017 *Inspector General, Defence Ministry
	Air Marshal Yuyu Sutisna (*promotion*) *June 10, 1962 *AAU 1986 *Aviators *January 17, 2018 *Deputy, Air Force Chief of Staff
	Air Marshal Fadjar Prasetyo (*promotion*) *April 9, 1966 *AAU 1988 *Aviators *May 20, 2020 *Commander, Kogabwilhan II
Deputy Chief of Staff (*Air Marshal*)	Air Vice-Marshal Bagus Puruhito (*promotion*) *October 3, 1962 *AAU 1984 *Aviators *May 12, 2014 *Assistant for Air Force Operation
	Air Vice-Marshal Hadiyan Sumintaatmadja (*promotion*) *January 5, 1961 *AAU 1983 *Aviators *November 9, 2015 *Commander, Kohanudnas

Position	Commanding Officer (*succession*)
	Air Vice-Marshal Yuyu Sutisna (*promotion*) *June 10, 1962 *AAU 1986 *Aviators *October 13, 2017 *Commander, Kohanudnas
	Air Vice-Marshal Wieko Syofyan (*promotion*) *April 4, 1964 *AAU 1986 *Aviators *March 2, 2018 *Expert Staff to Air Force Chief of Staff
	Air Vice-Marshal Fahru Zaini Isnanto (*promotion*) *September 19, 1963 *AAU 1986 *Aviators *January 25, 2019 *Assistant for Air Force Planning
	Air Vice-Marshal Agustinus Gustaf Brugman (*promotion*) *December 15, 1965 *AAU 1988 *Aviators *September 13, 2021 *Assistant for TNI Personnel
Assistant for Air Force Personnel (*Air Vice-Marshal*)	Air Vice-Marshal Bambang Samoedro *May 19, 1959 *AAU 1982 *Aviators *October 31, 2014 *Commanding General, TNI Academy
	Air Commodore Yadi Husyadi (*promotion*) *April 3, 1960 *AAU 1982 *Aviators *March 30, 2015 *Deputy, Wantanas
	Air Vice-Marshal Dedy Permadi *April 3, 1963 *AAU 1985 *Aviators *February 2, 2017 *Assistant for Air Force Security

continued

Position	Commanding Officer (*succession*)
	Air Vice-Marshal Anastasius Sumadi *January 20, 1962 *AAU 1984 *Aviators *June 2, 2017 *Expert Staff to TNI Commander
	Air Commodore I Nyoman Trisantosa (*promotion*) *December 20, 1963 *AAU 1988 *Aviators *January 7, 2020 *Deputy Assistant for Air Force Personnel to Air Force Chief of Staff
	Air Commodore Agustinus Gustaf Brugman *December 15, 1965 *AAU 1988 *Aviators *July 27, 2020 *Deputy Assistant for Air Force Personnel to Air Force Chief of Staff
	Air Commodore Elianto Susetio *November 29, 1966 *AAU 1984 *Aviators *April 26, 2021 *Deputy Assistant for TNI General Planing
	Air Vice-Marshal Mawardi *November16, 1958 *AAU 1981 *Aviators *April 18, 2013 *Assistant for Air Force Personnel
	Air Vice-Marshal Mochamad Safi'i (*promotion*) *November 11, 1957 *AAU 1983 *Navigators *March 30, 2015 *Director Defence Force Planning, Defence Ministry
	Air Vice-Marshal Suprianto Basuki (*promotion*) *May 28, 1961 *AAU 1983 *Aviators *December 2, 2015 *Deputy Assistant for Air Force Planning to Air Force Chief of Staff

Position	Commanding Officer (*succession*)
	Air Vice-Marshal Fahru Zaini Isnanto (*promotion*) *September 19, 1963 *AAU 1986 *Aviators *February 2, 2017 *Chief of Staff, Koopsau I
	Air Vice-Marshal Asep Dian Hermawan *November 15, 1962 *AAU 1986 *Aviators *January 25, 2019 *Assistant for Military Communication and Electronics
	Air Vice-Marshal Andyawan Martono (*promotion*) *April 30, 1967 *AAU 1989 *Aviators *May 26, 2020 *Commander, Koopsau II
	Air Vice-Marshal Purwoko Aji Prabowo *January 24, 1971 *AAU 1992 *Aviators *May 25, 2021 *Commander, Koopsau III
Assistant for Air Force Operation (*Air Vice-Marshal*)	Air Vice-Marshal Sudipo Handoyo *August 27, 1953 *AAU 1982 *Aviators *May 12, 2014 *Commander, Seskoau
	Air Vice-Marshal Ida Bagus Anom Manuaba *July 1, 1957 *AAU 1981 *Aviators *September 5, 2018 *Assistant for Air Force Logistics
	Air Vice-Marshal Barhim *May 8, 1960 *AAU 1984 *Aviators *June 15, 2015 *Commander, Koopsau II

continued

Position	Commanding Officer (*succession*)
	Air Vice-Marshal Johannes Berchman Surarso Wijayanto *July 14,1963 *AAU 1986 *Aviators *April 13, 2018 *Commander, Seskoau
	Air Vice-Marshal Umar Sugeng Hariyono *May 30, 1962 *AAU 1986 *Aviators *August 14, 2019 *Coordinator of Expert Staffs to Air Force Chief of Staff
	Air Vice-Marshal Henri Alfiandi *July 24, 1965 *AAU 1988 *Aviators *May 26, 2020 *Commander, Seskoau
	Air Vice-Marshal Muhammad Khairil Lubis *January5, 1968 *AAU 1990 *Aviators *February 23, 2021 *Commander, Kohanudnas
Assistant for Air Force Logistics (*Air Vice-Marshal*)	Air Vice-Marshal Sudipo Handoyo *August 27, 1953 *AAU 1982 *Aviators *September 5, 2014 *Assistant for Air Force Operation
	Air Vice-Marshal Moch. Nurullah *April 6, 1959 *AAU 1983 *Aviators *January 19, 2015 *Commander, Kodiklatau
	Air Vice-Marshal Yadi Husyadi *April 3, 1960 *AAU 1982 *Aviators *February 2, 2017 *Assistant for Air Force Personnel

Position	Commanding Officer (*succession*)
	Air Vice-Marshal Eko Supriyanto *May 28, 1961 *AAU 1983 *Aviators *February 14, 2018 *Coordinator of Expert Staffs to Air Force Chief of Staff
	Air Commodore Abdul Wahab (*promotion*) *August 9, 1962 *AAU 1986 *Air Force Electronics *May 14, 2019 *Head, Air Force Procurement Department
	Air Vice-Marshal Asep Dian Hermawan *November 15, 1962 *AAU 1986 *Aviators *May 26, 2020 *Assistant for Air Force Planning
	Air Commodore Djamaluddin (*promotion*) *November 27, 1963 *AAU 1988 *Aviators *November 27, 2020 *Deputy Assistant for Air Force Personnel
	Air Vice-Marshal M. Fadjar Sumarijadji *January 28, 1967 *AAU 1988 *Aviators *October 25, 2021 *Assistant for Air Force Security
Assistant for Air Force Security (Intelligence) (*Air Vice-Marshal*)	Air Vice-Marshal Zulhasymi (*promotion*) *May 29, 1959 *AAU 1982 *Aviators *March 1, 2013 *Commander, Air Force Police Centre
	Air Vice-Marshal Masmun Yan Manggesa (*promotion*) *April 6, 1958 *AAU 1983 *Air Force Electronics *January 19, 2015 *Deputy Assistant for Air Force Security

continued

Position	Commanding Officer (*succession*)
	Air Vice-Marshal Dedy Permadi *April 3, 1963 *AAU 1985 *Aviators *April 29, 2016 *Governor, Air Force Academy
	Air Commodore Kisenda Wiranatakusumah (*promotion*) *August 1, 1962 *AAU 1986 *Special Corps (Intelligence) *February 2, 2017 *Director D, BAIS TNI
	Air Vice-Marshal Dwi Fajariyanto (*promotion*) *September 25, 1961 *AAU 1985 *Aviators *December 19, 2017 *Deputy Assistant for Air Force Security
	Air Vice-Marshal Tamsil Gustari Malik *May 31, 1963 *AAU 1987 *Aviators *March 19, 2019 *Commander, Koopsau III
	Air Commodore M. Fadjar Sumarijadji (*promotion*) *January 28, 1967 *AAU 1988 *Aviators *October 21, 2020 *Secretary, BAIS TNI
	Air Commodore I Wayan Sulaba (*promotion*) *December 21, 1967 *AAU 1989 *Aviators *October 25, 2021 *Deputy Assistant for Air Force Security
Assistant for Aerospace Potential (*Air Vice-Marshal*)	Air Commodore Umar Sugeng Hariyono (*promotion*) *May 30, 1962 *AAU 1986 *Aviators *August 3, 2016 *Deputy Assistant for Air Force Operation

Position	Commanding Officer (*succession*)
	Air Vice-Marshal Agus Munandar *January 30, 1955 *AAU 1985 *Aviators *August 3, 2016 *Special Staff to Air Force Chief of Staff
	Air Vice-Marshal Iman Sudrajat *November 30, 1961 *AAU 1984 *Aviators *January 25, 2019 *Special Staff to Air Force Chief of Staff
	Air Commodore Nazirsyah (*promotion*) *January 9, 1962 *AAU 1985 *Aviators *June 25, 2019 *Deputy Assistant for Aerospace Potentials
	Air Vice-Marshal Hari Budianto *July 21, 1963 *AAU 1986 *Aviators *January 7, 2020 *Expert Staff to TNI Commander
	Air Vice-Marshal Suparmono *September 24, 1963 *AAU 1988 *Aviators *April 9, 2020 *Expert Staff to TNI Commander
	Air Vice-Marshal Irawan Nurhadi *December 8, 1962 *AAU 1986 *Aviators *June 20, 2020 *Deputy, National Disaster Management Agency (BNPB)
	Air Commodore Kusworo (*promotion*) *February 12, 1967 *AAU 1988 *Aviators *December 28, 2020 *Head, Air Force Operations and Training Department

continued

Position	Commanding Officer (*succession*)
	Air Vice-Marshal Bowo Budiarto *January 16, 1965 *AAU 1989 *Aviators *September 13, 2021 *Commander, Koopsau III
Commander, Air Force Doctrinal Development, Education and Training Command (Kodiklatau) (2013–20: *Air Vice-Marshal;* 2020–onward: *Air Marshal*)	Air Commodore Moch. Nurullah (*promotion*) *April 6, 1959 *AAU 1983 *Aviators *January 23, 2013 *Deputy Assistant for Air Force Operation
	Air Commodore Ras Rendro Bowo (*promotion*) *January 21, 1958 *AAU 1983 *Aviators *January 19, 2015 *Expert Staff to Air Force Chief of Staff
	Air Commodore Eko Supriyanto (*promotion*) *May 28, 1961 *AAU 1983 *Aviators *July 25, 2015 *Head of Air Force Education Department
	Air Commodore Chairil Anwar (*promotion*) *November 28, 1960 *AAU 1986 *Aviators *October 27, 2017 *Head of Air Force Aviation and Work Safety Department
	Air Commodore Andjar Sungkowo (*promotion*) *June 10, 1961 *AAU 1986 *Aviators *September 24, 2018 *Head of Air Force Education Department
	Air Commodore Diyah Yudanardi (*promotion*) *December 13, 1964 *AAU 1988 *Aviators *June 17, 2019 *Deputy Assistant for Air Force Personnel
	Air Vice-Marshal Tatang Harlyansyah (*promotion*) *January 25, 1964 *AAU 1987 *Aviators *September 24,2019 *Governor, Air Force Academy

Position	Commanding Officer (*succession*)
Commander, Air Force Command and Staff College (Seskoau) (*Air Vice-Marshal*)	Air Vice-Marshal Potler Gultom *March 12, 1957 *AAU 1981 *Aviators *May 12, 2014 *Expert Staff, Lemhannas
	Air Commodore Anang Murdianto (*promotion*) *August 10, 1959 *AAU 1983 *Aviators *January 19, 2015 *Head of Air Force Education Department
	Air Vice-Marshal Agus Dwi Putranto *August 27, 1959 *AAU 1983 *Aviators *January 5, 2016 *Commander, Koopsau I
	Air Vice-Marshal Dedy Nitakomara *June1, 1960 *AAU 1983 *Aviators *August 26, 2016 *Expert Staff, Lemhannas
	Air Commodore Johannes Berchman Widjayanto (*promotion*) *July 14,1963 *AAU 1986 *Aviators *August15, 2017 *Vice Governor, Air Force Academy
	Air Vice-Marshal Donny Ermawan Taufanto *December 12, 1965 *AAU 1988 *Aviators *April 13, 2018 *Special Staff to Air Force Chief of Staff
	Air Vice-Marshal Henri Alfiandi *July 24, 1965 *AAU 1988 *Aviators *August 14, 2019 *Commander, Koopsau II

continued

Position	Commanding Officer (*succession*)
	Air Vice-Marshal Samsul Rizal *February 23, 1969 *AAU 1990 *Aviators *May 26, 2020 *Head, Air Force Aviation and Work Safety Center
	Air Commodore Widyargo Ikoputra (*promotion*) *January 6, 1970 *AAU 1992 *Aviators *September 13, 2021 *Chief of Staff, Koopsau II
Governor, Air Force Academy (AAU) (*Air Vice-Marshal*)	Air Commodore Sugihardjo (*promotion*) *April 26, 1958 *AAU 1982 *Aviators *August 4, 2014 *Deputy Assistant for Air Force Personnel
	Air Vice-Marshal Abdul Muis *December 4, 1959 *AAU 1985 *Aviators *March 30, 2015 *Commander, Koopsau II
	Air Commodore Dedy Permadi (*promotion*) *April 3, 1963 *AAU 1985 *Aviators *October 28, 2015 *Commander, Atang Senjaya Airbase
	Air Commodore Iman Sudrajat (*promotion*) *November30, 1961 *AAU 1984 *Aviators *May 2, 2016 *Head of Air Force Personnel Wellbeing Department
	Air Vice-Marshal Tatang Harlyansyah *January 25, 1964 *AAU 1987 *Aviators *September 24, 2018 *Expert Staff to TNI Commander

Position	Commanding Officer (*succession*)
Commander, Air Force Operation Command (Koopsau) I (*Air Vice-Marshal*)	Air Vice-Marshal Nanang Santoso *July 10, 1964 *AAU 1988 *Aviators *September 24,2019 *Expert Staff to TNI Commander
	Air Commodore Agus Dwi Putranto (*promotion*) *August 27, 1959 *AAU 1983 *Aviators *July 15, 2014 *Commander, Air Defence Sector I
	Air Vice-Marshal Yuyu Sutisna *June 10, 1962 *AAU 1986 *Aviators *January5, 2015 *Expert Staff to Air Force Chief of Staff
	Air Commodore Imran Baidirus (*promotion*) *September3, 1964 *AAU 1988 *Aviators *February 23, 2017 *Deputy Assistant for Air Force Operation
	Air Commodore Nanang Santoso (*promotion*) *July 10, 1964 *AAU 1988 *Aviators *December 4, 2017 *Head, Air Force Operation and Training Department
	Air Vice-Marshal Fadjar Prasetyo *April 9, 1966 *AAU 1988 *Aviators *September 24, 2018 *Commander, Koopsau II
	Air Commodore Muhammad Khairil Lubis (*promotion*) *January 5, 1968 *AAU 1990 *Aviators *September 24,2019 *Deputy Assistant for TNI Operations

continued

Position	Commanding Officer (*succession*)
Commander, Koopsau II (*Air Vice-Marshal*)	Air Commodore Tri Bowo Budi Santoso (*promotion*) *November 24, 1965 *AAU 1989 *Aviators *May 26, 2020 *Commander, Silas Papare Air Force Base (Sentani)
	Air Commodore Tedy Rizalihadi (*promotion*) *July 18, 1970 *AAU 1991 *Aviators *February 23, 2021 *Deputy Assistant for TNI Operations
	Air Commodore Abdul Muis (*promotion*) *December 4, 1959 *AAU 1985 *Aviators *February 28, 2014 *Deputy Assistant for Air Force Operation
	Air Commodore Barhim (*promotion*) *May 8, 1960 *AAU 1984 *Aviators *March 30, 2015 *Chief of Staff, Kohanudnas
	Air Commodore Dody Trisunu (*promotion*) *July 19, 1962 *AAU 1986 *Aviators *June 15, 2015 *Chief of Staff, Koopsau II
	Air Commodore Umar Sugeng Hariyono *May 30, 1962 *AAU 1986 *Aviators *October 13, 2016 *Assistant for Aerospace Potential
	Air Commodore Yadi Indrayati Sutanandika (*promotion*) *September 29, 1963 *AAU 1986 *Aviators *April 25, 2017 *Expert Staff to TNI Commander

Position	Commanding Officer (*succession*)
	Air Commodore Fadjar Prasetyo (*promotion*) *April 9, 1966 *AAU 1988 *Aviators *February 14, 2018 *Commander, Halim Perdanakusuma Airbase
	Air Commodore Henri Alfiandi (*promotion*) *July 24, 1965 *AAU 1988 *Aviators *September 24, 2018 *Chief of Staff, Koopsau I
	Air Vice-Marshal Donny Ermawan Taufanto *December 12, 1965 *AAU 1988 *Aviators *August 14, 2019 *Commander, Seskoau
	Air Commodore Minggit Tribowo (*promotion*) *March 9, 1969 *AAU 1991 *Aviators *May 26, 2020 *Special Staff to Air Force Chief of Staff
Commander, Koopsau III (*Air Vice-Marshal*)	Air Commodore Tamsil Gustari Malik (*promotion*) *May 31, 1963 *AAU 1987 *Aviators *May8, 2018 *Head of Air Force Operation and Training Department
	Air Commodore Andyawan Martono Putra *April 30, 1967 *AAU 1989 *Aviators *March 19, 2019 *Chief of Staff, Koopsau I
	Air Vice-Marshal Novyan Samyoga *November 15, 1967 *AAU 1989 *Aviators *May 26, 2020 *TNI Deputy Inspector General

continued

Position	Commanding Officer (*succession*)
	Air Commodore Purwoko Aji Prabowo (*promotion*) *January 24, 1971 *AAU 1992 *Aviators *February 23, 2021 *Commander, Halim Perdanakusuma Airbase
	Air Vice-Marshal Bowo Budiarto *January 16, 1965 *AAU 1989 *Aviators *May 25, 2021 *TNI Deputy Inspector General
	Air Vice-Marshal Samsul Rizal *February 23, 1969 *AAU 1990 *Aviators *September 13, 2021 *Commander, Seskoau
Commander, National Air Defense Command (Kohanudnas) (*Air Vice-Marshal*)	Air Vice-Marshal Abdul Muis *December 4, 1959 *AAU 1985 *Aviators *October 15, 2015 *Governor, Air Force Academy
	Air Vice-Marshal Yuyu Sutisna *June 10, 1962 *AAU 1986 *Aviators *February 23, 2017 *Commander, Koopsau I
	Air Vice-Marshal Imran Baidirus *September 3, 1964 *AAU 1988 *Aviators *December 4, 2017 *Commander, Koopsau I
	Air Vice-Marshal Muhammad Khairil Lubis *January 5, 1968 *AAU 1990 *Aviators *May 26, 2020 *Commander, Koopsau I
	Air Vice-Marshal Novyan Samyoga *November 15, 1967 *AAU 1989 *Aviators *February 23, 2021 *Commander, Koopsau III

Position	Commanding Officer (*succession*)
Commander, Air Force Special Corps (Korpaskas) (*Air Vice-Marshal*)	Air Vice-Marshal Manimbul Manurung *November 13, 1957 *AAU 1981 *Special Force *October 31, 2014 *Expert Staff to TNI Commander
	Air Commodore Adrian Wattimena (*promotion*) *December29, 1959 *AAU 1983 *Special Force *March 30, 2015 *Director, State Intelligence Agency (BIN)
	Air Commodore T. Seto Purnomo (*promotion*) *October 20, 1961 *AAU 1985 *Special Force *November 15, 2016 *Deputy Commander, Korpaskhas
	Air Commodore Eris Widodo Y. (*promotion*) *June 11, 1964 *AAU 1988 *Special Force *October 15, 2018 *Deputy Commander, Korpaskhas Army HQ
Army Chief of Staff (*General*)	Lt. Gen. Gatot Nurmantyo (*promotion*) *March 13, 1960 *Akmil 1982 *Infantry *July 21, 2014 *Commander, Kostrad
	Lt. Gen. Mulyono (*promotion*) *March 13, 1960 *Akmil 1983 *Infantry *July 15, 2015 *Commander, Kostrad
	Lt. Gen. Andika Perkasa (*promotion*) *December 21, 1964 *Akmil 1987 *Infantry *November 22, 2018 *Commander, Kostrad
	Lt. Gen. Dudung Abdurrachman (*promotion*) *November 19, 1965 *Akmil 1988 *Infantry *November 17, 2021 *Commander, Kostrad

continued

Position	Commanding Officer (*succession*)
Deputy Chief of Staff (*Lieutenant General*)	Major General M. Erwin Syafitri (*promotion*) *April 9, 1959 *Akmil 1982 *Infantry *July 25, 2015 *Head of BAIS TNI
	Major General Hinsa Siburian (*promotion*) *October 28, 1959 *Akmil 1986 *Infantry *April 25, 2017 *Commander, Kodam XVII/Cendrawasih
	Major General Tatang Sulaiman (*promotion*) *April 1, 1962 *Akmil 1986 *Infantry *October 27, 2017 *Commander, Kodam IV/Diponegoro
	Major General Mochamad Fachrudin (*promotion*) *November14, 1962 *Akmil 1985 *Infantry *April 22, 2020 *Assistant for Army Operation
	General Andika Perkasa (*temporary replacement*) *December 21, 1964 *Akmil 1987 *Infantry *December 28, 2020 *Army Chief of Staff
	Major General Bakti Agus Fadjari (*promotion*) *August 1, 1964 *Akmil 1987 *Infantry *March 5, 2021 *Commander, Kodam IV/Diponegoro
Commander, Army Strategic Command (Kostrad) (*Lieutenant General*)	Major General Mulyono (*promotion*) *January 12, 1961 *Akmil 1983 *Infantry *September 5, 2014 *Commander, Kodam Jaya

Position	Commanding Officer (*succession*)
	Major General Edy Rahmayadi (*promotion*) *March 10, 1961 *Akmil 1985 *Infantry *July 25, 2015 *Commander, Kodam I/Bukit Barisan
	Lt. Gen. Agus Kriswanto *July 10, 1960 *Akmil 1984 *Infantry *January 4, 2018 *Commander, Kodiklatad
	Lt. Gen. Andika Perkasa *December 21, 1964 *Akmil 1987 *Infantry *July 13, 2018 *Commander, Kodiklatad
	Major General Besar Harto Karyawan (*promotion*) *May 31, 1963 *Akmil 1986 *Infantry *November 29, 2018 *Commander, Kodam III/Siliwangi
	Major General Eko Margiyono (*promotion*) *May 12, 1967 *Akmil 1989 *Infantry *July 27, 2020 *Commander, Kodam Jaya
	Major General Dudung Abdurachman (*promotion*) *November 19, 1965 *Akmil 1988 *Infantry *May 25, 2021 *Commander, Kodam Jaya
Commander, Army Doctrinal Development, Education and Training Command (Kodiklatad) (*Lieutenant General*)	Major General Agus Sutomo (*promotion*) *April 14, 1960 *Akmil 1984 *Infantry *July 25, 2015 *Commander, Kodam Jaya

continued

Position	Commanding Officer (*succession*)
	Major General Agus Kriswanto (*promotion*) *July 10, 1960 *Akmil 1984 *Infantry *January 26, 2016 *Commander, Kodam Iskandar Muda
	Major General Andika Perkasa (*promotion*) *March 13, 1960 *Akmil 1987 *Infantry *January 4, 2018 *Commander, Kodam XII/Tanjungpura
	Major General Anto Mukti Putranto (*promotion*) *February26, 1964 *Akmil 1987 *Infantry *July 13, 2018 *Commander, Kodam II/Sriwijaya
Assistant for Army Personnel (*Major General*)	Brigadier General Jaswandi (*promotion*) *March 12, 1960 *Akmil 1985 *Infantry *November8, 2013 *Chief of Staff, Kodam XIV/Hasanuddin
	Brigadier General Heboh Susanto (*promotion*) *December 4, 1962 *Akmil 1985 *Air Defence Artillery *July 25, 2015 *Commander, Air Defence Artillery Centre Kodiklatad
	Brigadier General Sonhadji (*promotion*) *December 29, 1961 *Akmil 1984 *Field Artillery *February 5, 2016 *Deputy Commander, Seskoad
	Brigadier General Subiyanto (*promotion*) *March 11, 1963 *Akmil 1988 *Infantry *March 27, 2017 *Chief of Staff, Kodam VI/Mulawarman
	Brigadier General Heri Wiranto (*promotion*) *November 23, 1967 *Akmil 1989 *Infantry *March 29, 2018 *Deputy Assistant for Military Personnel

Position	Commanding Officer (*succession*)
	Brigadier General Mulyo Aji (*promotion*) *July 28, 1964 *Akmil 1987 *Infantry *July 27, 2020 *Head, Army Research and Development Department (Dislitbangad)
	Major General Wawan Ruswandi *March 8, 1964 *Akmil 1987 *Cavalry *May 25, 2021 *Commander, Pussenkav TNI AD
Assistant for Army Planning (*Major General*)	Brigadier General Dominicus Agus Riyanto (*promotion*) *August 19, 1961 *Akmil 1985 *Combat Engineer *December 31, 2015 *Director for Programme and Budget Planning, Defence Ministry
	Brigadier General Hassanudin (*promotion*) *September 7, 1965 *Akmil 1989 *Air Defence Artillery *July 24, 2019 *Chief of Staff, Kodam I/Bukit Barisan
	Brigadier General Hendrasto Joko Saksono (*promotion*) *December 24, 1963 *Akmil 1988 *Infantry *March 31, 2020 *Secretary, Directorate Generale for Defence Power, Defence Ministry
Assistant for Army Operations (*Major General*)	Major General Sonny Widjaja *January 1, 1958 *Akmil 1982 *Infantry *March 21, 2014 *Coordinator of Expert Staffs to Army Chief of Staff
	Brigadier General Hinsa Siburian (*promotion*) *October 28, 1959 *Akmil 1986 *Infantry *August 15, 2014 *Chief of Staff, Kodam XVII/Cendrawasih

continued

Position	Commanding Officer (*succession*)
	Brigadier General Johny L. Tobing (*promotion*) *December 15, 1960 *Akmil 1983 *Infantry *September 5, 2014 *Director of Doctrine, Kodiklatad
	Brigadier General George Elnadus Supit (*promotion*) *July 22, 1962 *Akmil 1985 *Infantry *June 9, 2016 *Chief of Staff, Kodam VI/Mulawarman
	Major General Sudirman *March 5, 1963 *Akmil 1986 *Infantry *April 25, 2017 *Commander, Kodam II/Sriwijaya
	Major General Mochamad Fachrudin *November 14, 1962 *Akmil 1985 *Infantry *March 9, 2018 *Commander, Kodam Iskandar Muda
	Major General Surawahadi *March 26, 1963 *Akmil 1985 *Infantry *April 22, 2020 *Expert Staff Coordinator to Army Chief of Staff
	Major General Eka Wiharsa *September 11, 1963 *Akmil 1986 *Infantry *March 24, 2021 *Deputy Commander, Kodiklatad
	Major General Ainurrahman *July 4, 1965 *Akmil 1988 *Infantry *September 13, 2021 *Chief of Staff, Kostrad

Position	Commanding Officer (*succession*)
Assistant for Army Training (*Major General*)	Brigadier General Harianto (*promotion*) *January 1, 1965 *Akmil 1987 *Infantry *April 9, 2020 *Director for Training, Kodiklat TNI AD
Assistant for Army Logistics (*Major General*)	Brigadier General Suratmo (*promotion*) *April 24, 1958 *Akmil 1982 *Combat Engineer *September 22, 2014 *Special Staff to TNI Commander
	Brigadier General Gadang Pambudi (*promotion*) *September 4, 1959 *Akmil 1984 *Infantry *April 29, 2016 *Deputy Assistant for Military Logistics
	Brigadier General Irwan (*promotion*) *June 10, 1963 *Akmil 1987 *Combat Engineer *March 8, 2017 *Director of Combat Engineer
	Brigadier General Jani Iswanto (*promotion*) *January 25, 1964 *Akmil 1987 *Logistics (Material) *July 13, 2018 *Special Staff, Army Chief of Staff
	Brigadier General Saiful Rachiman (*promotion*) *August 2, 1965 *Akmil 1988 *Logistics (Material) *September 13, 2021 *Deputy Assistant for Army Logistics
Assistant for Army Security Affairs (*Major General*)	Brigadier General Yayat Sudrajat (*promotion*) *June 15, 1959 *Akmil 1982 *Infantry *October 10, 2014 *Director of Counterterrorism, BIN
	Brigadier General Ibnu Darmawan (*promotion*) *July 16, 1958 *Akmil 1983 *Infantry *July 25, 2015 *General Inspector, Army Inspector General

continued

Position	Commanding Officer (*succession*)

	Major General Rudy Yulius Huliselan
	  *February 17, 1959
	  *Akmil 1983
	  *Infantry
	  *June 4, 2016
	  *Expert Staff to TNI Commander

	Brigadier General Ilyas Alamsyah (*promotion*)
	  *April 11, 1966
	  *Akmil 1988
	  *Infantry
	  *February 23, 2017
	  *Chief of Staff, Kodam Jaya

	Major General Muhammad Nur Rahmad (*promotion*)
	  *November 25, 1965
	  *Akmil 1988
	  *Infantry
	  *October 27, 2017
	  *Chief of Staff, Kodam VI/Mulawarman

	Major General Santos Gunawan Matondang
	  *June 12, 1963
	  *Akmil 1987
	  *Infantry
	  *August 14, 2019
	  *Deputy Commander, TNI Academy

	Major General Widodo Iryansyah
	  *October 27, 1962
	  *Akmil 1987
	  *Infantry
	  *January 9, 2020
	  *Expert Staff Coordinator to Army Chief of Staff

	Major General Teguh Arief Indratmoko
	  *September 19, 1965
	  *Akmil 1988
	  *Infantry
	  *April 22, 2020
	  *Commander, Kodam Iskandar Muda

	Brigadier General Bambang Ismawan (*promotion*)
	  *July 31, 1966
	  *Akmil 1988
	  *Infantry
	  *May 25, 2021
	  *Deputy Commander, Pusterad

	Major General Suko Pranoto
	  *June 30, 1964
	  *Akmil 1987
	  *Infantry
	  *August 2, 2021
	  *Deputy Army Inspector General

Position	Commanding Officer (*succession*)
Assistant for Army Territorial Affairs (*Major General*)	Brigadier General Wiyarto (*promotion*) *October 3, 1959 *Akmil 1985 *Infantry *May 2, 2014 *Director for Operation and Education, Lemhannas
	Brigadier General Kustanto Widiatmoko (*promotion*) *March 16, 1965 *Akmil 1987 *Cavalry *January 19, 2015 *Chief of Staff, Kodam V/Brawijaya
	Brigadier General Komaruddin Simanjuntak (*promotion*) *January 10, 1960 *Akmil 1985 *Infantry *May 4, 2016 *Chief of Staff, Kodam II/Sriwijaya
	Brigadier General Widagdo H. Sukoco (*promotion*) *March 1, 1961 *Akmil 1983 *Combat Engineer *March 31, 2017 *Deputy Assistant for Army Logistics
	Brigadier General Supartodi (*promotion*) *April 17, 1964 *Akmil 1985 *Infantry *October 27, 2017 *Chief of Staff, Kodam XIV/Hasanuddin
	Brigadier General Bhakti Agus Fadjari (*promotion*) *January 8, 1964 *Akmil 1987 *Infantry *January 25, 2019 *Special Staff to Army Chief of Staff
	Major General Nurchahyanto *December 25, 1964 *Akmil 1987 *Air Defence Artillery *18 June 2020 *Expert Staff, Lemhannas

continued

Position	Commanding Officer (*succession*)
Commander, Army Command and Staff College (Seskoad) (*Major General*)	Brigadier General Agung Risdhianto (*promotion*) *April 22, 1961 *Akmil 1985 *Infantry *December 2, 2013 *Chief of Staff, Kodam Jaya
	Brigadier General Pratimun (*promotion*) *January 11, 1958 *Akmil 1982 *Infantry *January 25, 2015 *Deputy Commander, Seskoad
	Major General Dody Usodo Hargo S. *March 5, 1961 *Akmil 1984 *Infantry *November 23, 2016 *Special Staff to TNI Commander
	Major General Kurnia Dewantara *November 22, 1962 *Akmil 1980 *Infantry *January 4, 2018 *Deputy Commander, Seskoad
	Major General Anton Nugroho *September 27, 1966 *Akmil 1988 *Infantry *June 18, 2020 *Expert Staff, Lemhannas
Governor, Military Academy (Akmil) (*Major General*)	Major General Hartomo (*promotion*) *March 1, 1963 *Akmil 1986 *Infantry *July 25, 2015 *Commander, Army Intelligence Centre, Kodiklatad
	Brigadier General Arif Rahman (*promotion*) *April 22, 1966 *Akmil 1988 *Infantry *September 16, 2016 *Deputy Assistant for General Planning
	Brigadier General Eko Margiyono (*promotion*) *May 12, 1967 *Akmil 1989 *Infantry *October 27, 2017 *Chief of Staff, Kodam Jaya

Position	Commanding Officer (*succession*)
	Brigadier General Eka Wiharsa (*promotion*) *September 7, 1963 *Akmil 1986 *Infantry *March 2, 2018 *Director of Education, Kodiklatad
	Brigadier General Dudung Abdurachman (*promotion*) *November 19, 1965 *Akmil 1988 *Infantry *September 24, 2018 *Deputy Assistant for Army Territorial Affairs
	Brigadier General Totok Imam Santoso (*promotion*) *May 30, 1968 *Akmil 1989 *Field Artillery *July 27, 2020 *Head, TNI Center for Strategic Studies (Pusjianstra TNI)
	Brigadier General Candra Wijaya (*promotion*) *October 19, 1969 *Akmil 1991 *Air Defence Artillery *March 24, 2021 *Chief of Staff, Kodam IX/Udayana
	Brigadier General Robertus Legowo W. R. Jatmiko (*promotion*) *July 13, 1967 *Akmil 1988 *Infantry *December 6 2021 *Commander, Korem 161/Wira Sakti
Commander, Army's Territorial Centre (Pusterad) (Before 2020: *Major General; 2020–onward: Lieutenant General*)	Major General Meris Wiryadi *December 11, 1958 *Akmil 1983 *Infantry *January 19, 2015 *Commander, Kodam XIV/Hasanuddin
	Major General Agung Risdhianto *April 22, 1961 *Akmil 1985 *Infantry *September 10, 2015 *Deputy Commander, Kodiklatad

continued

Position	Commanding Officer (*succession*)
	Major General Heboh Susanto *December 4, 1962 *Akmil 1985 *Air Defence Artillery *February 5, 2016 *Assistant for Army Personnel
	Major General Purwadi Mukson *February 21, 1959 *Akmil 1982 *Cavalry *June 9, 2016 *Commander, Kodam II/Sriwijaya
	Major General Hadi Prasojo *November 17, 1959 *Akmil 1983 *Air Defence Artillery *February 24, 2017 *Commander, Kodam III/Siliwangi
	Major General Hartomo *March 1, 1963 *Akmil 1986 *Infantry *October 27, 2017 *Head of BAIS TNI
	Major General Arif Rahman *April 22, 1966 *Akmil 1988 *Infantry *January 25, 2019 *Commander, Kodam V/Brawijaya
	Major General Joppye Onesimus Wayangkau (*promotion*) *July 17, 1962 *Akmil 1986 *Infantry *April 30, 2020 *Commander, Kodam XVIII/Kasuari
	Lieutenant General R. Wisnoe Prasetija Boedi *January 5, 1964 *Akmil 1986 *Infantry *August 26, 2020 *Expert Staff Coordinator to Army Chief of Staff
	Major General Teguh Arief Indratmoko (*promotion*) *September 19, 1965 *Akmil 1988 *Infantry *May 25, 2021 *Assistant for Army Security

Position	Commanding Officer (*succession*)
Commander, Army Intelligence Centre (Pusintelad) (*Brigadier General*)	Col. Hartomo (*promotion*) *March 1, 1963 *Akmil 1986 *Infantry *December 3, 2013 *Commander, Army Officer Cadet School
	Col. Herianto Syahputra (*promotion*) *January 2, 1968 *Akmil 1990 *Infantry *July 25, 2015 *Commander, Korem 132/Tadulako Kodam XIV/Hasanuddin
	Col. Djaka Budhi Utama (*promotion*) *September 11, 1967 *Akmil 1990 *Infantry *October 27, 2017 *Middle-ranking officer, Army HQ Detachment
	Brigadier General Sonny Aprianto *September 4, 1969 *Akmil 1990 *Infantry *November 29, 2018 *Commander, Korem 031/Wirabuana Kodam I/Bukit Barisan
	Brigadier General Sudarji *February 13, 1965 *Akmil 1988 *Infantry *March 24, 2021 *Deputy Assistant for Army Security
Commander, Army Infantry Center (Pussenif TNI AD) (Before 2020: *Major General*; 2020–onward: *Lieutenant General*)	Major General Winston Simanjuntak *June 12, 1957 *Akmil 1981 *Infantry *January 30, 2014 *Assistant for Army Security
	Major General Hinsa Siburian *October 28, 1959 *Akmil 1986 *Infantry *September 5, 2014 *Assistant for Army Operation

continued

Position	Commanding Officer (*succession*)
	Major General Prihadi Agus Irianto *June 1, 1959 *Akmil 1982 *Infantry *August 18, 2015 *Special Staff to Army Chief of Staff
	Brigadier General Surawahadi (*promotion*) *March 26, 1963 *Akmil 1985 *Infantry *October 10, 2016 *Inspector, Kodiklat TNI
	Brigadier General Tri Soewandono (*promotion*) *December 21, 1963 *Akmil 1986 *Infantry *July 13, 2018 *Chief of Staff, Kodam XIV/Hasanuddin
	Brigadier General Teguh Pudjo Rumekso (*promotion*) *April 20, 1968 *Akmil 1991* *Infantry *November 29, 2018 *Chief of Staff, Kodam VI/Mulawarman
	Lieutenant General Besar Harto Karyawan *May 31, 1963 *Akmil 1986 *Infantry *July 27, 2020 *Commander, Kostrad
	Major General Arif Rahman (*promotion*) *April 22, 1966 *Akmil 1988 *Infantry *January 26, 2021 *Expert Staff to Army Chief of Staff
Commander, Army Aviation Centre (Pusnerbad) (Before 2016: *Brigadier General* 2016–onward: *Major General*)	Col. Benny Susianto (*promotion*) *December 10, 1963 *Akmil 1987 *Infantry *January 30, 2014 *Middle-ranking officer, Army HQ Detachment
	Brigadier General Suko Pranoto (*promotion*) *June 30, 1964 *Akmil 1987 *Infantry *June 9, 2016 *Head of Binda South Kalimantan

Position	Commanding Officer (*succession*)
	Brigadier General Besar Harto Karyawan (*promotion*) *May 31, 1963 *Akmil 1986 *Infantry *October 27, 2017 *Inspector, Kostrad
	Brigadier General Stephanus Tri Mulyono (*promotion*) *September 3, 1963 *Akmil 1986 *Infantry *March 19, 2018 *Chief of Staff, Kodam IX/Udayana
	Major General Teguh Pudjo Rumekso *April 20, 1968 *Akmil 1991 *Infantry *November 29, 2018 *Commander, Pussenif TNI AD
	Brigadier General Bueng Wardadi (*promotion*) *June 24, 1964 *Akmil 19867 *Cavalry *October 25, 2021 *Deputy Commander, Puspenerbad
Commander, Army Cavalry Center (Pussenkav TNI AD) (Before 2020: *Brigadier-General* 2020–onward: *Major General*)	Col. Anang Dwitono (*promotion*) *July 22, 1962 *Akmil 1985 *Cavalry *August 18, 2015 *Director of Education, Seskoad
	Col. Ana Supriatna (*promotion*) *April 16, 1963 *Akmil 1987 *Cavalry *March 7, 2017 *Deputy Commander, Pussenkav TNI AD
	Brigadier General Wawan Ruswandi (*promotion*) *March 8, 1964 *Akmil 1987 *Cavalry *May 25, 2021 *Director for Research, Kodiklatad

continued

Position	Commanding Officer (*succession*)
	Major General Sulaiman Agusto *August 11, 1966 *Akmil 1988 *Cavalry *June 23, 2021 *Expert Staff, Lemhannas
	Major General Gunung Iskandar *January 1, 1967 *Akmil 1989 *Cavalry *September 19, 2021 *Expert Staff, Lemhannas
Commander, Army Field Artillery Center (Pussenarmed) (*Brigadier General*) (Before 2020: *Brigadier-General* 2020–onward: *Major General*)	Col. Yudi Satriyono (*promotion*) *March 10, 1959 *Akmil 1983 *Field Artillery *September 10, 2015 *Middle-ranking officer to Expert Staff of Army Chief of Staff
	Col. Dwi Jati Utomo (*promotion*) *August 5, 1965 *Akmil 1988 *Field Artillery *March 1, 2017 *Deputy Commander, Pussenarmed
	Col. Purbo Prastowo (*promotion*) *October 5, 1966 *Akmil 1989 *Field Artillery *February 27, 2019 *Middle-ranking officer, Army HQ Detachment
	Brigadier General Dwi Jati Utomo (*promotion*) *August 5, 1965 *Akmil 1988 *Field Artillery *April 9, 2020 *Chief of Staff, Kodam III/Siliwangi
	Brigadier General Totok Imam Santoso (*promotion*) *May 30, 1968 *Akmil 1989 *Field Artillery *March 24, 2021 *Governor, Military Academy
Commander, Army Anti-Air Artillery Center (Pussenarhanud) (*Brigadier General*)	Brigadier General Heboh Susanto *December 4, 1962 *Akmil 1985 *Air Defence Artillery *December 30, 2014 *Director of Economic Research, Lemhannas

Position	Commanding Officer (*succession*)
	Col. Nurchahyanto (*promotion*) *December 25, 1965 *Akmil 1987 *Air Defence Artillery *July 25, 2015 *Commander, Korem 163/WS Kodam IX/ Udayana
	Col. Toto Nugroho (*promotion*) *June 3, 1966 *Akmil 1989 *Air Defence Artillery *April 13, 2018 *Inspector, Kodam Jaya
	Brigadier General Nisan Setiadi (*promotion*) *October 1, 1965 *Akmil 1988 *Air Defence Artillery *April 9, 2020 *Expert Staff, Lemhannas
Commander, Infantry Division-1, Kostrad	Brigadier General Fransen G. Siahaan (*promotion*) *May 27, 1958 *Akmil 1983 *Infantry *March 21, 2014 *Secretary of General Director for Defence Capability, Defence Minister
	Brigadier General Edy Rahmayadi (*promotion*) *March 10, 1961 *Akmil 1985 *Infantry *September 17, 2014 *Director for Strengthening State Defence, Lemhannas
	Brigadier General Lodewyk Pusung (*promotion*) *September 27, 1960 *Akmil 1985 *Infantry *January 19, 2015 *Chief of Staff, Kodam VI/Mulawarman
	Brigadier General Sudirman (*promotion*) *March 5, 1963 *Akmil 1986 *Infantry *August 18, 2015 *Vice Governor, Military Academy

continued

Position	Commanding Officer (*succession*)
	Brigadier General Anto Mukti Putranto (*promotion*) *February 26, 1964 *Akmil 1987 *Infantry *June 9, 2016 *Commander, Peacekeeping Centre
	Brigadier General Ainurrahman (*promotion*) *July 4, 1965 *Akmil 1988 *Infantry *April 25, 2017 *Chief of Staff, Kodam VI/Mulawarman
	Major General Agus Rohman (*promotion*) *August 15, 1953 *Akmil 1988 *Infantry *March 23, 2018 *Head of Army Physical Fitness Department
	Brigadier General Dedy Kusmayadi (*promotion*) *May 1, 1964 *Akmil 1987 *Infantry *July 27, 2020 *Inspector, Kostrad
Commander, Infantry Division-2, Kostrad (*Major General*)	Brigadier General Agus Kriswanto (*promotion*) *July 10, 1960 *Akmil 1984 *Infantry *July 15, 2013 *Chief of Staff, Kodam IV/Diponegoro
	Brigadier General Bambang Haryanto (*promotion*) *October 8, 1959 *Akmil 1984 *Infantry *May 19, 2014 *Commander, Korem 174/ATW Kodam XVII/ Cendrawasih
	Brigadier General Ganip Warsito (*promotion*) *November 23, 1963 *Akmil 1986 *Infantry *August 18, 2015 *Director of Training, Kodiklatad

Position	Commanding Officer (*succession*)
	Brigadier General Benny Susianto (*promotion*) *December 10, 1963 *Akmil 1987 *Infantry *June 9, 2016 *Commander, Puspenerbad
	Brigadier General Agus Suhardi (*promotion*) *July 24, 1965 *Akmil 1988 *Infantry *April 25, 2017 *Chief of Staff, Kodam V/Brawijaya
	Brigadier General Marga Taufik (*promotion*) *April 17, 1964 *Akmil 1987 *Infantry *March 23, 2018 *Chief of Staff, Kodam II/Sriwijaya
	Brigadier General Tri Yuniarto (*promotion*) *June 15, 1968 *Akmil 1989 *Infantry *December 20, 2018 *Director of Doctrine, Kodiklatad
	Brigadier General Andi Muhammad (*promotion*) *August 7, 1964 *Akmil 1988 *Infantry *April 12, 2021 *Chief of Staff, Kodam XIV/Hasanuddin
Commander, Infantry Division-3, Kostrad (*Major General*)	Major General Achmad Marzuki *February 24, 1967 *Akmil 1989 *Infantry *May 8, 2018 *Expert Staff, Lemhannas
	Brigadier General Wanti Waranei Franky Mamahit (*promotion*) *December 20, 1963 *Akmil 1987 *Infantry *April 9, 2020 *Director, Lemhannas

continued

Position	Commanding Officer (*succession*)
	Brigadier General Kunto Arief Wibowo (*promotion*) *December 20, 1963 *Akmil 1992 *Infantry *July 7, 2021 *Chief of Staff, Kodam III/Siliwangi
Commander General, Army Special Forces Command (Kopassus) (*Major General*)	Major General Doni Monardo *May 10, 1963 *Akmil 1985 *Infantry *September 5, 2014 *Commander, Paspampres
	Brigadier General Muhamad Herindra (*promotion*) *October 20, 1964 *Akmil 1987 *Infantry *July 25, 2015 *Chief of Staff, Kodam III/Siliwangi
	Brigadier General Madsuni (*promotion*) *February 14, 1964 *Akmil 1988 *Infantry *September 16, 2016 *Deputy Commander, Kopassus
	Major General Eko Margiyono *May 12, 1967 *Akmil 1989 *Infantry *March 2, 2018 *Governor, Military Academy
	Major General I Nyoman Cantiasa *June 26, 1967 *Akmil 1990 *Infantry *January 25, 2019 *Expert Staff to TNI Commander
	Brigadier General Mohamad Hasan (*promotion*) *March 13, 1971 *Akmil 1993 *Infantry *August 26, 2020 *Deputy Commander, Kopassus

Position	Commanding Officer (*succession*)
Commander, Military Region (Kodam) I/Bukit Barisan (*Major General*)	Major General Istu Hari Subagio *November 13, 1958 *Akmil 1983 *Infantry *November 8, 2013 *Assistant for Army Personnel
	Major General Winston Simanjuntak *June 12, 1957 *Akmil 1981 *Infantry *September 5, 2014 *Commander, Pussenif TNI AD
	Major General Edy Rahmayadi *March 10, 1961 *Akmil 1985 *Infantry *January 19, 2015 *Commander, Infantry Division-1, Kostrad
	Major General Lodewyk Pusung *September 27, 1960 *Akmil 1985 *Infantry *August 18, 2015 *Chief of Staff, Kodam VI/Mulawarman
	Major General Cucu Sumantri *November 5, 1961 *Akmil 1984 *Infantry *February 22, 2017 *Expert Staff, Lemhannas
	Major General Ibnu Triwidodo *November 9, 1961 *Akmil 1981 *Infantry *March 9, 2018 *Expert Staff, Lemhannas
	Major General Mohamad Sabrar Fadhilah *August 10, 1965 *Akmil 1988 *Infantry *July 31, 2018 *Head, TNI Public and Media Relations Centre
	Major General Irwansyah *November 10, 1962 *Akmil 1985 *Infantry *June 18, 2020 *Expert Staff, BIN

continued

Position	Commanding Officer (*succession*)
	Brigadier General Hassanudin (*promotion*) *September 7, 1965 *Akmil 1989 *Air Defence Artillery *November 18, 2020 *Commander, Kodam Iskandar Muda
Commander, Kodam II / Sriwijaya (*Major General*)	Major General Iskandar H. Sahil *February 7, 1959 *Akmil 1982 *Infantry *October 31, 2014 *Special Staff to Panglima TNI
	Major General Purwadi Mukson *February 21, 1959 *Akmil 1982 *Cavalry *July 25, 2015 *Deputy Commander, Kodiklatad
	Major General Sudirman *March 5, 1963 *Akmil 1986 *Infantry *June 9, 2016 *Commander, Infantry Division-1, Kostrad
	Major General Anto Mukti Putranto *February 26, 1964 *Akmil 1987 *Infantry *April 25, 2017 *Commander, Infantry Division-1, Kostrad
	Major General Irwan Zaini *June 10, 1963 *Akmil 1987 *Combat Engineer *July 13, 2018 *Assistant for Army Operation
	Major General Agus Suhardi *July 24, 1965 *Akmil 1988 *Infantry *July 27, 2020 *Special Staff to Army Chief of Staff
Commander, Kodam III / Siliwangi (*Major General*)	Major General Hadi Prasojo *November 17, 1959 *Akmil 1983 *Air Defence Artillery *August 18, 2015 *Special Staff to TNI Commander

Position	Commanding Officer (*succession*)
	Major General Muhamad Herindra *October 28, 1964 *Akmil 1987 *Infantry *September 16, 2016 *Commander, Kopassus
	Major General Doni Monardo *May 10, 1963 *Akmil 1985 *Infantry *October 27, 2017 *Commander, Kodam XIII/Merdeka
	Major General Besar Harto Karyawan *May 31, 1963 *Akmil 1986 *Infantry *March 19, 2018 *Commander, Puspenerbad
	Major General Tri Soewandono *December 21, 1963 *Akmil 1986 *Infantry *November 29, 2018 *Commander, Pussenif TNI AD
	Major General Nugroho Budi Wiryanto *March 23, 1964 *Akmil 1987 *Infantry *October 31, 2019 *Deputy, National Search and Rescue Agency (BASARNAS)
	Major General Agus Subiyanto *August 5, 1967 *Akmil 1991 *Infantry *August 2, 2021 *Commander, Pussenif TNI AD
Commander, Kodam IV / Diponegoro (*Major General*)	Major General Bayu Purwiyono *September 16, 1959 *Akmil 1982 *Infantry *September 22, 2014 *Assistant for Army Logistics
	Major General Jaswandi *March 12, 1960 *Akmil 1985 *Infantry *July 25, 2015 *Assistant for Army Personnel

continued

Position	Commanding Officer (*succession*)
	Major General Tatang Sulaiman *April 1, 1962 *Akmil 1986 *Infantry *March 31, 2017 *Commander, Kodam Iskandar Muda
	Major General Wuryanto *July 4, 1961 *Akmil 1986 *Infantry *October 27, 2017 *Head of TNI Public and Media Relations Centre
	Major General Mochamad Effendi *October 20, 1962 *Akmil 1986 *Combat Engineer *November 29, 2018 *Expert Staff to TNI Commander
	Major General Bakti Agus Fadjari (*promotion*) *August 1, 1964 *Akmil 1987 *Infantry *June 18, 2020 *Assistant for Army Territorial Affairs
	Major General Rudianto *March 7, 1967 *Akmil 1989 *Infantry *February 23, 2021 *Deputy, Coordinating Ministry for Political, Legal, and Security Affairs
Commander, Kodam V / Brawijaya (*Major General*)	Major General Eko Wiratmoko *October 18, 1958 *Akmil 1982 *Infantry *May 2, 2014 *Commander, Kodam XVI/Pattimura
	Major General Sumardi *February 20, 1959 *Akmil 1984 *Infantry *July 25, 2015 *Governor, Military Academy
	Major General I Made Sukadana *March 30, 1959 *Akmil 1982 *Combat Engineer *June 9, 2016 *Head, Baranahan, Ministry of Defense

Position	Commanding Officer (*succession*)
	Maj.Gen. Kustanto Widiatmoko *March 16, 1957 *Akmil 1987 *Cavalry *March 31, 2017 *Commander, Kodam IX/Udayana
	Major General Arif Rahman *April 22, 1966 *Akmil 1988 *Infantry *October 27, 2017 *Governor, Military Academy
	Major General R. Wisnoe Prasetja Boedi *April 20, 1964 *Akmil 1986 *Infantry *January 25, 2019 *Expert Staff to TNI Commander
	Major General Widodo Iryansyah *October 27, 1962 *Akmil 1987 *Infantry *April 22, 2020 *Assistant for Army Security
	Major General Suharyanto *September 8, 1967 *Akmil 1989 *Infantry *October 21, 2020 *Presidential Military Secretary
	Major General Nurchahyanto *December 25, 1964 *Akmil 1987 *Air Defence Artillery *December 9, 2021 *Assistant for Army Territorial Affairs
Commander, Kodam VI / Mulawarman (*Major General*)	Major General Benny Indra Pujihastono *December 2, 1961 *Akmil 1984 *Field Artillery *August 15, 2014 *Presidential Military Secretary
	Major General Johny L. Tobing *December 15, 1960 *Akmil 1983 *Infantry *June 9, 2016 *Assistant for Army Operation

continued

Position	Commanding Officer (*succession*)
	Major General Sonhadji *December 29, 1961 *Akmil 1984 *Field Artillery *March 8, 2017 *Assistant for Army Personnel
	Major General Subiyanto *March 11, 1963 *Akmil 1988 *Infantry *March 9, 2018 *Assistant for Army Personnel
	Brigadier General Heri Wiranto (*promotion*) *November 23, 1967 *Akmil 1989 *Infantry *July 25, 2020 *Assistant for Army Personnel
	Major General Teguh Pudjo Rumekso *April 20, 1968 *Akmil 1991 *Infantry *November 5, 2021 *Commander, Kodam VI/Mulawarman
Commander, Kodam IX / Udayana (*Major General*)	Major General Torry Djohar Banguntoro *September 14, 1957 *Akmil 1982 *Infantry *September 22, 2014 *Expert Staff, Lemhannas
	Major General Setyo Sularso *May 27, 1959 *Akmil 1982 *Infantry *September 10, 2015 *Chief of Staff, Kostrad
	Major General Kustanto Widiatmoko *March 16, 1957 *Akmil 1987 *Cavalry *May 4, 2016 *Assistant for Army Territorial Affairs
	Major General Komaruddin Simanjuntak *January 10, 1960 *Akmil 1985 *Infantry *March 31, 2017 *Assistant for Army Territorial Affairs

Position	Commanding Officer (*succession*)
	Major General Benny Susianto *December 10, 1963 *Akmil 1987 *Infantry *January 4, 2018 *Deputy Commander, TNI Academy
	Major General Kurnia Dewantara *November 22, 1962 *Akmil 1986 *Infantry *June 25, 2020 *Commander, Seskoad
	Major General Maruli Simanjuntak *February 27, 1970 *Akmil 1992 *Infantry *November 23, 2020 *Commander, Paspampres
Commander, Kodam XII / Tanjungpura (*Major General*)	Major General Toto Rinanto Soedjiman *January 12, 1960 *Akmil 1984 *Infantry *September 22, 2014 *Expert Staff, Lemhannas
	Major General Agung Risdhianto *April 22, 1961 *Akmil 1985 *Infantry *January 31, 2016 *Commander, Pusterad
	Major General Andika Perkasa *December 21, 1964 *Akmil 1987 *Infantry *May 20, 2016 *Commander, Paspampres
	Major General Achmad Supriyadi *March 5, 1961 *Akmil 1984 *Infantry *January 4, 2018 *Expert Staff to TNI Commander
	Major General Herman Asaribab *June 10, 1964 *Akmil 1988 *Infantry *March 19, 2019 *Special Staff to Army Chief of Staff

continued

Position	Commanding Officer (*succession*)
	Major General Muhammad Nur Rahmad *November 25, 1965 *Akmil 1988 *Infantry *September 2, 2019 *Assistant for Army Security
	Major General Sulaiman Agusto *August 11, 1966 *Akmil 1988 *Cavalry *September 29, 2021 *Commander, Pussenkav TNI AD
Commander, Kodam XIII / Merdeka (*Major General*)	Major General Ganip Warsito *November 23, 1963 *Akmil 1986 *Infantry *October 10, 2016 *Expert Staff to TNI Commander
	Major General Madsuni *February 14, 1964 *Akmil 1988 *Infantry *March 2, 2018 *Commander, Kopassus
	Major General Tiopan Aritonang *November 16, 1963 *Akmil 1986 *Infantry *July 13, 2018 *Expert Staff to TNI Commander
	Major General Santos Gunawan Matondang *June 12, 1963 *Akmil 1987 *Infantry *January 9, 2020 *Assistant for Army Security
	Major General Wanti Waranei Franky Mamahit *December 20, 1963 *Akmil 1987 *Infantry *June 30, 2021 *Commander, Infantry Division-3, Kostrad
Commander, Kodam XIV / Hasanuddin (former Kodam VII / Wirabuana) (*Major General*)	Major General Agus Surya Bakti *August 17, 1961 *Akmil 1984 *Infantry *October 28, 2015 *Deputy I, National Counterterrorism Agency (BNPT)

Position	Commanding Officer (*succession*)
	Major General Surawahadi *March 26, 1963 *Akmil 1985 *Infantry *July 13, 2018 *Commander, Pussenif TNI AD
	Major General Andi Sumangerukka *March 11, 1963 *Akmil 1987 *Air Defence Artillery *January 9, 2020 *Expert Staff, BIN
	Major General Mochamad Syafei Kasno *November 24, 1967 *Akmil 1990 *Field Artillery *April 1, 2021 *Expert Staff to TNI Commander
Commander, Kodam XVI / Patimura (*Major General*)	Major General Meris Wiryadi *December 11, 1958 *Akmil 1983 *Infantry *May 2, 2014 *Assistant for Army Territorial Affairs
	Major General Wiyarto *October 3, 1959 *Akmil 1985 *Infantry *January 19, 2015 *Assistant for Army Territorial Affairs
	Major General Doni Monardo *May 10, 1963 *Akmil 1985 *Infantry *July 25, 2015 *Commander, Kopassus
	Major General Suko Pranoto *June 30, 1964 *Akmil 1987 *Infantry *October 27, 2017 *Commander, Puspenerbad
	Major General Marga Taufik *April 17, 1964 *Akmil 1987 *Infantry *December 20, 2018 *Commander, Infantry Division-2, Kostrad

continued

Position	Commanding Officer (*succession*)
	Major General Agus Rohman *August 15, 1953 *Akmil 1988 *Infantry *July 24, 2020 *Commander, Infantry Division-1, Kostrad
	Brigadier General Jeffry Apoly Rahawarin (*promotion*) *January 21, 1964 *Akmil 1988 *Infantry *February 23, 2021 *Expert Staff, Coordinating Ministry for Politics, Law and Security Affairs
	Major General Bambang Isnawan (*promotion*) *July 31, 1966 *Akmil 1988 *Infantry *August 2, 2021 *Assistant for Army Security
	Major General Richard Horja Taruli Tampubolon *May 24, 1969 *Akmil 1992 *Infantry *December29, 2021 *Commander, TNI Special Operations Command
Commander, Kodam XVII / Cendrawasih (*Major General*)	Major General Fransen G. Siahaan *May 27, 1958 *Akmil 1983 *Infantry *September 15, 2014 *Commander, Infantry Division-1, Kostrad
	Major General Hinsa Siburian *October 28, 1959 *Akmil 1986 *Infantry *August 18, 2015 *Assistant for Army Operation
	Major General George Elnadus Supit *July 22, 1962 *Akmil 1985 *Infantry *April 25, 2017 *Assistant for Army Operation

Position	Commanding Officer (*succession*)
	Major General Yosua Pandit Sembiring *December 1, 1961 *Akmil 1986 *Infantry *September 24, 2018 *Deputy Commander, Kodiklatad
	Major General Herman Asaribab *June 10, 1964 *Akmil 1988 *Infantry *August 14, 2019 *Commander, Kodam XII/Tanjungpura
	Major General Ignatius Yogo Triyono *July 16, 1965 *Akmil 1988 *Infantry *November 18, 2020 *Commander, Army Officer Cadet School
Commander, Kodam XVIII / Kasuari (*Major General*)	Major General Joppye Onesimus Wayangkau *July 17, 1962 *Akmil 1986 *Infantry *December 19, 2016 *Expert Staff to TNI Commander
	Major General Ali Hamdan Bogra *January 6, 1963 *Akmil 1987 *Infantry *April 30, 2020 *Deputy Commander, Sesko TNI
	Major General I Nyoman Cantiasa *June 26, 1967 *Akmil 1990 *Infantry *August 20, 2020 *Commander, Kopassus
Commander, Kodam Jaya (*Major General*)	Major General Mulyono *March 13, 1960 *Akmil 1983 *Infantry *March 21, 2014 *Assistant for Army Operation
	Major General Agus Sutomo *August 14, 1960 *Akmil 1984 *Infantry *September 5, 2014 *Commander, Kopassus

continued

Position	Commanding Officer (*succession*)
	Major General Teddy Lhaksmana W. K. *February 1, 1959 *Akmil 1983 *Infantry *September 10, 2015 *Special Staff to Army Chief of Staff
	Major General Jaswandi *March 12, 1960 *Akmil 1985 *Infantry *February 23, 2017 *Commander, Kodam IV/Diponegoro
	Major General Joni Supriyanto *June 6, 1964 *Akmil 1986 *Infantry *March 2, 2018 *Vice Head of BAIS TNI
	Major General Eko Margiyono *May 12, 1967 *Akmil 1989 *Infantry *January 25, 2019 *Commander, Kopassus
	Major General Dudung Abdurrachman *November 19, 1965 *Akmil 1988 *Infantry *July 27, 2020 *Governor, Military Academy
	Major General Mulyo Aji *July 28, 1964 *Akmil 1987 *Infantry *May 25, 2021 *Assistant for Army Personnel
Commander, Kodam Iskandar Muda (*Major General*)	Major General Agus Kriswanto *July 10, 1960 *Akmil 1984 *Infantry *May 19, 2014 *Commander, Infantry Division-2, Kostrad
	Major General Luczisman Rudy Polandi *January 25, 1961 *Akmil 1985 *Infantry *January 26, 2016 *Expert Staff to TNI Commander

Position	Commanding Officer (*succession*)
	Major General Tatang Sulaiman *April 1, 1962 *Akmil 1986 *Infantry *September 16, 2016 *Chief of Staff, Kostrad
	Major General Mochamad Fachruddin *November 14, 1962 *Akmil 1985 *Infantry *March 31, 2017 *Special Staff to TNI Commander
	Major General Abdul Hafil Fudin *June 14, 1962 *Akmil 1985 *Field Artillery *March 9, 2018 *Expert Staff, Lemhannas
	Major General Teguh Arief Indratmoko *December 13, 1965 *Akmil 1988 *Infantry *July 31, 2018 *Expert Staff to TNI Commander
	Major General Hassanudin *7 September 1965 *Akmil 1989 *Air Defence Artillery *March 31, 2020 *Assistant for Army Planning
	Major General Achmad Marzuki *February 24, 1967 *Akmil 1989 *Infantry *November 18, 2020 *Inspector, Kostrad
	Major General Mohamad Hasan *March 13, 1971 *Akmil 1993 *Infantry *December 9, 2021 *Commander, Kopassus

Bérénice Bellina, Roger Blench, and Jean-Christophe Galipaud, editors. *Sea Nomads of Southeast Asia: From the Past to the Present*. Singapore: National University of Singapore Pres, 2021. 383.

Carol Warren

The Sea Nomads of Southeast Asia: From the Past to the Present offers impressive studies from an array of disciplines—archaeology, anthropology, history, linguistics, genomics—to piece together the *longue-durée* of "sea nomad" cultures in the Southeast Asian region.

There is a striking paradox that peoples so central to the deep history of globalization should find their cultures marginalized in the modern era. The collection of essays grapples with the relative "invisibility" of sea nomad cultures despite rich, although scattered, historical records of sightings and engagements from the 16th century among Western explorers and earlier still in Arabic and Chinese sources. Challenging also for interpretation are substantial differences in the socioeconomic status and political relationships reported in historical and contemporary ethnographic accounts.

The weight of evidence amassed in this volume goes some way toward revising the image of sea nomad populations as subordinated minorities within nation-states today. The sea nomads of Southeast Asia are shown in these studies to have contributed to linking together a Maritime Silk Road between South and East Asia in the ancient world and are credited with playing an important role in the earliest phases of the globalization of commerce. At the same time, evidence on the subsistence, trading, craft producing, and political arts of the sea peoples of the region in the historical and archaeological record leaves unresolved the questions of direct relationship with currently identified groups.

Case studies in the book cover multiple disciplines focused primarily on the main contemporary "sea nomad" populations—the Moken and Orang Laut off the Malay-Thai-Myanmar coasts and the Sama Bajau who inhabit the waters of eastern Indonesia, Malaysian Borneo, and southern Philippines. Yet much of the piecing together of material deposits from prehistory, recorded encounters, and contemporary ethnographies leave the tacit connections between past and present groups practicing a more or less mobile, boat-dwelling way of life an open question: Is this a cultural adaptation that saw groups and individuals move in and out of lives on the sea? Or has it been an enduring lifeway for distinctive groups whose cultural core revolved around maritime resources and relations that represent a largely intangible cultural heritage?

The chapter structure follows a roughly chronological trajectory, including early evidence of maritime movements as sea levels rose during the Pleistocene-Holocene transitional period that expanded the potential for this remarkable adaptation to the coastal cultural-ecological niche. The introductory chapter 1 by editors Bérénice Bellina, Roger Blench, and Jean-Christophe Galipaud sets out the themes around which core archaeological, historical, linguistic, genetic, and ethnographic questions are pursued in the following chapters: How should we understand the "sea nomads" and their relation to the wider traditions of maritime migration and exchange of goods, material, and intangible culture across the region? What are the relationships between mobile, boat-dwelling ethnic groups of island Southeast Asia and land-based groups of the estuaries and hinterlands? What roles have they played in the evolution of state societies and of the trading polities that mediated state-building among the emerging kingdoms that rose and fell across the region? How did they fit into the network of trading relations between state societies and the "stateless" cultures of the less controllable mountains and seas, who were more or less successful in practicing the arts of "not being governed."[1]

Chapters 2, 3, and 4, tease out the archaeological evidence on sea peoples in painstaking detail. They will be challenging for those outside the field, however. The technical vocabulary is unfortunately taken for granted and would have proved more accessible to scholars of other disciplines if a detailed glossary had been provided. Nonetheless the inferences drawn from assemblages of implements, pottery, and ornaments offer tantalizing interpretations and points of debate in these efforts to reconstruct a partially "invisible" world of seaborne fishers, foragers, guardians, pioneers, traders, and raiders.

Chapter 2 (co-authored by Sue O'Connor, Christian Reepmeyer, Mahirta, Michelle C. Langley and Elena Piotto) explores the distribution of obsidian and shell technology in the Lesser Sunda Islands of eastern Indonesia. The authors find what they term "communities of practice" reflecting distinct attributes of style and function in the concentric and J-shaped hooks crafted for use in waters with different depths, substrate features, and fish-types. Social networks among contiguous coastal communities appear tighter than between coast and hinterland on the basis of the distribution of these artifacts. Stylistic characteristics of crafted items offer a yet stronger basis for drawing conclusions about diffusion and cultural transmission than their functions, which can't exclude "the ambiguity of similarity" (44) that could equally be explained as independent adaptive uses. From subtle interpretation of such material traces, these scholars build convincing pictures of prehistorical networks of migration and exchange among coastal and hinterland populations.

David Bulbeck's chapter 3 reviews the earliest evidence that the archaeological record of the region presents for maritime exchange networks during the late Pleistocene and early Holocene transition. These date back at least 50,000 years as sea levels slowly rose to produce the island-studded, shallow seas of archipelagic Southeast Asia. This chapter is an encyclopedic effort to trace and interpret human movement, through seventeen maps that chart the distribution of sites of human habitation, through evidence of ground stone tools, rock art, fish hooks, ornaments, pottery, translocated fauna, and distinctive mortuary practices. The data, gleaned from 157 sources of precise site references to archaeological evidence, is presented in a six-page table (57ff) supplementing the densely annotated maps. These track the movement of technologies, resource use, and cultural traditions that point to extensive maritime interactions along several axes linking Malayo-Polynesian mariners from Taiwan with other groups through the northern Philippines, the Indonesian archipelago, and around the mainland Southeast Asian Malay-Thai peninsula. As different trajectories connected and overlapped over irregular time frames, the material culture distributions indicate the presence of local and

---

[1] James Scott, *The Art of Not Being Governed: An Anarchist History of Southeast Asia* (Singapore: National University of Singapore Press, 2009).

extended coastal exchange networks during the Pleistocene that become more coherent and continuous in later periods.

In chapter 4 Bellina, Aude Favereau, and Laure Dussubieux explore the complementarity of forager and nomadic adaptive strategies in the evolution of an early Maritime Silk Road that linked the Bay of Bengal with the South China Sea. Their focus on the integral role of forager-traders contrasts with more conventional treatments of mobile land and sea-based groups. Drawing inspiration from Scott's interpretation of active resistance to state incorporation among mainland Southeast Asian ethnic minorities as an active choice of autonomy, they argue the same ecological conditions on land and sea that enabled mobile peoples' independence from early lowland states also fostered economic specialization and trade with these settled centralizing polities and contributed to their rise. The archaeological evidence in trade goods and funerary deposits supports the theory that sea nomads played significant intermediary roles in the early maritime trading networks of the region, linking coastal traders and inland foragers across the Thai-Malay peninsula.

Cynthia Chou's contribution (chapter 5) on the Orang Suku Laut reorients portrayals of contemporary "tribal peoples of the sea" by shifting the center of attention to the marine domain as constructed territory. In focusing on the different spatial imaginings of an era when movement and mapping revolved around a maritime cultural landscape, the often-neglected sea peoples become central figures. Chou's chapter explores ethnographic accounts of movement-experience-knowledge that territorialized seascapes, creating places and spaces collectively "owned" by seafarers and entitled by their stories. Knowledge and movement authorize prominent relationships and provide vantagepoints to their agency as part of an otherwise "hidden transcript."[2] In this scenario the sea nomads could not be portrayed as subordinated outcasts except from a myopic land-biased perspective. Without assuming direct links of descent, ethnography then projects into prehistory a central acting role for the Orang Suku Laut, "or a population following the same way of life . . . who gained mastery of the seas, bridged the barrier between land and sea, and had the knowledge to realize this cultural variety to its full potential" (143).

Linguistic research explored by Blench in chapter 6 gives ambivalent evidence on the continuity and disruption of these maritime movements across a region that extends from the South China Sea through the Indian Ocean to Madagascar. Contemporary sea peoples' Austronesian languages show close connection with land-based cultures. While archaeological evidence suggests that the distinctive maritime nomadic lifestyle extended into deep antiquity, Blench argues its modern forms are no more than two thousand years old for the Moken and less for other groups, with both assimilation and adaptive replacements recurring regularly over time.

In his subsequent chapter 8, Blench discusses the evolution of technologies of ship construction and navigation to argue that small-scale sea dwelling cultures would have evolved in tandem with large seaborne trading empires, most importantly with China. The surprising aspect of this narrative of maritime evolutionary symbiosis is the

---

[2] James Scott, *Domination and the Arts of Resistance: Hidden Transcripts* (New Haven: Yale University Press, 1990).

evidence that it was massive Southeast Asian cargo ships with sophisticated rigging that inspired the later evolution of the Chinese junk, both vessel types dwarfing their European counterparts in early encounters. Ships from island Southeast Asia were reported in Chinese sources as carrying up to seven hundred pilgrims to China as early as the 1st millennium (202).

Chapters 10, 11, and 12 tackle the sweep of history and the resilience of the sea-going adaptations of Southeast Asians from past to present. In chapter 10, Jacques Ivanoff explores Moken notions of space and time, based on oral accounts and ethnographic work to reveal an egalitarian "nomad ideology" that encodes knowledge, meaning, and adaptive options. He uses local ethnographic data to propose a model illustrating the conditions of adaptation and assimilation that underpin Moken responses to political, economic, and environmental constraints. At different times and places these have impelled mobilization or settlement, marginalization or transformation. Ivanoff proposes a pan-Southeast Asian pattern of fluid identity formation, segmentation, integration, and renewal that engages multiple trajectories whose conjunctures leave identity markers and provide insights into a wider history of the region and its resilient sea-going peoples (250–51).

Ayesha Pamela Rogers and Richard Engelhardt continue the theme of resilience in their study of social and archaeological evidence of maritime-adapted populations of the Andaman Sea (chapter 11). The "Phuket Project" documented change among the Chaw Lay "sea gypsies" since the 1970s in the face of the dramatic transformation of the area into an international tourist destination. Seeking evidence of the intangible elements of cultures and community relations through retrievable material evidence of adaptations, they describe results of long-term, multidisciplinary research to learn what coastal archaeology could reveal about adaptation of sea-based coastal populations over time. The research combined archaeological with ethnographic explorations focused on social-ecological resilience in both historical and modern contexts. Like Ivanoff's study, this chapter takes the analysis of processes of cultural response to the limits posed by the contemporary enclosure of coastal land and sea resources. For the Chaw Lay of Phuket today this represents a threshold between a way of life that was able to respond to changes through mobility and deployment of ecological knowledge to one in which resilience in the sense of capacity to sustain both cultural identity and ecological integrity of the resources on which it is based, may no longer be possible. Nonetheless, cultural traces, place names, and local knowledge provide documentation of this important intangible heritage that may yet serve future adaptive response.

More optimistically, Galipaud et al. (chapter 12) retrace speculative theories on the early origins of sea nomad populations with Austronesian expansion and the development of large-scale trading. Their exploration of ethnic integration as well as the absorption and transformation of cultural traits and narratives gives close attention to interactions between boat dwellers and land-based populations. Their narrative positions trade rather than agriculture as the driving force dynamizing the region. The "sea nomads" were subsistence fishers, marine procurers, coastal traders, or pirates at various times and places, sometimes settling on land and becoming farmers. At other times and places the attractions of life at sea drew land-based peoples to a mobile maritime way of life. Paralleling a broad theme reiterated throughout the book, the pattern of sea peoples' remarkable adaptations feeds into what Andrew McWilliam refers to more broadly as "Austronesian cosmopolitanism."[3]

For a number of reasons, it seems logical to discuss the several chapters (7, 9, 13, 14) that primarily concern the Bajau in relation to one another. The Bajau (Bajo) of eastern Indonesia, east Malaysia, and the southern Philippines are the most widespread, numerous, and paradoxically most difficult ethnic group to characterize among the so-called "Sea Nomads." The research presented in these chapters poses provocative counternarratives alongside earlier interpretations of Bajau origins, cultural characteristics, and subsistence orientation.[4] Among the groups, which took on seafaring ways of life, it is only the Bajau that do not have a generally accepted common ancestral homeland or point of origin. The Bajau are today the most widely dispersed of the sea-oriented cultures and accordingly their languages, paralleling ethnological and genetic evidence, reflect diverse degrees of interaction with disparate land-based groups in a "creolization" process that Nagatsu (chapter 14) demonstrates continues into the present.

Chapter 7 provides a genomic perspective to add to linguistic and oral history accounts on the origin and dispersal of Bajau as part of the earliest migration and trade circulations connecting the Pacific and Indian Oceans as far as Madagascar (170, 180). Based on DNA samples from twenty-seven Bajau from the Kendari area of Sulawesi, the authors (Pradiptajati Kusuma, Nicolas Brucato, Murray Cox, Chandra Nuraini, Thierry Letellier, Philippe Grangé, Herawati Sudoyo and François-Xavier Ricaut) conclude that a statistically distinctive common genetic profile characterizes this Bajau sample that differs significantly from other ethnic populations. Their work found that intermarriage with land-based groups and assimilation in both directions took place over a long enough period of time to produce a common genetic profile with ancestry belonging to at least two genetically distinct parts of island Southeast Asia bisected by the Wallace line. The Kendari DNA samples show links to Bugis, Mandar, and other groups from Maluku and the Lesser Sunda islands, with sex-biased patterns indicating genetic links with South Asians through the male line and Papuans through the female line.

Kusuma et al. place the Kendari Sulawesi Bajau at the epicenter of island Southeast Asian genetic diversity. Combined genetic and ethno-linguistic evidence on similarities to the Ngaju Dayak leads the authors to support the southeastern Borneo origin thesis for the Bajau diaspora (191–93). That said, the largest Bajau population center recognized in current national census data is the distinctive Sulu (Philippines) cluster with almost four times the population of its Sulawesi counterpart (Nagatsu, this volume, 328). The merits of the Sulu versus South Bornean origin thesis for the Bajau are taken up by Illouz and Nuraini in chapter 13, where they show how the patterns of trade between the 9th and 14th centuries put the Sama Bajau in a position to control important trade arteries through the Sulu zone. They track a tentative milestone history of migrations

[3] Andrew McWilliam, "Austronesian in Linguistic Disguise: Fataluku Cultural Fusion in East Timor," *Journal of Southeast Asian Studies* 38, no. 2 (2007), quoted in Galipaud et al., this volume, 296.
[4] See the classic studies by David Sopher, *The Sea Nomads: A Study of the Maritime Boat People of Southeast Asia.* (1965; repr., Singapore: National Museum of Singapore, 1977); and Clifford Sather, *The Bajau Laut: Adaptation, History and Fate in a Maritime Fishing Society of South-Eastern Sabah* (Kuala Lumpur: Oxford University Press, 1997).

and alliances, culminating in colonial suppression of indigenous trade and postcolonial-imposed settlement. At this point the narrative of marginalization parallels those of Moken and Chaw Lay presented in chapters 10 and 11, as Bajau become caught up in a process of political, economic, and ecological enclosure that would require another volume to address.

Lance Nolde's Chapter 9 continues the revisionist theme, ascribing key economic and political roles to the Sama Bajau in early modern eastern Indonesia. He uses indigenous texts to tease out evidence of their historical role in maritime globalization. Nolde concludes their dispersion to be an indication of the cultural importance of these sea peoples in the rise and fall of the land-based kingdoms of the region. As procurers and traders of highly valued marine products, and as emissaries, guardians, and powerful actors in their own right, the picture painted of the Sama Bajau based on indigenous accounts is very different from the image of a marginalized and oppressed minority, restricted to a materially poor subsistence way of life as hunter-gatherers of the sea. Oral traditions and written texts give testimony to their importance to the rival Makassar and Bugis kingdoms into the 17th century. The particular role of the high-status Sama Bajau leader holding the title "Pupuq" is at the core of Nolde's counternarrative of Bajau history and cultural identity. The emergence of these elites of the Bajau polity points to their indispensable role in the movement of people and goods across the archipelago, at least in the Sulawesi regional context and until Dutch conquest brought an end to indigenous control over the region's bountiful seas.

The portrait Nolde paints of a highly regarded and relatively autonomous people with its own internal hierarchy apparently disappears with references to the Pupuq title in written records from the end of the 18th century (221). The title remains in oral tradition as a respectful term of address into the present, however. Questions arise from the Makassar manuscripts to what extent intermarriage with dominant cultures produced this elite intermediary class who were appointed to positions such as harbormaster and exercised control over territories but were apparently selected to the Pupuq position by the Sama Bajau themselves. The Makassar sources frequently refer to the prowess and expertise of Sama Bajau sailors, navigators, and warriors. Evidence of the significant role of this paramount Sama Bajau figure over a long period of time is found to have been "crucial to the political expansion and economic prosperity" of eastern Indonesian kingdoms (230), warranting reassessment of stereotypic images of the Sama Bajau as a subordinated people.

The revisionist treatment of Bajau history and identity is taken into the present in Nagatsu Kazufumi's remarkable ethnographic work in chapter 14, which concludes the book. This research is a comprehensive effort to track the genealogy of the Sama Bajau diaspora and attendant processes of hybrid cultural "creolization." Based on more than two decades of research, Nagatsu examines the processes of Bajau ethnic identity formation, creolization, and dispersal from extensive fieldwork in remote communities spread across Southeast Asia's shallow coral reef zones. His work on the island of Sapeken in the Kagean islands is particularly revealing of the fluidity of region-wide ethnogenesis. Here, Bajau language and identity have become dominant, as migrant Bugis, Makassar, and Madurese "become Bajau," leading Nagatsu to suggest that "syncretic ethnogenesis" may be "embedded in these diasporic processes of the maritime world" (354).

Sea Nomads of Southeast Asia offers rich interdisciplinary perspectives on cultures, which the cumulative evidence demonstrates contributed substantially to the importance of this region for more than a millennium. In doing so these diverse studies present stimulating insights into state formation and proto-globalization processes in which the maritime environment and cultures played an important and to date underappreciated role. Indeed, the extent of interaction and connectivity between land and sea across Southeast Asia justifies claims asserting the centrality of the maritime world and maritime cultures in global history long before the Eurocentric "Age of Discovery."

The array of evidence from different disciplines on the fluidity of seagoing adaptations suggests that the title of the book would have been better termed Sea "Peoples" rather than "Nomads," since only some groups in some periods were full-time boat dwellers and truly "nomadic." Constructions of cultures practicing an entirely boat-dwelling, mobile, and subsistence way of life never fit all the sea-oriented peoples of the region, or any of those explicitly identified as "nomads" at all times. This way of life has nearly disappeared with sedentarization and hardened borders in the post-WWII period of nation-state consolidation in the region.

The often-forced settlement of these cultures under contemporary nation-states raises other questions that deserve to be pursued. A second volume remains to be written that explores the impacts of national development policies, climate change, and the decline of marine resources on the Sea Peoples of the Southeast Asian region for the future. The editors and contributors to this volume have made a major contribution to our knowledge of the peoples of the island Southeast Asian world and the extraordinary richness of the socio-ecological environment and heritage they have pioneered for what we now know to have been millennia. The stage is set for a genuine effort to turn that heritage into rights.

Albert Schrauwers. *Merchant Kings. Corporate Governmentality in the Dutch Colonial Empire, 1815–1870*. New York: Berghahn, 2021.

G. Roger Knight

Merchant Kings is focused on an elite cadre of technocrats and their associates in government and business, something that Albert Schrauwers envisages as fusing colony and metropole into a single—in this instance Dutch—"corporate governmentality." It's an impressive and intriguing hypothesis, valuable not least for the way in which it draws attention, if not to the singularities of the Dutch empire, then at least to the dangers of conflating "empires" into an homogenous whole: clearly, the *Heeren* in Amsterdam, The Hague, and Rotterdam set out to run their vast Asian empire on lines considerably at variance from that of the Gentleman of London, Manchester, and Glasgow. The spotlight it plays on its subject in this respect illuminates what are arguably some substantial contrasts—as well as comparable features. All in all, it is a thought-provoking essay in trying to make sense of the interwoven history—a single, unified history—of what it has become increasingly threadbare to term merely as "core" and "periphery."

The Dutch empire in Asia, transformed in the middle of the last century into the Republic of Indonesia, has long attracted the attention of historians and others, above all on account of developments there during the middle decades of the nineteenth century on its centerpiece island of Java, far the most populous of the sprawling archipelagic territories that came to constitute what their colonial hegemon invariably referred to as "the Indies." It was there, in the shape of the Cultivation System (Dutch: *Cultuurstelsel*), that the colonial regime set about commandeering the land and labor of the island's peasantry for what became the highly profitable production of a "tropical" commodities for the world market, notably coffee, sugar, the dye-stuff indigo, and tobacco.

In respect to the forging and intermeshing of commodity chains linking metropole and colony, however, a crucial development was the fact that Java's extensive population (there were already perhaps as many as nine million Indonesians living on the island c. 1850) provided a potentially lucrative *market* for the manufactures of the metropolitan country. It was here that—as Schrauwers's account emphasizes—the heavily state-backed Netherlands Trading Society or NHM, one of the key entities in the evolution of the corporate regime that he identifies as coming into existence c. 1830 onward, played a key role. For not only did it transport and sell in Amsterdam the agricultural staples produced under the aegis of the system and act as banker to the colonial government, while subsequently playing a role (somewhat exaggerated in this account) in the industrialization of Java's sugar manufacture: the NHM also acted to bring into existence a "complimentary" cotton goods manufacturing industry in the Netherlands itself, especially in the "cheap labor" northeastern parts of the country.

The potential for an integrative analysis of the Dutch empire overseas with that of the empire at home, of course, was not lost on an earlier generation of scholars: Leiden professor Cees Fasseur, albeit from a potentially very different historical perspective from that of the book currently under review, might well have done so—building on series of publications beginning in the mid-1970s—had he not been deflected into the writing of a warmly received two-volume biography of the twentieth century Dutch Queen Wilhelmina. More recently, *Exploring the Dutch Empire* (ed. Antunes and Gommans, 2015) held out further early promise in that direction, but important work by historians writing in Dutch (as largely dictated by their funding bodies) on the imperial agents central to the Cultivation System, Governor-General Johannes van den Bosch (Sens 2019) and the state-backed Netherlands Trading Society of NHM (De Graaf 2012), has remained untranslated and hence unavailable to the academic community in general. In short, Schrauwers is filling an important gap for Anglophone readers, but he is doing much more than that.

The organic connection that he sets out to demonstrate—one between metropole and colony—begins with Van den Bosch, the individual who not only established the rudiments of the famous/notorious system on Java but, prior to that, had been closely associated with schemes in the Netherlands to alleviate pauperism in a country whose "Golden Age" was long over by the 1820s when Van den Bosch was active there. None of this is new, but what is refreshing is Schrauwers's reanalysis that merges Van den Bosch, his activities, and his ideas into a larger corporate entity headed by the Dutch king (Willem I was no means the merely titular head of "Netherlands Inc") and including not only the NHM but also the newly founded Royal Academy at Delft whose technocratic graduates came to form the basis for that de-politicized "rule of experts"—a term used here without the caustic irony inherent in Timothy Mitchell's eponymous book—that typified the regime both at home and on the colony.

Like any good thesis, *Merchant Kings* overstates and over-simplifies its case. Above all, Schrauwers's intellectually stimulating approach, while very welcome, suffers from being altogether too schematic, inter alia paying too little attention to nuancing the homogeneity and inner harmony of "corporate governmentality," while ignoring the potentially disruptive power and agency of individual economic and social actors. The infiltration of the corporate regime of Merchant Kings by an incipient colonial bourgeoise and its metropolitan affiliates may, as Schrauwers argues, be chimerical insofar as some (though by no means all) of the actors concerned remained creatures of the state, dependent on the regime for access to the basic factors of production along the relevant commodity chain.

Even so, there are major discrepancies: why, for example, if sugar was so central, was the lucrative trade in it from Java to Europe allowed to "slip away" from the NHM from the 1850s onward into the hands of mercantile interests whose affiliation to the corporate regime was not immediately obvious? By the 1880s, this had reached a stage where one such concern—the Batavia-based mercantile house of Maclaine Watson, founded in the 1820s and one of a number of similar entities whose position vis-à-vis the "corporate governmentality" schema remains somewhat problematic—had control (as the NHM acknowledged its Annual Reports) over more than 40 percent of the Java sugar crop. Of course, a historian's objections on this score might—quite properly perhaps—be dismissed as rooted in a conceptual misunderstanding of how the corporate regime of Merchant Kings analyzed by Schrauwers functioned. All the same, some other historical queries remain more worrying. Take the issue of railways, the development of which— in the Netherlands and on Java—Schrauwers quite correctly makes into an important plank of his argument. Yet it is a context in which matters, once again, do not quite fit together as neatly as he appears to suppose.

The railway in question—the first of its kind on Java—ran from Semarang on the island's central north coast through the mountains to the south port into the island's fertile and densely populated heartlands of South Central between the cities of Yogyakarta and Surakarta. The construction of the line is cited as an achievement that, in effect, brought "the area where the sugar industry was concentrated" (199) firmly into the orbit of the Merchant King complex and likewise identified as essentially the brainchild of the key NHM executive Willem Poolman and the merchant banking associates who backed this and much more extensive projects in the Netherlands. All this is no doubt correct up to a point, but a closer look reveals some problems. The railway in question took an awful long time to reach its completion in 1873—Poolman himself was already dead by the time it opened for business—and plans for its construction, first mooted more than two decades earlier, had been long in gestation, not least because of disagreements as to whether the state itself or entrepreneurial-investor interests outside the immediate competence of the Indies government should be responsible for building and running it. Furthermore, the area of sugar production that the railway serviced was *not* the island's most productive sector (that lay in East Java, several hundred kilometers from the railhead) and, most important of all, the sector that it *did* service was well outside the purview of the corporate regime that Schrauwers envisages, having never been incorporated into the Cultivation System that was so central to the evolution of the Merchant Kings paradigm. Just for good measure, moreover, it looks as if the railway was finally brought to realization by a big loan raised in the *London* financial market by Alexander Fraser, a former partner in Maclaine Watson (who had long been major backers of just this railway). He was certainly replete with good connections in the Netherlands and on Java (among them people identified, as Schrauwers makes very clear, as key players in the Merchant Kings' schema), but he was also someone whose transnational career, inter alia as the Southeast Asian chief executive of a major, British-owned regional shipping line, fits perhaps somewhat uneasily into the "corporate governmentality" of *Dutch* imperialism envisaged in this book.

These are perhaps no more than niggling problems about the historicity of what Schrauwers sets out to do and nowhere approach the tragic proportions of an interesting hypothesis knocked cold by a fact. But they do serve to temper enthusiasm a little for a book whose cerebral appeal remains, nonetheless, substantially undimmed. So much undimmed indeed, that it is apposite to call for more. The whole structure that Schrauwers so intricately delineates evolved during the middle decades of the nineteenth century and must, surely, have been sorely tested by the crisis that impacted massively on the sugar complex with which it was so closely bound up when, in the mid-1880s, the bottom fell out of the market for the industrially manufactured form of the commodity that Java produced. The existing historical literature on the subject is inclined to see the decade of the '80s as a watershed not only for the sugar industry but, understandably enough, for the Dutch empire as a whole. It would be good to hear Schrauwers's take on this and to see him carry his analysis through into the twentieth century.

The relevance of carrying it through is obvious enough, since an essential foundation of that analysis and of "corporate governmentality" per se is the presumption of reasonably harmonious relation existing among the several stakeholders concerned. This is an assumption that works well enough, perhaps, for the mid- and late nineteenth century, when the synergies between colony and metropole in respect to sugar and cotton, in particular, were obvious and uncontested. But, to leap ahead in time, what of the interwar decades of the twentieth century? By the 1930s, any notion of common interests holding together a corporate regime that fused the Netherlands with its great Southeast Asian colony was put under great pressure (to say the least) by the determination of Dutch cotton goods manufacturers to retain their hold on the Indies market by (in effect) denying entry there to cheap cottons from Japan, precluding thereby any hope that Java's sugar industry—whose markets were by then almost exclusively in Asia itself— might have had of selling their raw output to Japanese refineries as part of a wider trade agreement. Yet alluding to matters of this kind is not, of course, an indication of the present book's failings, but rather a tribute to its strengths in raising long-term questions about developments in the Dutch empire that arguably only began to play out more than half-a-century after *Merchant Kings'* avowed terminal date. As such, Schrauwers's new book stands out as an important and welcome contribution to a debate that still has some way to go.

Printed in the USA
CPSIA information can be obtained
at www.ICGtesting.com
LVHW021339170823
755531LV00012B/628

9 781501 769993